Lecture Notes in Computer Science 7896

Commenced Publication in 1973
Founding and Former Series Editors:
Gerhard Goos, Juris Hartmanis, and Jan van Leeuwen

T0218382

Hubert B. Keller   Erhard Plödereder
Peter Dencker   Herbert Klenk (Eds.)

Reliable Software Technologies – Ada Europe 2013

18th Ada-Europe International Conference
on Reliable Software Technologies
Berlin, Germany, June 10-14, 2013, Proceedings

 Springer

Volume Editors

Hubert B. Keller
Karlsruhe Institute of Technology
Institute of Applied Computer Science
Hermann-von-Helmholtz Platz 1, 76344 Eggenstein-Leopoldshafen, Germany
E-mail: hubert.keller@kit.edu

Erhard Plödereder
University of Stuttgart
Institute of Software Technology
Universitätsstr. 38, 70569 Stuttgart, Germany
E-mail: ploedere@informatik.uni-stuttgart.de

Peter Dencker
ETAS GmbH
Borsigstr. 14, 70469 Stuttgart, Germany
E-mail: peter.dencker@etas.com

Herbert Klenk
Cassidian – An EADS Company
Rechliner Straße, 85077 Manching, Germany
E-mail: herbert.klenk@cassidian.com

ISSN 0302-9743   e-ISSN 1611-3349
ISBN 978-3-642-38600-8   e-ISBN 978-3-642-38601-5
DOI 10.1007/978-3-642-38601-5
Springer Heidelberg Dordrecht London New York

Library of Congress Control Number: 2013938610

CR Subject Classification (1998): D.3, D.2, C.3, F.3, C.2, H.4, D.4, D.1

LNCS Sublibrary: SL 2 – Programming and Software Engineering

Cover picture: Thomas Wolf, www.foto-tw.de, modified by Hubert B. Keller

Typesetting: Camera-ready by author, data conversion by Scientific Publishing Services, Chennai, India

Printed on acid-free paper

Springer is part of Springer Science+Business Media (www.springer.com)

Introduction

After 13 years, the International Conference on Reliable Software Technologies, Ada-Europe, returned once again to Germany. In its 18th incarnation as a conference addressing software reliability issues, research, and experience, it is one of the premier conferences on this subject whose importance and actuality remain unbroken. It was also the 33rd annual Ada-Europe conference, with Ada being one of the foremost technologies that have focused specifically on software reliability. Editions of the conference with its focus on reliability were held in Switzerland (Montreux 1996 and Geneva 2007), the United Kingdom (London 1997, York 2005 and Edinburgh 2011), Sweden (Uppsala 1998 and Stockholm 2012), Spain (Santander 1999, Palma de Mallorca 2004 and Valencia 2010), Belgium (Leuven 2001), Austria (Vienna 2002), France (Toulouse 2003 and Brest 2009), Portugal (Porto 2006), Italy (Venice 2008), and Germany (Potsdam 2000 and now Berlin-Dahlem 2013).

Organized by Ada Deutschland e.V. and its scientific counterpart, the special interest group Ada of the Gesellschaft für Informatik (GI), the conference was sponsored by Ada-Europe, the European federation of national Ada societies, in cooperation with GI, ACM SIGAda, SIGBED, and SIGPLAN. We gratefully acknowledge additional sponsorship by DFG, the German Research Foundation. The conference took place in Berlin-Dahlem during June 11–15, 2013, at the Seminaris Conference Center Dahlem Cube. Before and after the conference, three ISO Working or Rapporteur Groups conducted their meetings at the conference location.

Thirteen years ago, we noted in the foreword of the proceedings of the conference in Potsdam: *"It is not an overstatement to note that our daily life is beginning to literally depend on the reliability of the software embedded in products. Yet such reliability does not come about by accident. It needs to be infused into the software and the processes of the software life cycle by the application of appropriate techniques and technologies."* These statements still hold true today, except that entrusting our lives and fortunes to software-based systems is no longer a vision of the future but daily reality as we drive in our cars, fly in airplanes, bank online, or are screened or operated upon by medical equipment with fascinating new capabilities most of which are the result of software support of ever-increasing complexity.

An added dimension in today's world is the advent of multi-core technologies or, to put it in software terms, the forced departure from fully deterministic execution models and the advent of systems in which computations occur in a non-deterministic parallel order. Design principles that for decades were applied to ensure certain reliability aspects in safety-critical software are no longer applicable when parallel executions become feasible and necessary.

The paper contributions to the conference mirrored these long-range issues as well as solutions to near-term problems.

Once again, the conference attracted submissions from around the world. Submissions were received from authors residing in Canada, China, Denmark, France, Germany, India, Israel, Italy, Macedonia, Mauritius, Portugal, Spain, Switzerland, Taiwan, Thailand, UK, and the USA. A total of 11 papers were accepted for the proceedings and five additional industry contributions were accepted for presentation at the conference. The overall acceptance rate was 38%. Two conference sessions were reserved for presentations by vendors of products supporting the development and management of reliable software.

As in past years, the conference comprised a three-day technical program at which the papers contained in these proceedings were presented, along with shorter presentations on related topics. The technical program was bracketed by two tutorial days when attendees had an opportunity to catch up on a variety of topics interesting to the field, at both introductory and advanced levels. Further, the conference was accompanied by an exhibition where vendors presented their reliability-related products.

Each conference day opened with a keynote presentation. The keynote speakers and their themes were:

- Bruce Powel Douglass, Chief Evangelist IBM Rational: Model-Based Ada Development for DO-178B/C and the Application of Agile Methods
- Jack G. Ganssle, The Ganssle Group: The Way Ahead in Software Engineering: Replacing Artists with Disciplined Grownups
- Giorgio C. Buttazzo, Scuola Superiore Sant'Anna of Pisa, Italy: Research Challenges in Exploiting Multi-Core Platforms for Real-Time Applications

In addition, Tucker Taft, the principal designer of Ada95, gave an invited overview of the new features of Ada 2012, the latest standard for Ada announced by ISO in December 2012.

We would like to express our sincere gratitude to these distinguished speakers, well known to the community, for sharing their insights and information with the audience.

The tutorial program featured international experts presenting introductory and advanced material on a variety of subjects relevant to software engineers:

- "Multicore programming using divide-and-conquer and work stealing," Tucker Taft
- "Designing and checking coding standards for Ada," Jean-Pierre Rosen
- "Effective requirements development practices and their role in effective design," William Bail
- "Understanding dynamic memory management in safety critical Java," Kelvin Nilsen
- "Developing code analysis applications with ASIS," Jean-Pierre Rosen
- "Verification and validation techniques for dependable systems," William Bail

- "Design of multitask software: The entity-life modelling approach," Bo Sanden
- "Testing real-time software," Ian Broster
- "Service-oriented architecture and enterprise service bus," Rick Sward
- "Developing high-integrity systems with GNAT GPL and the Ravenscar profile," Juan de la Puente
- "Maximize your application potential," David Sauvage

Many people contributed to the success of the conference. The Program Committee spent part of their Christmas vacation carefully reviewing all submitted papers and providing detailed evaluations. The Industrial Committee reviewed all proposals for experience reports submitted by industry. A subcommittee comprising Johann Blieberger, Jørgen Bundgaard, Hubert B. Keller, Ahlan Marriott, Jürgen Mottok, and Erhard Plödereder, met on a weekend in early February to compose the program based on the reviews.

We thank the committees for their dedication and hard work to get the reviews done in time. A significant help in organizing the paper review was the EasyChair system.

The Organizing Committee deserves special mention. Peter Dencker put together the exhibition where vendors presented their tools or services to make software more reliable and its production easier. Jürgen Mottok composed the attractive tutorial program. Jørgen Bundgaard dedicated extraordinary effort to soliciting contributions for the industrial sessions of the conference and coordinating their review. Erhard Plödereder organized the technical program together with Hubert Keller, who also put together the Preliminary and Final Program of the conference, along with the materials for the web presence. Dirk Craeynest did his usual best in contributing to the public relation material and in distributing the electronic calls for papers, contributions, and participation. Raúl Rochas helped with the local arrangements in Berlin. We also would like to thank Christine Harms who handled the registration and the local organization at Berlin.

Foremost, however, we wish to express our appreciation to the authors of the papers submitted to the conference, and to the participants who came to exchange their ideas and results. Without you, there would be no conference. We hope that you were satisfied by the technical program of the conference and enjoyed the social events of this 18th International Conference on Reliable Software Technologies.

April 2013   Hubert Keller
                                                                Erhard Plödereder

Organization

The 18th International Conference on Reliable Software Technologies - Ada-Europe 2013 was organized by Ada-Europe and Ada-Germany, in cooperation with ACM SIGAda, SIGBED, and SIGPLAN, GI, KIT, University of Stuttgart, VDE, VDI.

Organizing Committee

Conference and Program

Co-chairs

Hubert B. Keller   Karlsruhe Institute of Technology, Germany
Erhard Plödereder   University of Stuttgart, Germany

Tutorial Chair

Jürgen Mottok   Regensburg University of Applied Sciences, Germany

Industrial Chair

Jørgen Bundgaard   Ada in Denmark and Rambøll Danmark, Denmark

Exhibition Chair

Peter Dencker   ETAS GmbH, Germany

Publicity Chair

Dirk Craeynest   Aubay Belgium and K.U. Leuven, Belgium

Proceedings Chair

Herbert Klenk   Cassidian, Germany

Local Chair

Raúl Rojas   FU Berlin, Germany

Local Organizer

Christine Harms   ccH, Germany

Program Committee

Ted Baker
Johann Blieberger
Bernd Burgstaller
Alan Burns
Dirk Craeynest
Juan A. de la Puente
Franco Gasperoni
Michael González Harbour
Xavier Grave
Christoph Grein
J. Javier Gutiérrez
Peter Hermann
Jérôme Hugues
Hubert Keller
Pascal Leroy
Albert Llemosí
Kristina Lundqvist

Franco Mazzanti
John McCormick
Stephen Michell
Luís Miguel Pinho
Erhard Plödereder
Jürgen Mottok
Manfred Nagl
Laurent Pautet
Jorge Real
Jean-Pierre Rosen
José Ruiz
Ed Schonberg
Tucker Taft
Theodor Tempelmeier
Elena Troubitsyna
Tullio Vardanega
Juan Zamorano

Industrial Committee

Jørgen Bundgaard
Jacob Sparre Andersen
Jamie Ayre
Ian Broster
Dirk Craeynest
Peter Dencker
Michael Friess
Ismael Lafoz
Ahlan Marriott
Robin Messer

Steen Ulrik Palm
Paolo Panaroni
Paul Parkinson
Ana Isabel Rodríguez
Jean-Pierre Rosen
Alok Srivastava
Claus Stellwag
Jean-Loup Terraillon
Rod White

Supporting Organizations

The organizers of the conference would like to express their thanks to the exhibitors and supporters of the conference.

Exhibitors, at the time of writing, were:

AdaCore
Atego
Ellidiss
ETAS
Rapita Systems
Vector Software

Table of Contents

Session: Multicore and Distributed Systems

Experience with the Integration of Distribution Middleware into
Partitioned Systems 1
  Héctor Pérez and J. Javier Gutiérrez

Tasklettes – A Fine Grained Parallelism for Ada on Multicores 17
  Stephen Michell, Brad Moore, and Luís Miguel Pinho

Model-Based Deployment of Mission-Critical Spacecraft Applications
on Multicore Processors.. 35
  J. Reinier van Kampenhout and Robert Hilbrich

Session: Ada and Spark

A SPARK/Ada CubeSat Control Program 51
  Carl Brandon and Peter Chapin

Lady Ada Mediates Peace Treaty in Endianness War 65
  Thomas Quinot and Eric Botcazou

Session: Dependability

Provably Secure DNS: A Case Study in Reliable Software 81
  Barry Fagin and Martin Carlisle

Using Ontologies in the Integration of Structural, Functional, and
Process Perspectives in the Development of Safety Critical Systems 95
  Irene Bicchierai, Giacomo Bucci, Carlo Nocentini, and
  Enrico Vicario

Measuring the Odds of Statements Being Faulty 109
  Xiaozhen Xue and Akbar Siami Namin

Session: Real-Time Systems

A Model-Based Framework for Developing Real-Time Safety Ada
Systems 127
  Emilio Salazar, Alejandro Alonso, Miguel A. de Miguel, and
  Juan A. de la Puente

Towards a Time-Composable Operating System...................... 143
  Andrea Baldovin, Enrico Mezzetti, and Tullio Vardanega

Worst–Case Execution Time Analysis Approach for Safety–Critical
Airborne Software.. 161
    Esteban Asensio, Ismael Lafoz, Andrew Coombes, and Julian Navas

Author Index... 177

Experience with the Integration of Distribution Middleware into Partitioned Systems*

Héctor Pérez and J. Javier Gutiérrez

Computers and Real-Time Group
Universidad de Cantabria, 39005 - Santander, Spain
{perezh,gutierjj}@unican.es
http://www.ctr.unican.es/

Abstract. This paper proposes an architecture to enable the use of distribution middleware in partitioned systems based on a hypervisor. Partitioning is a widespread technique used in the development of high-integrity systems. In this kind of critical systems, software has to be as simple as possible in order to ease certification, and as the use of distribution middleware increases complexity, it has been avoided by developers. However, partitioning allows applications with different levels of criticality (mixed-criticality) to be executed in the same system. We propose the use of distribution middleware for the development of those applications with lower level of criticality, and present an experience in porting middleware based on CORBA and Ada DSA (Distributed Systems Annex) standards to the hypervisor XtratuM.

Keywords: distribution middleware, partitioned systems, CORBA, Ada DSA, real-time, communications.

1   Introduction

The traditional cyclic executive used mainly in high-integrity or safety-critical systems has evolved in the last years to a more sophisticated paradigm called partitioning or partitioned systems. In this kind of systems, the operating system manages a set of protected time frames called partitions, and also provides memory isolation. Each partition can contain one or more time windows that define the intervals during which the application allocated to that partition may execute. High-integrity software must pass a certification process that certifies compliance with certain requirements imposed by a regulatory authority (e.g., DO-178B for avionics [1]). Thanks to this time and space isolation, a set of applications can be certified all together even if they have been developed by different companies. As an example of partitioned system, ARINC-653 [2] is a standard for avionics systems which defines the interface of a partition-based operating system that allows multiple applications to execute in the same hardware platform, while maintaining time and space isolation among them.

---

* This work has been funded in part by the Spanish Government and FEDER funds under grant number TIN2011-28567-C03-02 (HIPARTES).

H.B. Keller et al. (Eds.): Ada-Europe 2013, LNCS 7896, pp. 1–16, 2013.

Distributed systems based on this sort of partitions are built interconnecting two or more monoprocessor partitioned systems through special purpose networks (e.g., AFDX [3] or SpaceWire [4]). Each processor is controlled by an operating system that supports partitioning (e.g., POK [5] for an ARINC-653 specification). Partitions execute simple activities in order to facilitate certification, and the use of distribution middleware is simply inconceivable. However, there are other approaches to partitioned systems that envisage the possibility of using distribution middleware; those based on a hypervisor, which is a layer of software that enables several independent execution environments to be run in a single computer. The hypervisor provides the basis of partitioning through a thin layer with a low overhead for switching between partitions. In this approach, each partition can execute a complete operating system providing a second level of scheduling in which applications with different tasks can be scheduled. Thus, a hypervisor can support partitions with different levels of criticality, which could be built on the top of operating systems with different purposes.

Our concern is that distributed applications with a low level of criticality can take advantage of common distribution middleware. This kind of application, possibly having real-time requirements, can be developed using common real-time operating systems, and may be executed together with other applications having a higher level of criticality in a partitioned system based on a hypervisor. Thus, distribution middleware can facilitate communication between subsystems, with the abstraction of complexity of network services, transparent management of communications, and interoperability [6]. Examples of distribution middleware standards that support different distribution paradigms are: CORBA [7] for object distribution, Ada DSA (Distributed Systems Annex) [8] for object distribution and RPCs (Remote Procedure Call), and DDS [9] for data-based distribution.

This paper deals with the use of distribution middleware technology in partitioned systems through the integration of communication middleware based on standards within XtratuM [10], which is an ARINC-653-like hypervisor especially designed for real-time embedded systems. The objective is to propose an architecture that enables partitioned distributed systems to be developed using distribution middleware on the top of the native communication services provided by XtratuM. This architecture will allow not only the communication of partitions in different processors through communication networks, but also the communication of those partitions allocated in different cores in a multicore processor. Additionally, a prototype has been developed in order to demonstrate the validity of the approach. It has been developed as a proof of concept over an x86 hardware, chosen due to availability of all the required technology for this architecture. This prototype enables XtratuM partitions, which communicate through distribution middleware following CORBA and Ada DSA standards, to be built on top of a real-time operating system.

The document is organized as follows. Section 2 presents the motivation of this research along with related work. In Section 3, the hypervisor XtratuM is introduced and relevant details of its architecture are described. Our proposal for the integration of distribution middleware with XtratuM is presented in Section 4. Section 5 deals with the implementation details of the proposed architecture for a specific middleware based on CORBA and Ada DSA, as well as an evaluation of the performance. Finally, Section 6 draws the conclusions and considers future work.

2   Motivation and Related Work

Using middleware technology in partitioned systems would have the following benefits:

- It would enable a transparent invocation of services allocated in partitions, independently of whether they are in the same processors (or core) or in a different one. On the one hand, middleware abstracts network services which allows the application code to be simplified while maintaining it independent from the communication subsystem. On the other hand, it facilitates the interoperability between two or more heterogeneous partitions, e.g., with different levels of criticality or using different data representations (e.g., endianness).
- We could schedule a multicore or a multiprocessor system as if it were distributed. This approach is reinforced by the fact that this kind of applications or partitions are statically allocated to the processors (migration is not allowed), and scheduling parameters are also fixed in advance.

Some works related to the integration of distribution middleware into high-integrity applications have been published in the last years, showing that this topic is attracting a high degree of interest, although research in this field is still in an early stage. One of the most notable efforts in this line is the work presented in [11], which proposes the integration of PolyORB-HI middleware into the TASTE framework [12]. PolyORB-HI is a minimal middleware that provides basic distribution services such as data marshalling/unmarshalling, request dispatching and network transport. Instead of following any distribution standard, this approach is based on the automatic generation of source code from architectural descriptions (i.e. system models). In this context, PolyORB-HI produces high-integrity code following the Ravenscar profile [13].

Regarding distribution standards, the use of CORBA [7] in high-integrity applications has previously been addressed in [14] and [15]. The former presents a real-time framework that uses ARINC-653 as the underlying platform, but extending the CORBA Component Model (CCM) [16] instead of relying on the standard real-time facilities. The latter is a European research project that defines an avionics platform using Java and CORBA (to communicate partitions) as the core technologies to reduce times and costs in software development.

There are other works for safety and security [17][18] based on the MILS (Multiple Independent Levels of Security) [19] architecture. It proposes the use of a separation kernel (guaranteeing the control of information flow and data isolation) with specific middleware to provide services to applications (e.g., interpartition communications, access to the network or system services).

One of the most important challenges that distribution standards should overcome to be used in high-integrity applications is complexity. This has motivated the attempt of distribution standards (1) to evolve towards safety-critical subsets of their full distribution facilities, such as the definition of a safety-critical profile for DDS (currently under discussion at OMG meetings), or (2) to adapt current

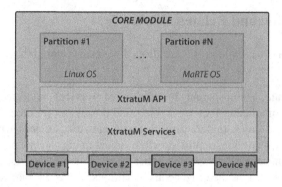

Fig. 1. XtratuM architecture

single-processor safety-critical profiles to distributed systems, as in the case of the Ada Ravenscar profile [20][21][22] or Safety Critical Java [23][24]. All these facilities are currently being investigated and will constitute a notable research field in the next years.

3   An Introduction to XtratuM

XtratuM [10] is an open source hypervisor designed for real-time embedded and high integrity systems. Although it does not follow a specific standard, its design is based on ARINC-653 so it provides the applications executing on top of it with time and space isolation. In XtratuM, the term *guest* or *partition* is used to reference a complete application which can be based on different operating systems, e.g., a general purpose OS (Linux), a real-time OS (MaRTE OS [25]), or an ARINC-653 OS (LithOS [26]). The general architecture of a system using XtratuM is shown in Fig. 1. Besides time and space isolation, XtratuM provides other facilities such as for example the virtualization of the basic resources of the system (clocks, timers, memory management, interrupts management, etc.), the static configuration of these resources, or specific communication services to enable the communication between two or more partitions.

Partitions are able to communicate by sending or receiving *messages* through the use of *ports*. A port can be configured to either send or receive messages, but not both. As in the case of the ARINC-653 standard, two types of ports are defined by XtratuM:

- *Sampling ports*, which provides sufficient storage for a single message so queuing is not required. The message remains available in the port until it is overwritten. This kind of port provides non-blocking communications and supports unicast, multicast and broadcast messages.
- *Queuing ports*, which provides sufficient storage for a fixed number of messages that are managed on a FIFO basis. Messages are buffered in the port until they are delivered. This kind of port provides non-blocking communications and only supports unicast messages.

As can be seen, any operation on a receiving port is non-blocking in XtratuM. Therefore, it is the partition's responsibility to retry the read/receive operation when the receiving buffer is empty.

Ports are virtually connected by *channels*, which represent a logical path between one sending port and one or more receiving ports. However, receiving ports can only receive messages from a single source at most (i.e., the source of messages is always known and fixed). A channel can connect ports that belong to partitions executing on the same *core module* (a hardware platform with one or more processors or cores). Channels, ports and queue properties are defined through a configuration file and so they cannot be changed at run-time.

Regarding the management of devices, partitions can access hardware by using specific XtratuM services to access the I/O ports. As in the case of the previous communication entities, partitions should be configured to access specific I/O ports before run-time. I/O ports can belong to only one partition, which means that specific I/O partitions should be created when more than one partition needs to access a particular device. Furthermore, I/O partitions are responsible for implementing the device drivers so devices shared among several partitions should be managed in a special way, as described in the next section.

4   Proposed Architecture

Our proposal will focus on the use of distribution middleware in partitioned systems in which a hypervisor is used to manage the hardware that could be formed by one processor with multiple cores. For this purpose, we perform an analysis to explore the various possible architectures for integrating a communication middleware within systems running on XtratuM. This analysis is divided into two levels: first, communications between core modules via the communications network, and secondly, communications between partitions through the communication services provided by XtratuM.

4.1   Communications between Core Modules and Middleware

Among the services offered by XtratuM are the virtualization of certain hardware components such as clocks or timers. However, XtratuM does not implement drivers at the hypervisor level, so sharing a device among multiple partitions should focus on handling the contention in order not to compromise the advantages of a partitioned system. In a distributed system, for example, multiple partitions may require access to the network card. A common strategy is the use of an I/O partition that has exclusive access to the network card. Under this approach, if one partition needs to communicate with another partition allocated in another processor, it must communicate with the I/O partition first, which will be responsible for redirecting messages to the communications network. Communication between an I/O partition and the other partitions in the same processor are performed through communication services provided by XtratuM as illustrated in Fig. 2.

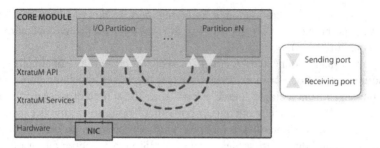

Fig. 2. XtratuM and the I/O partition

Since the main function of the I/O partition is redirecting messages, it can be designed by following two strategies:

- Considering the use of distribution middleware in this I/O partition, thus middleware will be responsible for performing routing transparently. In this case, messages are not opaque and can be processed by the I/O partition.
- Designing an I/O partition exclusively aimed at forwarding messages. In this case, messages are opaque to the I/O partition, and they would be routed through statically established connections. Therefore, each partition should know the destination of each of the remote requests beforehand.

4.2   Communications between Partitions and Middleware

Given the characteristics of the distribution middleware and the communication services provided by XtratuM, we have identified two aspects affecting the use of middleware:

- A receiving port can only receive messages from a sending port. Therefore, middleware must abandon the traditional concept of a shared port for listening to requests, since all communications have set the source and destination of the messages as static. This behaviour is similar to other approaches for real-time middleware [27].
- Asynchronous communication among ports; therefore, restricting the use of synchronous remote calls by middleware.

Considering both aspects, there are two possible configurations for communication between partitions. Without losing generality, we consider communication between the I/O partition and the remaining partitions as follows:

- A receiving port in the I/O partition for each partition in the core module. From a real-time perspective, this configuration serializes processing messages coming from a partition, regardless of the priorities assigned to each of the messages.
- Several receive ports in the I/O partition for each partition in the core module. That is, we define several communication channels between the I/O partition and the destination partition to enable the processing of messages according to their scheduling parameters (e.g., assigning the processing of messages coming from a

communication channel to a particular task). This configuration requires more system resources, but can respect the order of priorities by setting an appropriate configuration of the communications driver.

4.3 Discussion

From a communications perspective, the configuration of a partitioned distributed system using the hypervisor XtratuM should specify: (1) the assignment of partitions to each of the core modules of the distributed system, (2) the number and the type of ports (sampling or queuing, sending or receiving) of each partition, and (3) the communication channels between partitions within and outside the same core module, including the associated source and destination ports. The setting of these parameters is performed at two levels:

- The configuration of communications at partition level, so that they are independent with respect to the location of the source and destination partition. Specifically, at this level the number and type of sending and receiving ports available in each partition is set. More details are given in the appendix.
- The configuration of the communication channels at the level of the core module, within the same core module or between core modules. In this case, it is necessary to explicitly configure the source and destination of the messages (i.e., source and destination ports). When the communication is between core modules, it is also necessary to map communication ports to the underlying transport (see appendix).

Another important issue to be configured is the length of the time windows allocated to each partition. This is not a trivial problem, and it is even harder with inter-partitions dependencies as in the case of the I/O partition which should be executed with sufficient regularity to fulfil the I/O requirements of other partitions. This complexity can be reduced through the use of specialized tools such as Xoncrete [28]. The configuration of communications and time windows deserves a more detailed discussion that is beyond the scope of this paper.

Given the static nature of communications in this kind of partitioned systems, the use of middleware in the I/O partition is not strictly necessary. It would suffice that this partition routes received messages according to a previously generated configuration table. Furthermore, this approach may ease the certification process as the I/O partition should be certified at the same level as the highest level of criticality required by the partitions that use these I/O services.

From the point of view of minimizing the response time of remote calls, using multiple communication channels between two partitions prevents serialization of message processing by creating handling tasks with different scheduling parameters. However, a common strategy within distribution middleware lies in the definition of a single receiving port, where middleware initially deals with all requests coming from remote calls or from an automatic discovery of entities in the distributed system. Both aspects must be incorporated into distribution middleware for high-integrity systems, since the discovery of entities should be static, and for example, in the case of

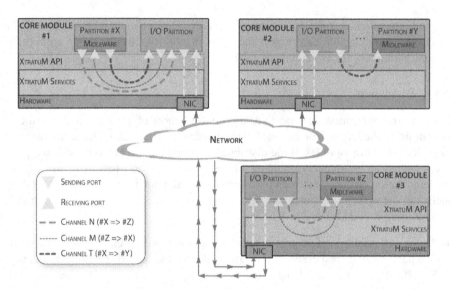

Fig. 3. Proposed architecture for integrating middleware with XtratuM

ARINC-like, communications between multiple sending ports and a single receiving port are not allowed.

Using synchronous remote calls in non-partitioned high-integrity systems has been discussed by several authors from several perspectives [20][21][22]. In the case of partitioned systems, it should be noted that a remote call could potentially be blocked and then it would create execution dependencies between partitions, i.e., an error in one partition may influence the behaviour of another partition. However, the ARINC-653-p1 standard does not preclude the use of synchronous communications if they are provided by the underlying system, as long as the partitioning is not violated. Therefore, this aspect is implementation dependent.

Finally, Fig. 3 shows an example of the proposed architecture for integrating distribution middleware with a partitioned system using XtratuM. The example consists of a distributed system comprising three core modules. Communications between partitions, belonging or not to the same core module, are performed via a communication middleware. In this case, we have defined three communication channels: channel N to interconnect a partition in core module # 1 with a partition in core module # 2, channel M to interconnect a partition in core module # 3 with a partition in core module # 1, and channel T to interconnect a partition in core module # 1 with a partition in core module # 3. As can be seen in the figure, each core module has an I/O partition, with exclusive access to the network card, that is responsible for routing the messages received by the underlying communications network.

5   Case Study

This section aims to validate the system architecture proposed in the previous section by integrating a specific distribution middleware in XtratuM. To this end, we will retrieve a distributed real-time platform previously developed [29] which consists of several software components: (1) PolyORB [30] as distribution middleware, (2) MaRTE OS [25] as the operating system and (3) RT-EP [31] as the real-time network. The integration of this platform with XtratuM is not straightforward and requires some extensions which are briefly described next.

5.1   Distributed Real-Time Platform Overview

PolyORB is introduced as middleware that can support different distribution standards such as CORBA, DSA or Web Services. It is distributed with the GNAT compiler and, in principle, it is envisaged for applications programmed in Ada. The architecture of PolyORB is divided into three separate layers: the application layer (referred to as application personality), the neutral layer or microkernel and the protocol layer (called protocol personality).

Since the proposed approach uses the ARINC-like communication services provided by XtratuM, a new protocol personality called ICMC (Intra Core Module Communication) has been developed in PolyORB. This new protocol personality allows the transparent use of XtratuM services for inter-partition communications. Furthermore, the XtratuM API is written in C so the corresponding Ada *bindings* have also been developed in order to call it from Ada applications.

Regarding concurrency patterns, PolyORB has been configured to create a handler task for each reception port defined in the partition. As XtratuM does not include blocking calls to listen for incoming messages, each handler task performs a periodic polling on the targeted receiving port.

To enable the communication among core modules, the previous platform relied on the RT-EP protocol [31], which is based on a token-passing scheme. However, this kind of networks could not fit well in partitioned systems as it demands intense processing times to manage the token and perform the scheduling, and partitioning increases the token rotation time excessively. This may require a significant increase of the slot time assigned to the I/O operations which can influence the overall performance. To better focus on middleware and hypervisor incurred overheads, we decided to use point-to-point communications for this case study.

5.2   Evaluation Scenario: Video-Surveillance

Performance and interoperability capabilities are evaluated by applying it to a simulated video-surveillance example, where multiple display monitors may request video captures from the recording application. A key feature for this kind of systems resides in the reliability of the recording application, as it must keep recording data continuously, so it can benefit from strong isolation capabilities and can be executed together with local display monitors or other third-party applications. The architecture for the proposed system is depicted in Fig. 4 and it is composed of:

- One node or core module with two partitions called "Video_Recorder" and "IO_Server": the first partition is responsible for obtaining data from the attached video cameras and serving the requested video captures to other partitions; the

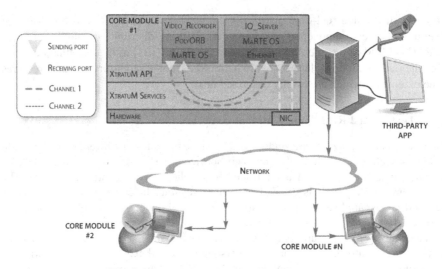

Fig. 4. Scheme of a video-surveillance example

second partition is in charge of routing the request/replies from/to other core modules spread across the distributed system.

- A variable number of nodes N or core modules representing the remote clients that may request the current live video stream or a previous recording. These nodes or core modules may or may not be partitioned systems. In our example remote clients will not be partitioned.

The hardware platform consists of two 800 MHz embedded nodes connected through a 100 Mbps Ethernet. The software platform was previously developed and integrates PolyORB (the CORBA personality), MaRTE OS, XtratuM and direct communications over Ethernet, as can be seen in Fig. 4.

We have carried out a test in this scenario to quantify the overhead introduced by using the hypervisor and the proposed architecture with respect to the non-partitioned case. The test will measure the execution time of a remote operation that sends the requested video frames. This evaluation has a twofold objective: on the one hand, it provides a rough idea about the overhead introduced by the hypervisor; on the other hand, it proves the interoperability between partitioned and non-partitioned distributed systems by using the same distributed real-time software platform developed in [29].

As mentioned in Section 4, the optimal configuration of partitions to meet their deadlines and maximize the processor's utilization is a complex problem, especially in the case of the I/O partition. In our example, it is expected that the execution time of middleware operations will be much greater than the ones associated with the routing operations. Therefore, the length of the time window allocated to the IO_Server should be enough to execute all its operations in one go in order to minimize idle times in the middleware partition. To this end, a set of measurements have been taken to estimate this length, which results in times below 90μs. Hence, the video-surveillance application has been configured to have a dedicated time window of 100μs for the IO_Server, and 400μs for the Video_Recorder partition, resulting in a scheduling plan repeated every 500μs (this is the major frame).

We measure the operation carried out from the time when the request of a video capture is made until the image is returned. This operation is executed 1000 times, and the average, maximum, and minimum times are estimated, together with the standard deviation and the 90th percentile (i.e., the value below which 90 percent of the measurements are found). To avoid additional overheads in the measurements, the test is executed without requiring network fragmentation (the payload is bounded to 1 kilobyte). We have also estimated the temporal cost of using the network (transmitting and receiving a message) by implementing the test over Ethernet in isolation.

Table 1. Performance metrics for the video-surveillance example

	MAX.	AVG.	MIN.	STD. DEV.	PER90
NETWORK	321	305	298	2	308
NON-PARTITIONED	5728	5691	5689	2	5694
SINGLE PARTITION	5862	5740	5716	36	5790
PARTITIONED	7944	7334	7130	184	7282

Table 1 shows the results for the measurements taken for the test. As can be seen, the network provides a communication link with sufficiently low dispersion to allow a suitable evaluation. The distributed operation takes less than 6 ms for both the non-partitioned (without using the hypervisor) and the single partition (using the hypervisor without the I/O partition) scenarios. In this case, XtratuM adds a minimum overhead to the non-partitioned scenario. Under the proposed system architecture (partitioned scenario), the operation takes less than 8 ms. On average, the performance decrease of the partitioned system is around 29%: 25% is inherent to the selected partition configuration, i.e., an extra time of 100μs is added every 400μs of the execution of the Video_Recorder partition; and the remaining 4% can be explained by different overheads (e.g., context switches between partitions, the use of ARINC-like communication ports or the intermediate routing performed).

The maximum time found in the partitioned system can be explained by the extra delay that the IO_Server partition can undergo when: (1) the message is received but cannot be processed immediately because the Video_Recorder partition is executing, or (2) the message is sent by the Video_Recorder partition at the beginning of its time window. Both cases could add a worst-case delay of 400μs each. Finally, it is worth noting that most of the measurements are closer to the minimum value for the partitioned system, as can be deduced from the 90th percentile, while the rest of the measures remain in the same range as the maximum.

As a consequence of the response times obtained in the case study, it can be observed that the overhead of using middleware together with a partitioned system could be reasonable for the kind of applications we have in mind, although a significant improvement is expected when using less complex middleware. In any case, our approach presents a low standard deviation as expected for this scenario.

6   Conclusions and Future Work

This work has explored the integration of standard distribution middleware into partitioned systems. This integration does not only enable a transparent communication among partitions in different processors through communication networks, but it also allows partitions allocated in the same core or in different cores in a multicore processor to communicate. Furthermore, it eases the interconnection between partitioned and non-partitioned distributed systems.

Our research has addressed the potential communication issues of this integration at two different levels: the first one dealt with the communication among core modules while the second refers to the inter-partition communication. For the former, the design of XtratuM imposes the creation of an I/O partition in charge of handling all the incoming/outcoming network messages. Hence, whether this partition may or may not include middleware depends on the nature of the distributed application (i.e. static or dynamic) and the certification requirements. For the inter-partition communication level, the use of middleware would be restricted to using asynchronous communications and to having as many reception ports as there are possible senders.

Mixed-criticality distributed applications can take advantage of the proposed system architecture. As partitions have space and temporal isolation capabilities, their determinism can only be jeopardized by the sharing of I/O services. In our approach, the I/O partition has been kept simple and it is exclusively aimed at forwarding messages, although other approaches could be explored.

Although this integration can facilitate the use of partitioned systems within a distributed environment, further investigation is required to fully determine which features of distribution standards can be applied, i.e., the suitability of distribution models or the applicability of some QoS configurations. Furthermore, other approaches could also be explored, e.g., middleware could benefit from having a virtual network card available in each partition. This approach would avoid the required modification of middleware to use the ARINC communication services, as the complexity of these services can be abstracted by a virtual network which interconnects the I/O server with the other partitions.

References

1. Radio Technical Commission for Aeronautics (RTCA). DO-178B Software Considerations in Airborne Systems and Equipment Certification, http://www.rtca.org/
2. Airlines Electronic Engineering Committee, Aeronautical Radio INC. Avionics Application Software Standard Interface. ARINC Specification 653-1 (March 2006)
3. Airlines Electronic Engineering Committee, Aeronautical Radio INC. ARINC Specification 664P7: Aircraft Data Network, Part 7 - Avionics Full Duplex Switched Ethernet (AFDX) Network (June 27, 2005)

4. European Cooperation for Space Standardization (ECSS), European Space Agency (ESA). SpaceWire Standard, http://spacewire.esa.int/
5. Delange, J., Lec, L.: POK, an ARINC653-compliant operating system released under the BSD license. In: Proc. of the 13th Real-Time Linux Workshop, Prague (Czech Republic) (2011)
6. Uchenick, G.M.: Partitioning Communications System for safe and secure distributed systems. In: Proc. of the 26th Digital Avionics Systems Conference, Texas (EEUU) (2007)
7. Object Management Group. CORBA Core Specification. OMG Document, v3.0 formal/02-06-01 (2003)
8. Tucker Taft, S., Duff, R.A., Brukardt, R.L., Plödereder, E., Leroy, P. (eds.): Ada 2005 Reference Manual. LNCS, vol. 4348. Springer, Heidelberg (2006)
9. Object Management Group. Data Distribution Service for Real-time Systems. OMG Document, v1.2, formal/07-01-01 (2007)
10. Masmano, M., Ripoll, I., Crespo, A., Metge, J.J.: Xtratum a hypervisor for safety critical embedded systems. In: Proc. of the 11th Real-Time Linux Workshop, Dresden (Germany) (2009)
11. Hugues, J., Zalila, B., Pautet, L., Kordon, F.: From the prototype to the final embedded system using the Ocarina AADL tool suite. ACM Tr. Embedded Computer Systems 7(4), 1–25 (2008)
12. Perrotin, M., Conquet, E., Dissaux, P., Tsiodras, T., Hugues, J.: The TASTE toolset: Turning human designed heterogeneous systems into computer built homogeneous software. In: Proc. of the 5th Int. Congress on Embedded Real-Time Software and Systems - ERTS2 (2010)
13. Burns, A., Dobbing, B., Vardanega, T.: Guide for the Use of the Ada Ravenscar Profile in High Integrity Systems. Technical Report YCS-2003-348, University of York (UK). Approved as ISO/IEC JTC1/SC22 TR 42718 (2003)
14. Dubey, A., Karsai, G., Mahadevan, N.: A component model for hard real-time systems: CCM with ARINC-653. Software: Practice and Experience (SPE) 41(12), 1517–1550 (2011)
15. Coutinho, R.M.A.: Aspects on Architecture for Independent Distributed Avionics (AIDA). In: Proc. of the 27th Digital Avionics Systems Conference (DASC), Minnesota (EEUU) (2008)
16. Object Management Group. Common Object Request Broker Architecture (CORBA) Specification - Part 3: CORBA Component Model. OMG Document, v3.3 formal/2012-11-16 (2012)
17. Uchenick, G.M.: Middleware for security and safety critical systems. Embedded Systems Europe, 24–26 (2006)
18. Vanfleet, W.M., Beckwith, R.W., Calloni, B., Luke, J.A., Taylor, C., Uchenick, G.M.: MILS: Architecture for High-Assurance Embedded Computing. CROSSTALK The Journal of Defense Software Engineering, 12–15 (August 2005)
19. Rushby, J.: From DSS to MILS - (Extended Abstract). In: Jones, C.B., Lloyd, J.L. (eds.) Dependable and Historic Computing. LNCS, vol. 6875, pp. 53–57. Springer, Heidelberg (2011)
20. Audsley, N., Wellings, A.: Issues with using Ravenscar and the Ada distributed systems annex for high-integrity systems. In: Proc. of the 10th International Real-Time Ada Workshop, pp. 33–39. ACM Press, New York (2001)
21. Urueña, S., Zamorano, J., de la Puente, J.A.: A Restricted Middleware Profile for High-Integrity Distributed Real-Time Systems. In: Kordon, F., Kermarrec, Y. (eds.) Ada-Europe 2009. LNCS, vol. 5570, pp. 16–29. Springer, Heidelberg (2009)
22. Pérez Tijero, H., Javier Gutiérrez, J., González Harbour, M.: Adapting the end-to-end flow model for distributed Ada to the Ravenscar profile. In: Proc. of the 15th International Real-Time Ada Workshop, Liébana (Spain), to appear in ACM Ada-Letters (2013)

23. Tejera, D., Alonso, A., de Miguel, M.A.: RMI-HRT: remote method invocation - hard real time. In: Proc. of the 5th International Workshop on Java Technologies for Real-Time and Embedded Systems, pp. 113–120. ACM, New York (2007)
24. Higuera-Toledano, M.T.: Adaptive Distributed Embedded and Real-Time Java Systems Based on RTSJ. In: Proc. of the 15th International Symposium on Object/Component/Service-Oriented Real-Time Distributed Computing Workshops, pp. 164–171 (2012)
25. Aldea Rivas, M., González Harbour, M.: MaRTE OS: An Ada Kernel for Real-Time Embedded Applications. In: Strohmeier, A., Craeynest, D. (eds.) Ada-Europe 2001. LNCS, vol. 2043, pp. 305–316. Springer, Heidelberg (2001)
26. Masmano, M., Valiente, Y., Balbastre, P., Ripoll, I., Crespo, A., Metge, J.J.: LithOS: a ARINC-653 guest operating for XtratuM. In: Proc. of the 12th Real-Time Linux Workshop, Nairobi (Kenya) (2010)
27. Pérez Tijero, H., Gutiérrez, J.J., González Harbour, M.: Support for a Real-Time Transactional Model in Distributed Ada. In: Proc. of the 14th International Real-Time Ada Workshop (IRTAW 14), Portovenere (Italy), ACM Ada-Letters, vol. 30(1), pp. 91–103 (2010)
28. Brocal, V., Masmano, M., Ripoll, I., Crespo, A., Balbastre, P.: Xoncrete: a scheduling tool for partitioned real-time systems. In: Proc. of the 5th Int. Congress on Embedded Real-Time Software and Systems - ERTS2 (2010)
29. Pérez Tijero, H., Gutiérrez, J.J.: Experience in integrating interchangeable scheduling policies into a distribution middleware for Ada. ACM Ada-Letters 29(3), 73–78 (2009)
30. Vergnaud, T., Hugues, J., Pautet, L., Kordon, F.: PolyORB: A Schizophrenic Middleware to Build Versatile Reliable Distributed Applications. In: Llamosí, A., Strohmeier, A. (eds.) Ada-Europe 2004. LNCS, vol. 3063, pp. 106–119. Springer, Heidelberg (2004)
31. Martínez, J.M., González Harbour, M.: RT-EP: A Fixed-Priority Real Time Communication Protocol over Standard Ethernet. In: Vardanega, T., Wellings, A.J. (eds.) Ada-Europe 2005. LNCS, vol. 3555, pp. 180–195. Springer, Heidelberg (2005)

Appendix

This appendix describes the way to configure communication channels using the XML configuration scheme followed by XtratuM. Fig. 5 shows the symbols that are used in the XML diagrams and their interpretation:

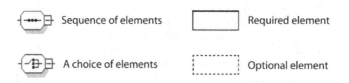

Fig. 5. Symbols used in the XML diagrams

Partition Level Configuration

At the partition level configuration, ARINC-like communications are based on the independence of (1) the underlying transport mechanism used and (2) the source/destination of messages.

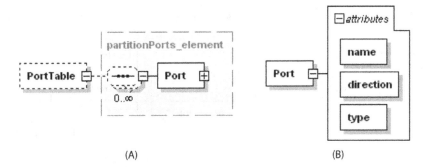

Fig. 6. Partition level configuration of ports

Each partition is configured independently by specifying the number of available ports (Fig. 6-A). Additionally, the name, type (i.e., sampling or queuing) and direction (i.e., source or destination) of each port are set (see Fig. 6-B).

Core-Module Level Configuration

At the core module level, the configuration of ARINC-like communications requires the specification of the number and type of channels. Each channel describes a route connecting one source port to one or several destination ports through intermediate ports. For instance, Fig. 7 shows the attributes required to configure a sampling channel whose source, destination or intermediate ports are defined by a pair of values (partitionId, portName). Furthermore, extra port attributes may be specified to map them to the underlying transport mechanism by means of the input and output transport links, as described in Fig. 8.

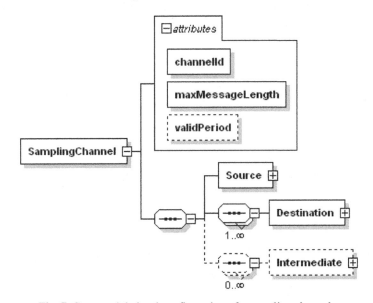

Fig. 7. Core-module level configuration of a sampling channel

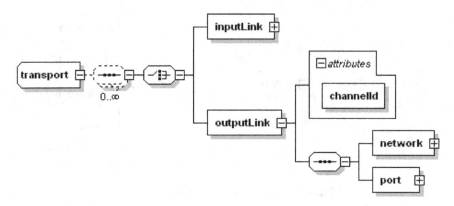

Fig. 8. Core-module level configuration of the underlying transport mechanism

Tasklettes – A Fine Grained Parallelism
for Ada on Multicores

Stephen Michell[1], Brad Moore[2], and Luís Miguel Pinho[3]

[1] Maurya Software Inc, Canada
stephen.michell@maurya.on.ca
[2] General Dynamics, Canada
brad.moore@gdcanada.com
[3] CISTER/INESC-TEC, ISEP, Polytechnic Institute of Porto, Portugal
lmp@isep.ipp.pt

Abstract. The widespread use of multi-CPU computers is challenging programming languages, which need to adapt to be able to express potential parallelism at the language level. In this paper we propose a new model for fine grained parallelism in Ada, putting forward a syntax based on aspects, and the corresponding semantics to integrate this model with the existing Ada tasking capabilities. We also propose a standard interface and show how it can be extended by the user or library writers to implement their own parallelization strategies.

1 Introduction

The development of ubiquitous multi-CPU computers has led to a more pressing need to be able to express parallel computational algorithms effectively in general purpose programming languages.

The development of programs that capture concurrent properties of algorithms has been a focus of many research papers (since [1, 2]) and has been implemented in operating systems, such as DEC RT-11, HP, Unix, POSIX and Microsoft Windows, and programming languages concurrent Pascal [1], Ada [3] and Java [4]. Most approaches focused either on concurrency in the small (a few of threads or interrupts) or specialized processor domains, such as SIMD (Single Instruction Multiple Data) environments. Recently, other languages, such as C# and C++ have added or are investigating methods of implementing fine grained concurrency, which is the subject of this paper. We are ignoring much of the work for SIMD machines for now as they use specialized toolsets and techniques.

Unfortunately, the perception of the general threading or tasking environment is that the threads or tasks are too expensive in resource usage, cumbersome (in terms of being easy to use by average programmers), not easily mapped to the physical resources at hand at the time of program execution, and divergent from the problem space when attempting to apply concurrency to computationally intensive activities [5, 6].

Arguably, the Ada tasking model with its first-class task types and well defined syntax/semantics for inter-task interactions [7] simplifies the expression of many

H.B. Keller et al. (Eds.): Ada-Europe 2013, LNCS 7896, pp. 17–34, 2013.
© Springer-Verlag Berlin Heidelberg 2013

concurrent properties and solutions. However, other models, such as loop-level parallelism or parallel subprogram execution are not easily expressed in the current Ada model. In addition, the resource consumption issues and cost of dynamic task creation and destruction of Ada tasks when used in undisciplined ways still begs for a better approach to map the concurrency power available at the hardware level to algorithms written at the below-subprogram level.

Parallel programming in Ada was considered several years ago ([8,9,10]). Mayer and Jahnichen [8] introduce a `parallel` keyword, which applies to for loops, allowing a specific compiler to optimize loop iterations, targeted to a multiprocessor platform. Hind and Schonberg [9] also targeted the optimization of parallel loops, introducing the concept of lightweight (mini) tasks, to reduce the overhead of using tasks for parallelism. Thornley [10] proposes two extension keywords to standard Ada: `parallel` and `single`, where `parallel` is used for declaring that a block or a `for loop` will be executed in parallel.

More recent proposals have been made to extend Ada's capabilities by using generics [11], pragmas [11], and language constructs [12]. This work builds upon these to present a more unified proposal.

In this paper we address these issues as they relate to the Ada programming language; propose syntax for Ada that more closely matches the need for fine grain concurrency than exists at present; and propose semantics for the syntax presented that seamlessly integrates the existing Ada tasking capabilities and the new fine grain concurrency.

2   Problem Analysis

Concurrency as a discipline has been the subject of intense research from the days of Per Brinch Hansen [13]. The most common usage was to handle external events, to manage the progression of work and to ensure that work was scheduled according to the importance (priority) of the work. For the majority of systems there was a single CPU that was the resource to be scheduled, and for the rest there were a few CPUs that were shared between many more tasks.

As long as CPU speed was increasing exponentially, the pressure to increase throughput by increasing CPU count was overwhelmed by that speed increase. When maximum CPU speed became capped in the mid-2000's, the pressure to increase performance by adding cores became overwhelming. We now stand on the threshold of "too many cores", where chip manufacturers prepare to deliver hundreds or thousands of cores, each with tens or hundreds of "lanes" for parallel work.

With these changes, there will be many more cores than tasks ready to execute at any one time. These cores are available to subdivide heavy calculations when the algorithms can be effectively parallelized.

There is an apparent belief that we can create lightweight threads and that a program can detect how many cores are available at any one time and allocate the lightweight threads to cores to execute a parallel algorithm. This belief ignores the fact that the operating system schedules all resources, memory, threads, and cores. A program cannot schedule cores without scheduling the threads that could be using them.

An approach institutionalized by MIT [14, 15] and now commercialized by Intel [16] and being used by ParaSail [17], Intel's Threading Building Blocks [18], Java Fork/Join [19], OpenMP [20], Microsoft's Task Parallel Library [21], is to put lightweight "tasks" on top of thread pools. This is a promising approach that we investigate further to implement the model that we develop here.

Another issue that must be addressed for such distribution is the nature of the algorithm being distributed. Any algorithm that is a candidate for parallel execution must calculate a deterministic result independently of the order in which the fragments are combined. This is simple if there is only a single operation (such as "+" or "*") and the operation is commutative, but may not be trivial for non-commutative operations such as "-" or for more complex combinations of such functions or operations.

Often, the algorithm must be rewritten to add partial temporary accumulator variables and to combine these temporary variables correctly to produce the correct result. In some cases, the compiler may be able to perform such rewrites, but it is ultimately the programmers' responsibility to be aware of such issues and to ensure that when parallelism is applied to a programming construct, the algorithm as written will not be incorrect when executed in parallel.

3   Semantic Model

In order to effectively describe the new concurrent behavior, we introduce a unit of concurrency called a "tasklette". Unlike tasks, tasklettes are not nameable or directly visible in a program. A tasklette carries the execution of a subprogram or of a code fragment in parallel with other tasklettes executing the same code fragment (with different variables) and possibly in parallel with other tasklettes executing code fragments from other Ada tasks.

Tasklettes come in two types. The first type is invisible to the programmer and is created by the compiler when it can determine that an operation can be parallelized and submitted to multiple CPUs. Example of such usage could be the default initialization or assignment of values to arrays of records or the copy of a large structure using the Ada assignment operator.

The second tasklette type is the subject of this paper and requires the programmer to use explicit syntax to guide the compiler and runtime. This syntax will include the use of aspects on subprograms or on loops. This syntax will be specified in the next section, followed by examples.

A major impetus behind making tasklettes not declarable is to separate the programmer from the implementation of the parallel constructs [1]. Programmers will declare an intent that code fragments be executable in parallel, but need not concern themselves with the details of the parallelism itself. Tasklettes are meant to augment, not replace tasks as the visible unit of concurrency.

---

[1]   This is the opposite of tasks, where the decision was to make the parallel computation obvious, since tasks are used to express concurrent activities while tasklettes are used to map the application to the underlying platform.

Tasklettes behave as if each one is executed by a single Ada task that is explicitly created for the execution of the tasklettes and terminated immediately after execution of the code fragment. Instead of attempting to map tasklettes to cores, we map them to tasks and use the Ada tasking model to express the concurrency since tasks in Ada already have a computationally sound model that addresses priority and scheduling on multicore platforms. To not base this concurrency on tasks could mean extreme difficulty in using tasks and tasklettes in the same partition.

Any such tasks that execute the tasklettes are usually hidden from the programmer, and the only interface that the compiler exposes (even if we create our own task pool) is a set of packages and generics to let the pool provide the service. This interface is specified in section 5.

At the present time we are working to extend the model to include real-time behaviors, task priorities, and the Ravenscar tasking model. To date we have found no fundamental limitations that would prevent this extension.

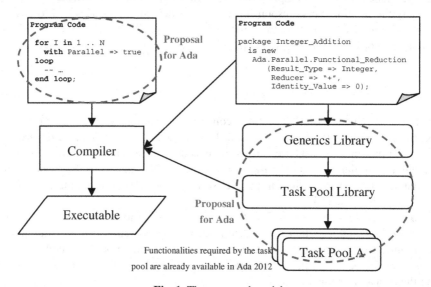

Fig. 1. The proposed model

We propose a runtime model where the execution of code fragments executed by multiple tasklettes is restricted to producing the same result as would happen if executed sequentially. This has some obvious constraints on the user code:

— Parallel code fragments must not update any non-atomic variable read by another code fragment that is executed in parallel, without making special language measures to protect the variable [2].

— Program execution must not proceed beyond the parallelized code until tasklettes executing that fragment have completed and delivered their results.

---

[2] If the underlying implementation does not use tasks, then protected operations and potentially blocking operations cannot be called directly from user code. As the proposed model is based on mapping tasklettes to tasks this restriction is not needed.

Our proposal includes an Ada interface to implement the semantic model provided in this paper. Compilers and runtimes would be free to provide an implementation that does not use the interface as long as the execution of the tasklettes has the same semantic effect given here. However, if a task pool is provided for the default, then it must be used as specified here. Figure 1 provides an overview of the proposed model.

4   Syntax

In this section we present the addition of parallelization abilities to subprograms and loops [3]. The most relevant addition to the language is the introduction of the `Parallel` aspect, which, when applied to a specific construct instructs the implementation that parallelization should be provided.

It is important to note that the programmer must also be able to specify the underlying behavior of the runtime, both controlling the scheduling of tasklettes and the parameters of the task pool. This is achieved through the programmer being able to interact with the underlying library as will be detailed in Section 5.

4.1   Parallel Subprograms

Subprograms are a natural candidate for parallelization, in particular for the case of pure functions, which are not intended to present side effects. Nevertheless, even subprograms that operate on shared data can be parallelized as it may be possible for the programmer to control contention, to verify that contention is controlled, or to verify that parallel access is on non-overlapping areas of data [4].

Two possibilities are provided for the placement of the aspect specification. One is to place `with Parallel` in the specification of the subprogram, and the second is for the syntax to be placed in the actual call.

The first method (on the subprogram specification) can be used to create default behavior and make the parallel nature visible to callers. The second approach supports legacy libraries, and allows the programmer to have a fine-grained control of the parallel behavior (at the time of call, e.g. due to different execution conditions).

In its simple form, if the programmer accepts the default behavior of the underlying task pool and tasklette scheduling, she just needs to include the Parallel aspect in the call to the subprogram:

```
Ret := Call (Parameters)
   with Parallel => True;
```

---

[3] We also considered the parallelization of blocks, but after analyzing we found that the syntax required to make them effective would be similar to declaration of "anonymous" subprograms, e.g. with in and out parameters, so we decided to propose that programmers specify parallel subprograms in these cases.

[4] Access even on non-overlapping areas of data may cause contention as a write into a variable may cause a cache line to be invalidated, thus impacting on variables in the same line.

Note that, in accordance to the rules for aspects [22], the => true can be omitted. In case **with** Parallel is not included the value of the aspect is false, so the subprogram cannot be executed asynchronously.

In order for the return of the parallel call to be "safe", and so that no waiting needs to be implemented explicitly by the programmer, the asynchronous call waits either on (what comes first):

— Access to the variable holding the call result, or
— The end of the enclosing scope of the call.

This restriction implements fully-strict parallelism [23], and guarantees that the asynchronous subprogram has access to the stack frame of the enclosing scope of the call in its execution, a similar approach as determined for Cilk, and which has been proposed for C++ [24]. An example for instance is a parallel solution for the Fibonacci series, which could be written as [5]:

```
function Fibonacci(N: Natural) return Natural is
   function Sequential_Fibonacci (N: Natural)
        return Natural is
      ... -- Some implementation of iterative fibonacci
   end  Sequential_Fibonacci;
begin
   if N < Cut then -- to stop parallelism (efficiency)
      return Sequential_Fibonacci(N);
   else
      return
        Fibonacci (N-1) with Parallel => True
        + Fibonacci (N-2) with Parallel => False;
   end if;
end Fibonacci;
```

We also considered that a way to control parallel actions is necessary, including (i) "select"ing on multiple alternative parallel actions, continuing after getting the first result, and (ii) directly requesting the abort of all tasklettes still pending in the current scope (for scope exit). We have identified this as future work.

4.2   Parallel Loops

Parallelizing loops is one of the best known examples of the advantages of parallel execution. A simple loop that can be parallelized is:

```
for I in 1 .. N
   with Parallel => True
loop --... end loop;
```

---

[5]   To increase efficiency this solution parallelizes one of the branches, since the existing task can do the N-2 branch, and stops parallelization when it is more efficient to go sequentially.

In the simple case the compiler could create *N* tasklette objects, one per iteration, which would be placed in the queue of the default task pool. This approach is only appropriate if each iteration is computationally intensive (e.g. ray tracing). In most cases, the advantages of parallelization are only obtained if some partitioning is used.

This partitioning could be performed by the compiler, dividing the range in P "chunks" (even with variable or varying dimensions), with P < N, e.g. based on the number of available cores.

Nevertheless, in most cases loop iterations are not independent, and some sort of reduction may be required. As an example, if the loop was calculating a sum, then each chunk would produce a partial value which would need to be reduced to one result. Generalizing, for some code:

```
X : User_Type := Some_Default;
for I in 1 .. N loop
  X := Func(X, I);
end loop;
```

the programmer could express the loop in terms of a formal parallel model, being able to identify to the compiler the reduction operation, the variable which will be partially calculated in each chunk of iterations and then accumulated (or reduced), and the identity value, which is used to initialize each partial result:

```
function G (Accumulator, Iteration_Result: User_Type)
  return User_Type is
  ... -- some function
begin
 X : User_Type := Some_Default;
 for I in 1 .. N
  with   Parallel => True, Reduction => G,
         Accumulator => X,
         Identity => Some_Identity_Value
 loop
    X := Func(X, I);
 end loop;
end;
```

Nevertheless, for the general case, the compiler may not be able to parallelize a sequential loop without the help of the programmer (e.g. even in simple aggregation loops, if the operation is not associative). One approach would be for the programmer to rewrite the loop in terms of the associative operation. For instance:

```
for I in 1 .. N loop
  Sub := Sub - Buffer(I);
end loop;
```

could be rewritten in order to have an associative operation being performed (Sub := Sub + (-Buffer(I)) [6]. This would nevertheless require the programmer to change the code. Instead, our proposal allows for the programmer to directly identify reduction and identity:

```
for I in 1 .. N
  with  Parallel => True, Reduction => "+",
        Accumulator => Sub, Identity => 0
loop
  Sub := Sub - Buffer(I);
end loop;
```

4.3   Explicit Control of Partitioning

For the cases that the partitioning is not easy to understand or the reduction operation is not as simple to identify (or the programmer prefers to explicitly handle it in the loop), we also allow for the explicit control of partitioning.

In its simple form, the programmer may partition the loop into "chunks", using a sequential iteration in each chunk. For example (for simplicity assuming that N is divisible by Chunk_Size):

```
for I in 1 .. N/Chunk_Size with Parallel => True
loop
  for J in I*Chunk_Size .. (I+1)*Chunk_Size-1
                with Parallel => False loop
    --...
  end loop;
end loop;
```

The Parallel => False in the inner loop is not necessary, but can be given for higher clarity. Chunk_Size can be a constant, a user variable (e.g. the user queries the number of cores in the platform) or even a function supplied by the task pool (e.g. how many tasks in the task pool are available).

The chunk policy can also be provided as an aspect of the loop. This allows more advanced partitioning approaches, with variable chunk sizes depending on the system load, dynamically managed by the underlying runtime. In this case, the start and finish of the chunk is obtained using attributes on the appropriate loop control variable:

```
for I in 1 .. N
        with Parallel => True,
             Chunk_Size => [N_Core | auto | dynamic]
loop
  for J in I'Chunk_First .. I'Chunk_Last loop
```

---

[6] Compilers may eventually be able to perform many automatic parallelizations in these simple examples being shown. Nevertheless the model is for the general case.

```
    -- Other attributes could give size and range
    -- No aspect in the inner loop so it is sequential
  end loop;
end loop;
```

Dependencies and reduction can be supported by declaring local variables inside the loop [7], and aggregating the result in a global variable (would need to be protected).

```
Sub := ...;
for I in 1 .. N loop
  Sub := Sub - Buffer(I);
end loop;
```

could become:

```
Sub := ...;
for I in 1 .. N with Parallel => True,
                     Accumulator => Sub
loop
  declare
    Local_Sub : Integer := 0;
  begin
    for J in I'Chunk_First .. I'Chunk_Last loop
      Local_Sub := Local_Sub - Buffer(I);
    end loop;
    Sub := Sub + Local_Sub;
  end;
end loop;
```

The Sub variable can now be updated in parallel. Therefore, the Accumulator aspect in the loop also signals the compiler that Sub must be protected.

A more complex case is when the code presents a loop-carried dependency, where subsequent iteration of a loop requires the computed value of the previous iteration:

```
Cumulative(1) := Histogram(1);
for I in 2 .. N loop
  Cumulative (I) := Cumulative (I-1) + Histogram(I);
end loop;
```

This code cannot be automatically converted into a parallel loop. It can nevertheless be parallelized using a prefix-sum algorithm [25], since the operation is associative.

The proposed approach also considers another level of abstraction, where the programmer is able to specify and control the underlying scheduling, manipulating more directly the operations being performed by the runtime. To support this control, an

---

[7] This could also allow the compiler to optimize the placement of variables in Non Uniform Memory Architectures (NUMA), as these variables will only be used in one core.

aspect `Parallel_Manager` is used, to specify the object that controls parallelism. This is presented in the next section.

5   Interface to the Runtime

The goal of the parallel runtime is to define an interface that provides flexibility to the application programmer, yet minimizes the implementation burden for the compiler writer. The desire is also to provide an interface that could be standardized so that a parallel library writer could plug in different parallelism strategies and allow the application programmer to have fine-grained control over the parallelism. The runtime consists of the task pool interface and the parallelism generics.

5.1   Task Pool Interface

We define an interface (partly shown below) to a task pool facility that provides the abstraction of managing a set of tasks as general purpose workers where a worker can be dispatched to a tasklette. The parallelism strategy implemented by a library writer interacts with the task pool. The model is that the parallelism manager offers work (procedure `Offer_Work`) to the task pool in the form of a work plan object defined by the library writer. The task pool releases a worker which calls the `Engage` method of the plan to perform the work. The `Engage` call is essentially the tasklette code that is executed, which ultimately calls out to execute the users' parallel algorithm.

```
package Ada.Parallel.Task_Pools is
   -- A Work Plan defines the work strategy
   type Work_Plan is limited interface;

   procedure Engage (Plan : Work_Plan) is abstract;
   -- When a worker starts executing, it engages the
   -- work plan. This call represents the tasklette
   -- code. Engage executes the plan. Upon returning,
   -- the Worker returns to the task pool

   type Task_Pool_Interface is limited interface;

   procedure Offer_Work
     (Pool : in out Task_Pool_Interface;
      Item : aliased in out Work_Plan'Class;
      Worker_Count : Positive_Worker_Count)
   is abstract;
   -- Allows a work plan to request workers from the
   -- task pool. The Work plan is offered to the task
   -- pool, which is then engaged by each worker
end Ada.Parallel.Task_Pools;
```

The task pool interface shown above can be implemented by extending the interface by any number of implementations that could be provided by library writers. Some possible candidates are unbounded task pools, where the number of workers can dynamically increase to accommodate the load, bounded task pools where the number of worker tasks is statically defined, and Ravenscar tasks pools that are compatible with the Ravenscar profile tasking restrictions.

5.2   Parallelism Control

Having presented the task pool interface, we now consider the parallelism generics that interact with the task pool. We have identified a need for two forms of parallelism in an application; non-recursive parallel subprograms, and divide and conquer parallelism, which covers both parallel loops and recursive subprograms.

5.3   Non-recursive Subprograms

The non-recursive subprogram case is perhaps the simplest, since there is only one call involved and thus there is no need for a parallelism strategy such as work-sharing, work-seeking, or work-stealing [8], nor is there a need for reduction. In addition, there are no specific restrictions on the parameter profile of the subprogram, and the compiler writer can implement the calls without the need for library support [9]. For example, the compiler can create a wrapper for each non-recursive subprogram to be called in parallel. The wrapper declares a tasklette which obtains a worker task from a task pool, and then invokes the real call from the context of the worker task. Since the tasklette is declared within the stack frame of the wrapper, it can issue the call to the real subprogram simply passing the parameters passed to the wrapper straight through to the real subprogram. The parallel non-recursive call is simple enough that it warrants no further discussion.

5.4   Divide and Conquer Parallelism

The other types of parallelism in our proposal are parallel loops and parallel recursion. These apply parallelism by utilizing a divide and conquer strategy. There are several possible sub-strategies. For instance, a load balancing sub-strategy might be utilized if the effort to process items in the loop varies through the iteration or if the recursion is unbalanced. Work-sharing might be chosen if the work can be divided more evenly. Regardless of the sub-strategy chosen, reduction may be needed if the parallelism produces a result. For these forms of parallelism, a library approach is proposed. Such a library implemented in Ada would involve generics, since the data types, loop iteration index types, and result types are user-defined and may range from simple elementary types such as Integer and Float, to complex user-defined record structures and tagged types.

---

[8]   More details on these strategies can be found in [26].
[9]   If a library for this strategy is provided, the compiler will implement the calls to this library.

The runtime library model for divide and conquer parallelism consists of a hierarchy of packages that can be selected for specific purposes. These libraries provide the parallelism, while the compiler performs a transformation from the syntax features described above.

The run time interface consists of a three stage generic instantiation (shown later):

— Stage 1 => Reduction primitives
— Stage 2 => Work type + Strategy Interface
— Stage 3 => Parallelism Strategy

The first instantiation allows the application programmer to specify the result type, the reducing function, and the identity value for the result type.

The second instantiation defines the data type describing the work to be processed in parallel, and defines the interface to be implemented by library writers for the third level instantiation. There are two possibilities here. If the parallelism is a parallel loop, then the work type is the iteration index type. This may be any user-defined scalar type. If the parallelism is for a recursive subprogram, then the work type is the data type that represents the work to be performed.

The third instantiation defines the parallelism strategy and how the work is to be performed in parallel. While the first two stages establish the parallelism framework and are proposed for standardization, the third level libraries implement the level 2 interface and may be provided by third-party library writers.

Level one Instantiation Interface

```
generic
  type Result_Type is private;
  with function Reducer (Left, Right : Result_Type)
               return Result_Type;
  Identity_Value : Result_Type;

package Ada.Parallel.Functional_Reduction is
end Ada.Parallel.Functional_Reduction;
```

As can be seen, the first instantiation is trivial, defines no operations, and requires no body [10]. This instantiation is only used if a result is to be generated, and allows a programmer to specify the reducing operation needed for the parallelism opportunity.

Level two Generic Interface for Parallel Loops

```
generic
   type Iteration_Index_Type is (<>);
package Ada.Parallel.Functional_Reduction.Loops is

   type Parallelism_Manager is limited interface;
```

---

[10] More complex situations, such as where the reducers are of different type from the result value, can be handled by other generics, with more parameters.

```
procedure Execute_Parallel_Loop
   (Manager : Parallelism_Manager;
    From    : Iteration_Index_Type
         := Iteration_Index_Type'First;
    To      : Iteration_Index_Type
         := Iteration_Index_Type'Last;
    Process : not null access procedure
         (Start, Finish : Iteration_Index_Type;
          Item : in out Result_Type);
    Result : in out Result_Type)
 is abstract;

end Ada.Parallel.Functional_Reduction.Loops;
```

The level two instantiation for parallel loops is a child package of the Functional_Reduction package of level 1. This package allows the programmer to specify the data type associated with the loop index as the Iteration_Index_Type. The manager type defines the interface to be implemented by the library writer for the level 3 instantiation. The library writer must also provide a constructor function called Create (with defaulted parameters) that returns a Manager object [11].

Level two Generic Interface for Recursive Subprograms

```
generic
   type Work_Type is private;
   -- Data type to be processed recursively

package Ada.Parallel.Functional_Reduction.Recursion is

   type Parallelism_Manager is limited interface;

   function Execute_Parallel_Subprogram
      (Manager : in out Parallelism_Manager;
       Item : Work_Type;
       Worker_Count : Worker_Count_Type :=
                             Default_Worker_Count;
       -- Top level item to process recursively
       Process : not null access function (
           Item : Work_Type) return Result_Type)
       return Result_Type
    is abstract;
end Ada.Parallel.Functional_Reduction.Recursion;
```

---

[11] This function is to be used by the compiler to create a manager object for each parallelism opportunity. The function must provide the parameters to match the aspects specified at the parallelism opportunity.

Similarly, the level 2 instantiation for recursive subprograms defines the interface that the library writer needs to implement and is proposed for standardization. The Execute_Parallel_Subprogram is invoked by a wrapper function generated by the compiler, which manages the parallelism opportunity. As before, a Create constructor function returns a manager object, which is called by compiler generated code to initialize an object declared in the declaration section of the wrapper function for the programmers' code.

5.5   Example: Parallel Loops

To demonstrate the 3 stage process, consider the earlier example to calculate the sum of integers from 1 to N.

The first stage generic instantiation sets up the reduction needed for Integer addition.

```
with Ada.Parallel.Functional_Reduction;
package Integer_Addition is new
   Ada.Parallel.Functional_Reduction
      (Result_Type => Integer,
       Reducer => "+",
       Identity_Value => 0);
```

For the second phase instantiation, we need to decide if the parallelism applies to a loop or to a recursive subprogram. In this case, we are interested in a loop. The package instantiation from the first phase is used to create the parallel loop generic.

```
with Integer_Addition;
with Ada.Parallel.Functional_Reduction.Loops;
package Integer_Addition_Loops is new
      Integer_Addition.Loops
         (Iteration_Index_Type => Integer);
```

For the third and final phase instantiation, we need to specify the parallelism strategy. For this phase, we can instantiate a generic library provided by a library writer, which may be a third party developer, a library provided by the compiler vendor, or a library written by the application programmer.

Assuming that a work sharing library is of interest for this loop, one might instantiate the third phase at library level to look something like:

```
with Integer_Addition_Loops;
with Ada.Parallel.Functional_Reduction.Loops.
                                          Work_Sharing;
package Work_Sharing_Integer_Addition_Loops is new
   Integer_Addition_Loops.Work_Sharing;
```

Now that the parallelism package has been fully instantiated, it can be used in an application program, to generate the parallelism.

```
with Work_Sharing_Integer_Addition_Loops;
with Ada.Parallel.Task_Pools.Bounded;
use Ada.Parallel;
package WSIA renames
                Work_Sharing_Integer_Addition_Loops;

-- ...
  declare
     Sum : Integer := 0;
  begin
    for I in 1 .. N
      with Parallel => True, Worker_Count => 4,
           Task_Pool => Task_Pools.Bounded.Default_Pool,
           Parallel_Manager => WSIA.Parallelism_Manager,
           Accumulator => Sum
    loop
        Sum := Sum + I;
    end loop;
    -- ...
```

Another example is provided in Appendix, illustrating how one might instantiate the parallelism generics to solve the parallel fibonacci problem recursively in parallel.

6   Conclusion and Future Work

We have shown a powerful model that permits fine grained concurrency to be added to Ada and is consistent with the Ada tasking model, which we intend to propose to the Ada standardization committee as an extension of Ada.

Our research indicates that we can not only add a fine-grained concurrency mechanism to Ada, as shown in this paper, but this fine grained concurrency can be specialized to behave correctly in situations where Ada must meet difficult constraints, such as in hard real-time systems. These additional capabilities are being refined and will be presented in other works (an initial model is provided in [27]).

The programmer should also have the ability to control execution of parallel tasklettes, aborting loop iterations that are no longer necessary (e.g. in a search operation). This will be further investigated. Other constructs that can be provided with parallelism annotations are select statements, which are identified as future work.

Acknowledgments. We would like to thank the anonymous reviewers for their valuable comments. This work was partially supported by Portuguese Funds through FCT (Portuguese Foundation for Science and Technology) and by ERDF (European Regional Development Fund) through COMPETE (Operational Programme 'Thematic Factors of Competitiveness'), within VIPCORE (ref. FCOMP-01-0124-FEDER-015006) and AVIACC (ref. FCOMP-01-0124-FEDER-020486) projects.

References

1. Hansen, P.B.: The Programming Language Concurrent Pascal. IEEE Transactions on Software Engineering 1(2), 199–207 (1975)
2. Hoare, C.A.R.: Communicating Sequential Processes. Prentice Hall (1985)
3. Ada Programming Language, ANSI/MIL-STD-1815A-1983 (1983)
4. Java Language Specification, http://www.oracle.com/java (last accessed February 2013)
5. Sutter, H., Larus, J.: Software and the concurrency revolution. Queue 3, 54–62 (2005)
6. Asanovic, K., Bodik, R., Catanzaro, B.C., Gebis, J.J., Husbands, P., Keutzer, K., Patterson, D.A., Plishker, W.L., Shalf, J., Williams, S.W., Yelick, K.A.: The landscape of parallel computing research: A view from Berkeley. Technical Report UCB/EECS-2006-183, EECS Department, University of California, Berkeley (December 2006)
7. Ada 83 Rationale, http://www.adaic.org/ada-resources/standards/ada83/ (last accessed February 2013)
8. Mayer, H.G., Jahnichen, S.: The data-parallel Ada run-time system, simulation and empirical results. In: Proceedings of Seventh International Parallel Processing Symposium, Newport, CA, USA, pp. 621–627 (April 1993)
9. Hind, M., Schonberg, E.: Efficient Loop-Level Parallelism in Ada. In: Proceedings of Tri-Ada 1991 (October 1991)
10. Thornley, J.: Integrating parallel dataflow programming with the Ada tasking model. In: Engle Jr., C.B. (ed.) Proceedings of TRI-Ada 1994. ACM, New York (1994)
11. Moore, B.: Parallelism generics for Ada 2005 and beyond. In: Proceedings of the ACM SIGAda Annual Conference (SIGAda 2010) (October 2010)
12. Ali, H., Pinho, L.M.: A parallel programming model for Ada. In: Proceedings of the ACM SIGAda Annual Conference (SIGAda 2011) (November 2011)
13. Hansen, P.B.: Structured Multiprogramming. Communications of the ACM 15(7) (July 1972)
14. Frigo, M., Leiserson, C.E., Randall, K.H.: The implementation of the cilk-5 multithreaded language. SIGPLAN Notice 33, 212–223 (1998)
15. Leiserson, C.: The Cilk++ concurrency platform. In: Proceedings of the 46th Annual Design Automation Conference. ACM, New York (2009)
16. Intel, Cilk Plus, http://software.intel.com/en-us/articles/intel-cilk-plus/ (last accessed February 2013)
17. Taft, T.: Designing ParaSail, a new programming language, http://parasail-programming-language.blogspot.pt/ (last accessed February 2013)
18. Intel. Threading Building Blocks, http://threadingbuildingblocks.org/ (last accessed February 2013)
19. Lea, D.: A Java fork/join framework. In: Proceedings of the ACM 2000 Conference on Java Grande, JAVA 2000, pp. 36–43. ACM, New York (2000)
20. Marowka, A.: Parallel computing on any desktop. Communications of the ACM 50, 74–78 (2007)
21. Microsoft. Task parallel library, http://msdn.microsoft.com/en-us/library/dd460717.aspx (last accessed February 2013)
22. Barnes, J.G.P.: Rationale for Ada 2012: 1 Contracts and aspects. Ada User Journal 32(4) (December 2011)
23. Blumofe, R.D., Leiserson, C.E.: Scheduling multithreaded computations by work stealing. Journal of the ACM 46(5), 720–748 (1999)
24. Halpern, P.: Strict Fork-Join Parallelism. JTC1/SC22/WG21 N3409 (September 2012)

25. Ladner, R.E., Fischer, M.J.: Parallel Prefix Computation. Journal of the ACM 27(4), 831–838 (1980)
26. Moore, B.: A comparison of work-sharing, work-seeking, and work-stealing parallelism strategies using Paraffin with Ada 2005. Ada User Journal 32(1) (March 2011), http://www.ada-europe.org (last accessed February 2013)
27. Moore, B., Michell, S., Pinho, L.M.: Parallelism in Ada: General Model and Ravenscar. In: 16th International Real-Time Ada Workshop, York, UK (April 2013)

Appendix - Parallel Recursive Subprogram Example

In the main part of the paper, an example was provided that illustrated the approach for fine grained parallelism control for parallel loops. This appendix provides a similar example that is intended to show the recursive subprogram case.

Once again a three state generic instantiation can be applied if the recursion needs to generate a result.   Here we consider the recursive Fibonacci example.

As with the parallel loop example, the reducing operation is integer addition, therefore the first stage instantiation from the loop example can be reused.

For the second stage instantiation, the recursive subprogram generic needs to be instantiated. In this case, the work type, `Integer`, is the type of the top level work item to be processed, which corresponds to the `Value` parameter of the Fibonacci function. We can then provide the following instantiation for the second phase.

```
with Integer_Addition; -- from Section 5
with Ada.Parallel.Functional_Reduction.Recursion;
package Integer_Addition_Recursion is new
      Integer_Addition.Recursion (Work_Type => Integer);
```

For the third phase, we will assume that a parallel library writer has provided a work-seeking library for recursion. As with the parallel loop case, the instantiation is straightforward, since there are no formal parameters to the generic.

```
with Integer_Addition_Recursion;
with Ada.Parallel.Functional_Reduction.
                            Recursion.Work_Seeking;
package Work_Seeking_Integer_Addition_Recursion is new
   Integer_Addition_Recursion.Work_Seeking;
```

Now that the third phase instantiation exists, the application programmer can rewrite the Fibonacci example as follows to obtain a parallel result with fine-grained control of the parallelism.

```
with Work_Seeking_Integer_Addition_Recursion;
with Ada.Parallel.Task_Pools.Bounded;
package WSeIA renames
             Work_Seeking_Integer_Addition_Recursion;
```

```
function Fibonacci (Value : Natural) return Natural
   with Parallel => True, Worker_Count => 4,
        Parallel_Manager => WSeIA.Parallelism_Manager,
        Task_Pool => Parallel.Task_Pools.Default_Pool;
```

As seen, the `Parallel_Manager` aspect can be provided in the spec (or body) of the subprogram, but can be overridden by the caller code. It specifies a manager to be used when the subprogram is called with `Parallel => True`.

The body of Fibonacci can be written in very much the same style as it would have been for the sequential case. In this case, the implementer of the Work-seeking abstraction declares an atomic boolean variable [26], `Seeking_Work`, which is referenced from the users' code to see if there are idle workers looking for more work. Note that an attribute must be provided that permits access to the parallelism manager object for the local scope.

```
function Fibonacci (Value : Natural) return Natural is
   Sequential_Cutoff : constant Integer := 22;
begin
   if Value < 2 then
      return Value;
   elsif  Parallel'Manager.Seeking_Work and then
         Value > Sequential_Cutoff then
      return
        Parallel_Fibonacci (Value - 2)
           with Parallel => True
         + Parallel_Fibonacci (Value - 1);
   else
      return Fibonacci (Value - 2) +
             Fibonacci (Value - 1);
   end if;
end Fibonacci;
```

Model-Based Deployment of Mission-Critical Spacecraft Applications on Multicore Processors

J. Reinier van Kampenhout and Robert Hilbrich

Fraunhofer FOKUS
Kaiserin-Augusta-Allee 31
10589 Berlin Germany
{j.r.van.kampenhout,robert.hilbrich}@fokus.fraunhofer.de
http://www.fokus.fraunhofer.de

Abstract. A variety of complex spacecraft applications, such as autonomous maneuvers based on image recognition, can benefit from the increased performance of multicore processors. On the other hand the redundant cores can also be used for fault-tolerance. Spacecraft missions more and more require a balanced trade-off between power, performance and reliability. Finding an optimal trade-off for each mission phase leads to new engineering challenges, especially regarding the efficient and safe deployment of software applications to hardware resources. We propose a model-based approach for the construction of software deployment schemes, and apply it to a spacecraft use case with two different mission phases to illustrate the benefits of such model-based software deployment.

Keywords: avionics, deployment, multicore, model-based engineering.

1 Introduction

After being widely adopted in the server, desktop and hand held markets, multicore processors now start to appear in the domain of safety-critical and mission-critical embedded systems. At the same time an ongoing trend to integrate functionality on shared platforms becomes apparent from initiatives such as Integrated Modular Avionics (IMA) [26,25] and AUTOSAR [2].

Similar ideas slowly start to emerge in the domain of spacecraft avionics. A holistic engineering approach to combine the two trends and exploit the full potential of multicores is required for the successful adoption of such processors. At the same time there is a significant increase in complexity that threatens the system reliability, and poses the challenge of managing this complexity to system architects, system engineers and software developers. In this work we propose a model-based systems engineering approach with software architecture deployment at its center.

In Section 2 we present the motivation for the use of multicore processors in spacecraft avionics and describe our own use case: a multicore based computing platform for space applications. Section 3 then describes the challenges that

H.B. Keller et al. (Eds.): Ada-Europe 2013, LNCS 7896, pp. 35–50, 2013.

arise by the use of multicore processors in complex space applications, and why existing engineering methods are at their limits. In Section 4 we describe our approach to model-based deployment, and present a first implementation that we apply to an example mission with two phases in Section 5.

Related Work

Recently the use of multicore processors in safety-critical domains has received much attention [11,23,12]. Of particular interest for these domains is the improvement of reliability by using the available parallelism [6,17]. Real-time scheduling has been an active research domain for decades, and recently several approaches to dynamic [4] and static [7,3] scheduling of mixed-criticality software tasks on multicores have been proposed. In the deployment process however the hardware usage and runtime scheduling are affected by the allocation and mapping of tasks [24,9]. Therefore these should be addressed in a unified systems engineering methodology in order to arrive at an integrated result in which the key properties are balanced [21,18]. Model-driven systems engineering offers the appropriate mechanisms to address these challenges [10]. Apart from that, *partitioning* is indispensable to guarantee the absence of interference between applications in the deployment of safety-critical systems [27,22]. One way to achieve this which currently receives much attention is by virtualization of resources [19,20,13,12].

2   Multicore Processors for Spacecraft Avionics

2.1   Space Mission Requirements

We recognize that the complexity of spacecraft applications in modern space missions has risen significantly over the last years. The widespread use of high-resolution sensors leads to the generation of large amounts of data. There is a clear trend to process these data on board in order to relieve the pressure on space-to-ground communications. In the imaging domain we see applications such as hyperspectral imaging, earth observation and synthetic-aperture radar systems. In communication, antennae arrays and broadband communication can benefit from advanced encoding algorithms. Another cluster of applications are solutions for autonomous Entry, Descent and Landing (EDL) or docking maneuvers in space. These can be based on advanced imaging processing algorithms. All these applications need a significant amount of computational power.

State-of-the-art systems often use highly specialized FPGA or DSP solutions. These are costly and limited to a relatively low functional complexity, and cannot be reconfigured easily once in flight. Such benefits are only offered by software-defined systems, which can execute complex dissimilar workloads and offer a flexibility that can be used to balance power, performance and fault tolerance. While specialized single-core processors are currently used in spacecraft avionics, their performance and energy consumption lags behind that of commercially available processors. Especially *multicore* processors provide an increase in processing power by exploiting the parallelism that is inherent to many applications, while combining energy-efficient semiconductor technologies, moderate clock rates and advanced power management functions. Such processors provide a major increase in versatility besides power and performance benefits. In the following sections we focus on the benefits and challenges of the use of multicore processors for space applications.

2.2 The MUSE Platform

As an answer to the increasing demand for computing power in space applications, we developed a satellite payload computer that builds on COTS multicore technology in the context of the MUSE project [5]. We employed the Freescale QorIQ P4080 processor, which features eight PowerPC e500 cores operating at 1.5 GHz. An additional advantage is the use of power saving silicon-on-insulator technology, which is less susceptible to single-event upsets that are due to the background radiation in space applications. Especially when using COTS components, the high reliability and availability demands for space computing can only be guaranteed when sufficient redundancy is provided on the system level.

The MUSE platform consists of two P4080 nodes on separate boards, connected by an additional I/O board that also contains the logic and connectors to other instruments. Thus a dual redundant symmetric 1-out-of-2 setup with several high-speed I/O channels is achieved (see Figure 1).

Each processing board furthermore contains DDR3 memory, radiation tolerant flash memory, and an FPGA that together with its symmetrical counterpart controls the worker/monitor configuration of the boards. The two FPGA's are connected to the processors over the Enhanced Local Bus (ELB) and implement watchdog functionality to monitor the status of the processor, as well as a synchronizing voter to generate reliable control outputs. Because the FPGA's are radiation tolerant and their logic is triple-mode redundant, the implementation as a whole is radiation-hardened. All large memory areas such as the DRAM, L3 and L2 caches are protected by error correction logic. Thus a design with multiple complementary mechanisms for fault-tolerance is achieved, with the ultimate safety net of a node switch where the monitor becomes worker if a fault in the latter can not be handled locally.

We implemented the software for the mission that was previously discussed in Section 2.1, namely that of autonomous EDL, which builds on an advanced image processing algorithm called *MoonDetect* [5]. Using a pre-loaded map of the moon's surface, the landing zone is recognized with help of one or more high-resolution cameras. The application was implemented on top of a standard embedded operating system and uses the redundant cores of the multi-core processor not only to maximize computing power, but also to increase fault tolerance by the redundant execution of critical functions.

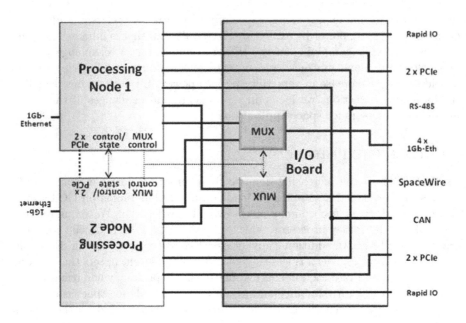

Fig. 1. The architecture of the MUSE platform with one I/O board and two redundant processing nodes

3 Emerging Engineering Challenges

3.1 Dynamic Mission Requirements

The increasing functional requirements that we described in Section 2.1 translate to novel and more complex resource requirements for space missions. Mission requirements especially become more dynamic, there are three main drivers for this.

Firstly, missions become more and more complex and thus include multiple applications with different criticality levels that each have unique requirements regarding power, performance and reliability. The engineering process must ensure that the tasks of each application are mapped and scheduled so that there is no unintended interference during simultaneous execution. We will elaborate on this in Section 3.2.

Secondly, deep-space and planet exploration missions usually consist of different phases. To execute multiple functions with different criticality levels in each phase of the mission, the deployment of software-based platforms must be *dynamically reconfigured.*

Thirdly, support for online software updates is desirable for both maintenance and configuration changes caused by a revision of the mission targets. This again requires dynamic reconfiguration, we focus on this subject in Section 3.3.

3.2   Multi-function Integration within a Mission Phase

The requirements for the spacecraft missions that we previously described have a complexity that requires an implementation based on multiple applications. In our example, an image recognition algorithm is executed in parallel with a camera driver and a control task that monitors the system status. As these applications have different requirements, we are dealing with *mixed criticality* software for which the use of time and space partitioning is indispensable, as described in [29]. This publication also mentions a reduced integration effort, hardware savings, fault containment and increased security between applications as additional advantages of a partitioning approach. Partitioning in time assures that the execution of a software application in one partition does not affect timely behaviour of a software application in another partition.

Partitioning in space on the other hand protects the data and private devices of partitions by exclusively allocating memory and other hardware resources such as busses and I/O interfaces. Thus partitioning isolates applications from each other. This functionality is usually provided by the operating system [27]. Correct partitioning can however not be achieved with mere isolation, as safety requirements such as redundancy also impose constraints on the deployment. A deployment only based on safety requirements however would lead to inefficient resource usage, because simultaneous access to shared resources will be blocked by the isolation mechanism. Therefore we propose a method for optimizing the deployment according to the changing resource requirements.

3.3   Dynamic Reconfiguration between Multiple Mission Phases

A spacecraft mission comprises multiple phases which are executed over time during the mission. Each phase has different requirements so that the resource utilization trade-off between power, performance and reliability may need to be re-balanced at run-time. Dynamic reconfiguration allows to exploit the flexibility of multicore processors to switch from one phase to another. These transitions require a change and perhaps transformation of partitions, which is not accounted for in classical time and space partitioning. Thus an extension of these concepts is required in order to deal with data integrity and security, and to minimize and control the disruption of service. The phase-based ("mode-based") partitioning that we proposed in [16] is a first step in this direction. A reconfiguration mechanism furthermore simplifies maintenance and allows online software updates.

We conclude that the versatility of multicore processors can be exploited with existing methods such as partitioning, but enhancements are necessary to deal with the extended spatial dimension and to better support varying requirements of multiple mission phases as well as online updates.

4   Model-Based Software Deployment

Software deployment refers to the assignment of hardware resources, such as CPU time, memory, and I/O access to software tasks. This assignment process results in a *deployment scheme*. We distinguish between spatial and temporal deployment. The former leads to the mapping of a task to a set of hardware resources, such as a processor or electronic control unit. The latter concerns the execution schedule of each hardware resource in time. A deployment is correct if the proper type and amount of resources is assigned to all tasks at the right time. The operating system must ensure that the temporal deployment is properly executed at runtime.

There are two prerequisites for successful deployment: software must be *distributable* and *isolatable*. The trend towards function-oriented development ensures the dependencies between software and hardware are dissolving. This is enabled by standardized interfaces such as described in the ARINC 653 Apex [1] and integrated modular avionics (IMA) [26,25] for the avionics domain, and in AUTOSAR [2] for the automotive domain. The ability to distribute tasks on its own however is not sufficient for building cost-effective mission-critical embedded systems, this capability must be complemented with time and space isolation. There are commercially available hypervisors and tools that provide such isolation on modern multicore architectures.

The correctness of a software deployment scheme has a direct impact on the extra-functional requirements of embedded software, such as real-time behaviour and reliability. Furthermore the deployment scheme determines the amount of resources that are required, and thus its efficiency has a significant influence on the hardware costs for a system. Because the trend towards integrating software from different vendors on one electronic control unit increases, a deployment scheme is the central asset and synchronization point for different development teams during the system integration phase. Therefore we address these issues by exploring an automated deployment approach based on models.

4.1   Engineering Methodology

Traditional engineering methodologies for software-based systems require a high number of development iterations and prototypes, and the correctness of the system is often primarily assured by observing the system behaviour after it has been built [21]. This becomes more and more difficult as the complexity of the system and software architecture increases, and analytical approaches to assure correct timing behaviour do not suffice for modern multicore processors [28].

In our research we explore an alternative engineering methodology, which is rooted in the "Correctness by Construction" (CbyC) principle. CbyC is based on the observation that the correctness of a complex system should be argued "*in terms of the manner in which it had been produced, rather than just observing operational behaviour*" [8,14].

We applied this approach to the construction of software deployment schemes. In order to assure correctness, we use models to capture deployment requirements as well as architectural properties and capabilities in a clear and unambiguous way. The explicit distinction between problem statement, solution construction strategy and solution proves to be beneficial to achieve optimized, re-usable architectures.

Our approach for the construction of a deployment scheme is depicted in Fig. 2a. Due to the complexity of the solution space, the spatial and temporal deployment are addressed consecutively. Therefore our methodology comprises two steps that distinctly focus on the spatial ("mapping") and temporal deployment ("scheduling"). Within each step, different types of deployment requirements and engineering constraints are addressed. Several iterations between these two steps may be required before valid a deployment scheme is obtained.

However, in order to account for the knowledge of experts, we distinguish between *valid* and *desired* solutions (see Fig. 2b). Valid solutions are all those that are correct with regard to the specified requirements. This set might be very large. The desired solutions on the other hand are valid, but also optimal with respect to certain optimization criteria provided by a domain expert. Thus we achieve solutions that are not only formally correct, but also incorporate valuable knowledge and experiences from those experts.

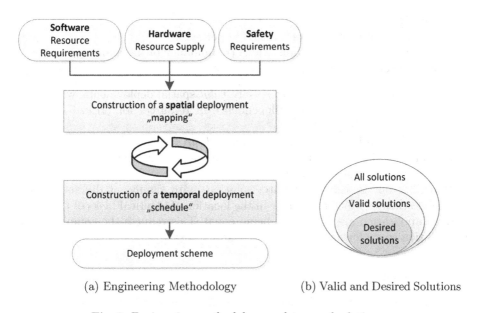

(a) Engineering Methodology   (b) Valid and Desired Solutions

Fig. 2. Engineering methodology and types of solutions

This methodology was implemented in a prototype tool suite (see Section 5). It allows us to automatically construct a correct and optimized deployment scheme for our use-case within minutes.

4.2   Construction of Mappings

Where spatial deployment could be performed manually for a handful of single-core processors, it is not viable for complex systems with hundreds of cores spread over dozens of processors. This is especially true when we consider the need for a safe dynamic reconfiguration to optimize the resource utilization. Besides, the mapping of safety-critical systems does not only depend on the schedulability, but also on the satisfaction of other safety-related criteria, such as redundancy, dissimilarity and independence.

Applications that belong to two redundant partitions for instance are usually not allowed to be mapped on the same core or processor, because that would violate safety requirements. Some safety critical applications contain partitions that feature a dissimilar implementation of the same functionality. Depending on the criticality level, these partitions may need to be mapped onto dissimilar processors and configured to use dissimilar communication channels to account for undetected design errors.

Our prototype tool generates all valid mappings of software components onto processor cores. It matches the resources offered by the underlying hardware architectures to the resource requirements of the applications.

Currently the following *matching criteria* are implemented:

– type of processors, cores and I/O interfaces;
– capacity of processors, cores and I/O interfaces;
– safety relations between applications (redundancy or dissimilarity);
– communication intensity between applications, in order to express proximity.

The first three criteria are used to specify *valid* spatial deployments, where the correct type, amount and the independence of resources for critical software components has to be guaranteed.

Metrics and optimization strategies for a *desired* spatial deployment on the other hand are based on criteria such as minimizing average communication distances and equal load distribution.

Note that our tool only generates solutions with significant difference. Deployment schemes which only differ in the location of identical tasks of the same parallel application are treated as being equal. This reduces the complexity of the solution space for applications with parallel tasks.

4.3   Construction of Schedules

Our model-based approach for the construction of static operating system schedules for multicores is based on the following assumptions. To achieve predictable and deterministic real-time behaviour for a system that relies only on periodical tasks with known periods, the following information (or at least an estimation) must be available at design time:

1. timing characteristics such as the worst case execution time (WCET), period and jitter, of all tasks within an application;
2. dependencies between tasks;
3. the access patterns of external resources of all applications.

A key aspect of static scheduling is that all conflicts that may appear at run-time and lead to unpredictable timing are resolved at design time. Our approach aims to construct and optimize the schedule beforehand to avoid cumbersome timing analysis afterwards.

For this we developed a prototype scheduling tool [15]. It automatically generates a valid static schedule that satisfies the timing characteristics of a given set of applications on a given hardware architecture. As the underlying problem is NP-hard, there are many solutions and the user can adjust the generated schedules for specific needs and purposes. Our scheduler ensures that no constraints are violated during the adjustment process.

Based on constraint-solving strategies specifically tuned for the problem, our scheduler constructs a schedule that satisfies the constraints defined in the input model. This model and the problem specifications have been developed to suit the needs of the safety-critical aerospace domain. All execution times for software tasks should be based on a worst-case analysis.

The resulting schedule is input for a time-triggered OS dispatcher that executes the tasks at run-time. External resources can be separately modelled and incorporated in the schedule construction process. After being approved by the certification authority, the schedule is used in the final configuration of the operating system.

5 Use-Case: Spacecraft Software Deployment on the MUSE Platform

In this section we describe our use-case, a real mission consisting of two phases to show our approach to model-based software deployment on the fault-tolerant MUSE hardware platform.

5.1 Mission Description

We implemented one of the previously discussed missions, namely that of autonomous EDL based on images provided by a Camera Driver (CamDr). An optimal performance can be achieved if MoonDetect (MD), our image recognition application, is executed on eight cores in parallel, as depicted on the left hand side of Figure 3. Here, one instance of MoonDetect is executed, its result are saved with triple redundancy and checked for plausibility by independent tasks (Plausibility Check, PC). The ELB driver (ELBDr) collects these results and transfers them shifted in time after which they are voted in the FPGA, our radiation hardened component.

Furthermore we consider the supervisor system application, which consists of two redundant tasks in a worker/monitor configuration (SVWorker/SVmonitor). This application has a higher criticality than MoonDetect, and thus we are dealing with mixed-criticality as discussed in Section 3.2.

The main goal in this phase is to recognize the landing area from a great distance, for which high performance is necessary because of the large area that must be covered. At a resolution of 800x600 pixels we achieved a frame rate of 23 fps when MoonDetect was executed on eight cores.

In the second phase the spacecraft descends for landing, and reliability becomes more important because a fault might lead to loss of the spacecraft. The frame rate can however be reduced because the target area is already recognized and the algorithm is only used for course alterations that are performed every few seconds or so. Thus in this phase an architecture such as depicted on the right hand side of Figure 3 is more suitable. Here two cameras are used, there are two (possibly dissimilar) instances of MoonDetect on four cores each, and the data path of each instance still has triple-mode redundancy. We expect that in this case the overhead will reduce the frame rate to less than half than that of the eight-core solution, and indeed we measured 11 fps at 800x600 in the actual setup.

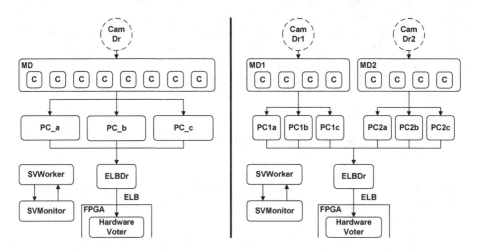

Fig. 3. Two mission phases: on the left an eight-core solution with triple redundant datapath is shown, the solution on the right features two redundant instances of the algorithm that use four cores each

Our example mission consists of two phases. Both contain mission-critical applications and the phases must be dynamically switched over time. The mission thus contains the challenges we initially described in Section 3. In the remainder of this section we will describe our approach to automatically deploy these two phases on the MUSE hardware. As the software on both processors is identical in this mission, we will show the workflow for one processor only. Our tools however can handle multiple (distributed) processors with dissimilar workloads as well.

5.2   Spatial Deployment - "Mapping"

As described in Section 4.2, the generation of correct mappings requires modelling the resources provided by the hardware architecture and the demands of software components. In our use-case, we employ an eight core processor (see Section 2.2).

Although all cores on the P4080 are physically connected to all I/O interfaces, we imposed additional access constraints on I/O interfaces for reliability purposes. Therefore Ethernet connections are allowed on core 1 and 2 only, and ELB connections only on core 3. The resulting hardware model is contained in Listing 1.1. The computational capacity and I/O access capabilities are specified for each core within a processor.

```
 1   Hardware {
 2       Processor QorIQ_P4080 {
 3       Core C1 {
 4           Capacity = 100;
 5           Provides IO access = Ethernet;
 6       };
 7
 8       [...]
 9
10       Core C3 {
11           Capacity = 100;
12           Provides IO access = EnhancedLocalBus;
13       };
14
15       [...]
16   }
17   }
```

Listing 1.1. Modelling the QorIQ P4080 hardware architecture

The software architecture is modelled similarly (see Listing 1.2). Applications are modelled per task, thus each "*Application*" is mapped onto a single core. An "*Application*" requires a certain amount of computational capacity, as well as access to specific I/O interfaces.

```
 1   Software {
 2       Application CamDr {
 3           Core Utilization = 2;
 4           Requires IO access = Ethernet;
 5       };
 6
 7       Application ELBDr {
 8           Core Utilization = 2;
 9           Requires IO access = EnhancedLocalBus;
10       };
11
12       Application MD_a {
13           Core Utilization = 90;
14       };
15
16       Application MD_b {
17           Core Utilization = 90;
18       };
19
20       [...]
21
22       Application PC_a {
23           Core Utilization = 1;
24       };
25
26       [...]
27   }
```

Listing 1.2. Modelling the software architecture

In addition to the matching of resource supply and demand, the correctness of a mapping depends on reliability criteria. Using *independent* resources is a significant prerequisite for robustness and reliability.

In our use-case we limit our focus to independence on the core level, which means that two redundant applications are not allowed to be deployed on the same core. These redundancy requirements are specified in Listing 1.3.

```
1  Relations {
2      MD_a, MD_b, MD_c, MD_d, MD_e, MD_f, MD_g, MD_h redundant;
3      SVWorker, SVMonitor, CamDr, ELBDr redundant;
4      PC_a, PC_b, PC_c redundant;
5  }
```

Listing 1.3. Modelling reliability relations for spatial deployment (phase 1)

With this modelling approach we generated mappings for both phases. The results for each phase are shown in Table 1. The generation process took about 1 second on a standard laptop.

Table 1. Result of the spatial deployment for phase 1 (upper half) and 2 (lower half)

Phase	Cores							
	C_1	C_2	C_3	C_4	C_5	C_6	C_7	C_8
1	MD_a	CamDr	ELBDr	MD_d	MD_e	MD_f	MD_g	MD_h
	PC_a	MD_b	MD_c	SVMonitor				
	SVworker	PC_b	PC_c					
2	MD_1a	MD_1b	MD_1c	MD_1d	MD_2a	MD_2b	MD_2c	MD_2d
	PC1a	PC1b	PC1c	SVMonitor	SVWorker	PC2a	PC2b	PC2c
	CamDr1	CamDr2	ELBDr					

5.3 Temporal Deployment - "Static Scheduling"

In order to initiate the scheduling process, several input parameters are required. Global parameters include the hyperperiod duration and switching time between applications (OS overhead), which we fixed at 0.5 milliseconds. Then the processor is modelled as follows:

```
1  def_processor
2      id('1'),
3      name('P4080'),
4      cores(8).
```

Listing 1.4. The processor model

For the modelling of applications timing information is needed, the execution time of MoonDetect can be deduced from the frame rate. Although we measured that the camera and ELB drivers, the supervisor and the plausibility checks have execution times in the order of microseconds, we will model them all with 1 millisecond to be able to depict them on the same scale. An application model looks as follows:

```
1  def_application
2    id(CamDr),
3    processor('1'),
4    cores_possible(3),
5    period(500),
6    duration(10).
```

Listing 1.5. The model of the CamDriver application

We see that this process is only allowed to be executed on core C_3, which is the result of the mapping process. Finally the dependencies that are needed for the scheduling must be specified. They are implied by Figure 3. Such dependencies may be specified in the following way.

```
1  def_after
2    id1(CamDr),
3    id2(moondetect),
4    distance(0,10).
```

Listing 1.6. Specifying a dependency

Figure 4 shows the schedules of one execution period of each phase. The first phase is shown in the upper eight horizontal bars, time is on the horizontal axis. We see that MoonDetect, as expected, requires the bulk of the processing power. Shorter tasks are executed in parallel to each other whenever possible.

In the second phase depicted in the lower eight bars we see that two instances of MoonDetect are executed in parallel and subsequently have a longer execution time, and that there are six instances of the plausibility check task instead of three. Because of the parallel instances of MoonDetect the frame rate deteriorates. In the first phase it is 20 fps (or a hyperperiod of 50 ms), in the second we achieve 10.4 fps (hyperperiod is 96 ms).

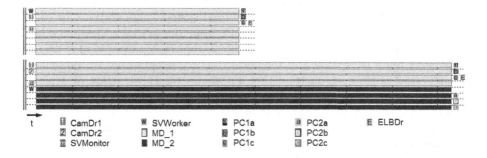

t	1 CamDr1	W SVWorker	8 PC1a	a PC2a	E ELBDr
	2 CamDr2	☐ MD_1	5 PC1b	☐ PC2b	
	⊞ SVMonitor	■ MD_2	⊠ PC1c	⊠ PC2c	

Fig. 4. The schedule of one period of phase 1 (upper eight bars) and 2 (lower eight bars). The horizontal axis represents time, on the bottom the task identifiers are indexed.

Between the two phases dynamic reconfiguration is necessary as both the mapping and scheduling change because tasks are started and migrated. Startup and migration times in our system are negligible with these execution times, and thus a phase switch can take place without noticeable disruption of service. A switch could however also be modeled as separate phase in which the startup and migration times are precisely indicated.

While our example is somewhat simplified and the final deployment scheme could have been produced manually, the benefit of using a model-based approach becomes especially apparent when more tasks and more resources have to be incorporated. With the advent of manycore processors comes the likelihood that the system complexity will significantly rise in the near future. At this point, manual processing of problems with such orders of magnitudes is costly, error prone and inefficient. Our automated approach completes in mere seconds, its result is *correct by construction* and a new iteration can be started with one click. Furthermore, optimization criteria can be easily modified so that existing models can be efficiently re-used.

6   Conclusions

In this paper we discussed the advantages of using multicore processors in spacecraft avionics, and recognized that many missions can benefit from the increased computing power. We introduced our MUSE hardware platform that comprises two eight-core processors and focused on the engineering challenges that come with increasingly diverse mission requirements. Multicore processors seem a future-proof platform for space applications as they offer the flexibility to support these requirements. The push towards multi-function integration leads to new challenges that are created by applications with different criticality levels.

Safe integration requires the operating system to offer time and space partitioning extended to support multicores, in concert with correct deployment. Comprehensive mission requirements result in multiple mission phases and corresponding mode-switches that must be accounted for. Such dynamic reconfiguration furthermore allows online software updates.

Exploiting the potential of multicores in spacecraft avionics requires an engineering method that efficiently builds optimized system configurations for each phase of a mission. The challenge to profit from the available flexibility becomes apparent in the software deployment. A correct deployment of software components relies on spatial and temporal resource assignment. We presented a model-based engineering method that automates the construction of deployments. It facilitates the efficient design of complex software architectures and has a result that is "Correct by Construction".

Finally we presented an example mission consisting of two phases which contain mixed-criticality applications. We deployed these phases onto the MUSE hardware platform and showed the advantages of our engineering approach, namely that, once a phase is modelled, a correct deployment scheme can be generated almost instantly. This allows quick feedback and easy balancing of parameters in the development process. In concert with the operating system, isolated execution of mission-critical applications along with non-critical applications and can be handled. Multiple deployment schemes allow multi-phase missions provided that mode-switches are well-defined.

References

1. ARINC. ARINC Specification 653P1-2: Avionics Application Software Standard Interface Part 1 - Required Services. Technical report, Aeronautical Radio Inc., Maryland, USA (December 2005)
2. AUTOSAR. Layered Software Architecture (November 2010), http://autosar.org/download/R4.0/AUTOSAR_EXP_LayeredSoftwareArchitecture.pdf
3. Baro, J., Boniol, F., Cordovilla, M., Noulard, E., Pagetti, C.: Off-line (Optimal) multiprocessor scheduling of dependent periodic tasks. In: Proceedings of the 27th Annual ACM Symposium on Applied Computing, SAC 2012, pp. 1815–1820. ACM, New York (2012)
4. Baruah, S., Bonifaci, V., D'Angelo, G., Li, H., Marchetti-Spaccamela, A., Megow, N., Stougie, L.: Scheduling Real-Time Mixed-Criticality Jobs. IEEE Transactions on Computers 61(8), 1140–1152 (2012)
5. Behr, P.M., Haulsen, I., van Kampenhout, J.R., Pletner, S.: Multi-Core Technology for Fault Tolerant High-Performance Spacecraft Computer Systems. In: DASIA (2012)
6. Borkar, S.: Designing reliable systems from unreliable components: the challenges of transistor variability and degradation. IEEE Micro 25(6), 10–16 (2005)
7. Brocaly, V., Masmanoy, M., Ripolly, I., Crespoy, A., Balbastrey, P., Metge, J.-J.: Xoncrete: a scheduling tool for partitioned real-time systems. In: Proceedings of the Embedded Real Time Software and Systems Conference, ERTS2 2010 (May 2010)
8. Chapman, R.: Correctness by construction: a manifesto for high integrity software. In: Proceedings of the 10th Australian Workshop on Safety Critical Systems and Software, SCS 2005, vol. 55, pp. 43–46. Australian Computer Society, Inc., Darlinghurst (2006)
9. Chou, C.-L., Marculescu, R.: User-Aware Dynamic Task Allocation in Networks-on-Chip. In: 2008 Design, Automation and Test in Europe, pp. 1232–1237. IEEE (März 2008)
10. Deng, G., Schmidt, D.C., Gokhale, A.: Addressing crosscutting deployment and configuration concerns of distributed real-time and embedded systems via aspect-oriented & model-driven software development. In: Proceedings of the 28th International Conference on Software Engineering, ICSE 2006, pp. 811–814. ACM, New York (2006)
11. Fuchsen, R.: How to address certification for multi-core based IMA platforms: Current status and potential solutions. In: 2010 IEEE/AIAA 29th Digital Avionics Systems Conference, DASC, pp. 5.E.3-1–5.E.3-11 (October 2010)
12. Gaska, T., Werner, B., Flagg, D.: Applying virtualization to avionics systems – The integration challenges. In: 2010 IEEE/AIAA 29th Digital Avionics Systems Conference, DASC, pp. 5.E.1-1–5.E.1-19 (2010)
13. Heiser, G.: The role of virtualization in embedded systems. In: Proceedings of the 1st Workshop on Isolation and Integration in Embedded Systems, IIES 2008, pp. 11–16. ACM Press, New York (2008)

14. Hilbrich, R.: How to Safely Integrate Multiple Applications on Embedded Many-Core Systems by Applying the "Correctness by Construction" Principle. Advances in Software Engineering 2012(354274), 14 (2012)
15. Hilbrich, R., Goltz, H.-J.: Model-based generation of static schedules for safety critical multi-core systems in the avionics domain. In: Proceeding of the 4th International Workshop on Multicore Software Engineering, IWMSE 2011, pp. 9–16. ACM, New York (2011)
16. Hilbrich, R., van Kampenhout, J.R.: Partitioning and Task Transfer on NoC-based Many-Core Processors in the Avionics Domain. In: 4. Workshop: Entwicklung zuverlässiger Software-Systeme (Stuttgart, Deutschland) and Journal "Softwaretechniktrends" (2011)
17. Jacobs, A., Cieslewski, G., George, A.: Adaptive Software-based Fault Tolerance for Space Multicore Processing. In: Workshop for Multicore Processors For Space - Opportunities and Challenges, IEEE International Conference on Space Mission Challenges for Information Technology, SMC-IT (2009)
18. Jamshidi, M.: System of systems engineering: innovations for the 21st century. Wiley series in systems engineering and management. Wiley (2009)
19. Kaiser, R.: Alternatives for scheduling virtual machines in real-time embedded systems. In: Proceedings of the 1st Workshop on Isolation and Integration in Embedded Systems, IIES 2008, pp. 5–10. ACM, New York (2008)
20. Kaiser, R.: Virtualisierung von Mehrprozessorsystemen mit Echtzeitanwendungen. Dissertation, Universität Koblenz-Landau (June 2009)
21. Kossiakoff, A., Sweet, W., Seymour, S., Biemer, S.: Systems Engineering Principles and Practice. Wiley Series in Systems Engineering and Management. Wiley (2011)
22. Leroux, P.N., Johnson, K.: Using Resource Partitioning to Build Secure, Survivable Embedded Systems. Technical report, QNX Software Systems (2009)
23. Nowotsch, J., Paulitsch, M.: Leveraging Multi-Core Computing Architectures in Avionics. In: 2012 European Dependable Computing Conference (2012)
24. Pinello, C., Carloni, L., Sangiovanni-Vincentelli, A.: Fault-Tolerant Distributed Deployment of Embedded Control Software. IEEE Transactions on Computer-Aided Design of Integrated Circuits and Systems 27(5), 906–919 (2008)
25. Prisaznuk, P.J.: ARINC 653 role in Integrated Modular Avionics (IMA). In: 2008 IEEE/AIAA 27th Digital Avionics Systems Conference, pp. 1.E.5-1–1.E.5-10. IEEE (2008)
26. RTCA. Integrated Modular Architecture – Development Guidance and Certification Considerations (2005)
27. Rushby, J.: Partitioning for Safety and Security: Requirements, Mechanisms, and Assurance. NASA Contractor Report CR-1999-209347, NASA Langley Research Center (June 1999)
28. Wilhelm, R., Grund, D., Reineke, J., Schlickling, M., Pister, M., Ferdinand, C.: Memory Hierarchies, Pipelines, and Buses for Future Architectures in Time-Critical Embedded Systems. IEEE Transactions on Computer-Aided Design of Integrated Circuits and Systems 28(7), 966–978 (2009)
29. Windsor, J., Hjortnaes, K.: Time and Space Partitioning in Spacecraft Avionics. In: Third IEEE International Conference on Space Mission Challenges for Information Technology, SMC-IT 2009, pp. 13–20 (July 2009)

A SPARK/Ada CubeSat Control Program

Carl Brandon[1] and Peter Chapin[2]

[1] Vermont Technical College, Randolph Center VT 05061, USA
[2] Vermont Technical College, Williston VT 05495, USA
{CBrandon,PChapin}@vtc.edu

Abstract. With software's increasing role in safety-critical and security sensitive infrastructure it is of paramount importance to educate the next generation of software engineers in the use of high integrity development methods. In this paper we discuss our experience training undergraduate students in the use of SPARK toward the construction of a mission-critical embedded system. In particular the students designed and implemented the control program for a CubeSat nano-satellite that will orbit the Earth as the first step toward the ultimate goal of building a prototype CubeSat that will go to the Moon. Our work shows that inexperienced undergraduates can learn to use SPARK to produce more robust software than might otherwise be the case, even in the environment of a volatile student project.

Keywords: SPARK, student project, CubeSat.

1 Introduction

We received a 2009 NASA Consortium Development Grant for work on prototyping and analyzing technologies for a self propelled CubeSat to the Moon that will orbit or land on it. No CubeSat has yet left low earth orbit. The Consortium Development Grant is to have several institutions work together on a project with cooperation with one or more NASA centers. Carl Brandon, as the Scientific Principal Investigator, is leading the project from Vermont Technical College (VTC), with groups at the University of Vermont, Norwich University, and students from St. Michaels College. The construction of the CubeSat and the production of the control software and translation of the navigation software are begin done at Vermont Technical College at both our Randolph Center (main) and Williston campuses. This software work is being done mostly by students under the direction of Peter Chapin. The star tracker camera analysis of near body images is being done at Norwich University by students under the direction of Danner Friend and Jacques Beneat. The analysis of low energy transfer paths to the Moon and radiation exposure analysis is being done at the University of Vermont with students under the direction of Jun Yu.

The eventual goal of the project is to build and get launched a triple CubeSat which will be self propelled to the Moon. Two paths are being investigated. Both will start with a piggy-back ride on a geosynchronous communications satellite

H.B. Keller et al. (Eds.): Ada-Europe 2013, LNCS 7896, pp. 51–64, 2013.

launch. One option will be for a double CubeSat "booster" with four mono-propellant (hydroxyl ammonium nitrate – methanol (HAN)) thrusters carrying a single CubeSat lander (also with four mono-propellant thrusters) from the apogee of the geosynchronous transfer ellipse on a direct Hohmann transfer orbit to the Moon, à la the Apollo missions. The booster would then insert into a Lunar orbit with the lander after a trip of about a week. The lander would then separate from the booster and use its own thrusters for a descent and soft landing on the Moon.

The second option, and more likely due to the hazard of flammable chemical propellants on an expensive communication satellite launch, would be for a xenon ion drive. It would contain 0.5–0.75 kg of xenon in a carbon fiber tank at 200–300 atmospheres. This triple CubeSat would also get a ride to a geosynchronous transfer ellipse, but would stay in the ellipse with a burn of the xenon ion engine near perigee during each orbit of the Earth. This would gradually increase the size of the ellipse over a period of about 10 months when the apogee would reach the Lagrange point, L_1, about three quarters of the way to the Moon. The ellipse would then be "flipped" to an orbit about the Moon, and the xenon ion drive would burn at perilune during each orbit over a period of about 6 months until the final, relatively low orbit is obtained.

We were selected by NASA for a test flight as part of the ELaNa IV (Educational Launch of Nano-satellites) mission. We will be testing the navigation and other systems that would be used on a Lunar mission. The test spacecraft, a single CubeSat (10 cm x 10 cm x 10 cm, 1.33 kg) will be launched in October, 2013, into a 500 km orbit, as a secondary payload on the U. S. Air Force ORS-3 (Office of Responsive Space) mission on a Minotaur 1 [10] launch vehicle from Wallops Island, Virginia. The navigation portion will use the NASA Goddard Space Flight Center developed GEONS (Goddard Enhanced Onboard Navigation System) software package. We have started to rewrite that C program in SPARK, which would be completed for the Lunar mission. If we are successful in obtaining additional funding, the Lunar flight would follow the test flight by about six years.

The control program for the ELaNa IV CubeSat is being written in SPARK for greatly increased reliability over the C language software used in almost all CubeSats to date. Most CubeSat failures are believed to be software related. The success of the fairly complicated software on the ELaNa CubeSat will give us confidence for the much more complicated and expensive Lunar mission.

2   System Overview

The CubeSat system has several components that are controlled by software, either running on their own hardware or by the overall control software running on the main MSP430 processor. There are components of the control program described in Section 3.3 that interact with each of the hardware components of the CubeSat. The CubeSat requires a power system consisting of photovoltaic cells on all six sides of the CubeSat and the Electrical Power System (EPS) which controls the charging of the batteries from the photovoltaic cells, generates the required system voltages, and protects the batteries from over and under voltage. The motherboard mounts the Pluggable Processor Module with the CPU. The radio board contains a receiver and transmitter for satellite communications. There are deployable antennas for transmitter and receiver. The Position and Time Board (PTB) mounts the GPS board, whose CPU we use to run the GEONS navigation software and there is a patch antenna for the GPS. Finally, there is the Inertial Measurement Unit (IMU) and camera board which mounts them and the hysteresis rods for magnetic damping. The CubeSat Kit structure, which mounts everything also has magnets for passive magnetic stabilization along the Earth's magnetic field lines. Figure 1 shows a photograph of our completed CubeSat.

Fig. 1. Photograph of our CubeSat

2.1   Structure, Motherboard and CPU

The CubeSat structure is an aluminum frame made by CubeSat Kit [6]. It contains their Motherboard (MB) and Pluggable Processor Module (PPM). Our PPM contains a Texas Instruments MSP430F2618 16-bit micro-controller (MCU) with 116 KB program memory, 8 KB on-chip SRAM, 2 USCI, 8-channel 12-bit ADC, 2-channel 12-bit DAC, 16-bit Timer, 3-channel DMA and on-chip comparator. The motherboard also contains a 2 GB SD card for storage of GPS, IMU, GEONS and camera data prior to transmission to our ground station. In each corner of the structure, we are epoxying Alnico V magnets for passive magnetic stabilization of the CubeSat which will align itself with the earth's magnetic field.

2.2   GPS and Position and Time Board

The primary purpose of testing the navigation system will make use of a Novatel OEMV-1 GPS board, previously used on the University of Michigan RAX triple

CubeSats[12], which has had the CoCom speed and altitude limits removed so it can be used in orbit. We also have the Novatel API activated, which allows us to run software on the GPS board's ARM processor. It is mounted on a University of Michigan designed RAX Position and Time Board (PTB) [13] which allows GPS board access through an SPI bus and the real time clock through an I^{2}C bus. The board also supplies a variety of telemetry items about the GPS power, temperature, etc., over the I^{2}C bus. The PTB access of the GPS will allow communication with the GEONS software running on the GPS ARM CPU. The GPS receiver gets the GPS satellite signals via an Antcom 1.5G15A3F-XT-1 GPS patch antenna [1] with a built in 33 dB gain low noise amplifier (LNA).

2.3   Radio

Communication with the CubeSat will be done from our ground station to the Astrodev Helium-100 transceiver [7] on the CubeSat. This radio has a 2 m band receiver and 70 cm band transmitter with a power of 2.8 W. We have frequencies assigned by the International Amateur Radio Union (IARU) which does frequency coordination for non governmental satellites. These frequencies are 145.960 MHz for our uplink, and 437.305 MHz for our downlink. We will send commands to the satellite via the uplink, and receive data (images, GPS output, inertial measurement unit (IMU) output, system state telemetry and GEONS output) via the downlink. We will have a ground station with 2 m circularly polarized crossed Yagi and 70 cm circularly polarized crossed Yagi antennas mounted on altitude and azimuth rotors on top of a 50 foot tower. Our ground station radio is an Icom IC-910H satellite radio with 2 m, 70 cm and 25 cm transceivers controlled by SatPC32 software [14]. The radio will use a protocol described below that will ensure non corrupted data. The data will have first been stored on the on-board SD card.

2.4   Antennas

Our CubeSat will have deployable antennas for both the 2 m and 70 cm bands. The ISIS AntS antenna system [8] has dual microprocessors and can supply telemetry data as to its state, and receive commands to first arm the antenna, and then to deploy the antennas. The four spring elements are coiled up behind spring hinged doors, held closed by nylon thread which passes over surface mount resistors internally. When the deploy command is received over the I^{2}C interface, the resistors are heated up to melt the thread and release all four antenna elements. The elements on opposite sides of the CubeSat make up a dipole antenna, and the two antennas are perpendicular to each other. The antenna module is mounted on the bottom of the satellite, just outside the internal motherboard.

2.5   Electrical Power System

Electrical Power for the CubeSat is supplied by high efficiency photo-voltaic cells (28.3% efficient) made by Spectrolab [16]. These 1 W cells are arranged with two cells on three sides and the bottom of the CubeSat, and one cell on the top, leaving room for the GPS patch antenna and an aperture for our camera, and one cell on one of the sides leaving room for a charging port, USB port and remove before flight pin. Power from the cells goes to the Clyde Space 1U Electrical Power system board [4]. This board controls the charging of the attached 10 Wh 8.2 V lithium polymer battery. The board also has regulated voltage outputs of 3.3 V and 5.0 V as well as the unregulated battery voltage (used in the power amplifier of the radio transmitter). It has protection circuitry for the battery and provides telemetry data as to battery voltage, current and temperature over I^2C. It also controls a battery heater to maintain the battery temperature above $0°$ C.

2.6   Camera and Inertial Measurement Unit Board

This board has various capabilities not contained on the other commercial boards above. The second part of the magnetic stabilization consists of two HyMu 80 hysteresis rods, perpendicular to each other on this board and the corner Alnico magnets on the main structure. There is a Microstrain 3DM-GX3-25 miniature Attitude Heading Reference System (IMU) [9], utilizing MEMS sensor technology. It combines a triaxial accelerometer, triaxial gyro, triaxial magnetometer, temperature sensors, and an on-board processor running a sophisticated sensor fusion algorithm to provide static and dynamic orientation, and inertial measurements. The C329 color VGA camera module [3] with an f6.0mm F1.6 lens which performs JPEG compression and communicates via an SPI interface. The images of stars and near bodies (sun, earth and moon) will be downloaded for navigation analysis by the GEONS software.

3   Project Description

In this section we describe the organization of the project including the tool chain we used, the system architecture, and our approach to testing.

3.1   SPARK

SPARK is an annotated sub-language of Ada designed for the development of high integrity software [17]. It has been used successfully in industry to construct mission-critical systems [18].

SPARK is a sub-language of Ada in the sense that it omits numerous Ada features that are not amenable to static analysis. The major omitted features include exception handling, access types, dynamic memory allocation, dynamic dispatch, and recursion. SPARK also restricts Ada in numerous additional ways to ensure that programs have fully specified, unambiguous semantics.

SPARK extends Ada with annotations embedded in comments that enrich interfaces with declarations of information flow and with pre- and post-conditions. The main SPARK tool, the Examiner, uses the annotations, together with the code itself, to statically check that no uninitialized data is used and that all results computed by the program are consumed in some way. Furthermore the Examiner generates *verification conditions* stating conjectures about the runtime checks and the pre- and post-conditions used in the program. These verification conditions are discharged by an automatic theorem prover, the Simplifier, sometimes with human assistance. This provides static assurance that in all cases no runtime checks will fail and that pre- and post-conditions will be honored.

In our project SPARK was used by undergraduate student workers. Although undergraduate use of SPARK has been documented previously [20], this project differs from that earlier work in that here the students are building a "real life" system that will actually fly in space and not just a carefully managed class project.

Our policy was to keep the code submitted to our version control repository examinable at all times with full information flow analysis enabled. Exceptions to this policy were made so that incomplete stubs could be committed in order to facilitate testing. Proofs of freedom from runtime errors were deferred until a particular package was deemed to be stable enough to justify the effort involved in discharging all verification conditions associated with that package.

3.2 Tool Chain

The tool chain we used was largely the same as described in [19]. For convenience we briefly summarize the tool chain in Figure 2.

Ada source files were first analyzed using SPARK and then compiled to standard C with an Ada to C translator [15]. The C was then compiled, along with hand written low level C modules, using a commercial C compiler for our target platform [5]. This approach allowed us to develop SPARK programs for targets on which Ada is not otherwise well supported.

One important disadvantage of our approach is that the underlying C compiler is now a source of potential errors in our system. Although compilers are generally robust, silent mis-compilation of correct source code is certainly possible. In our system this concern is particularly acute since the Ada to C translator relies on a human generated configuration file describing the characteristics of the underlying C compiler.

For example, the underlying C compiler for our MSP430 target uses 16 bit integers. We made this known to the Ada to C translator by way of its configuration file so that the Ada type Integer was also taken to be 16 bits. In addition, the SPARK configuration file was used to convey this information to the SPARK tools. A mistake in either level of configuration could result in an undetected error reaching the object code.

We dealt with this problem in part by being cautious; the configuration files are small and amenable to careful review. We also wrote several small programs that exercised some of the issues covered by the configuration files. By manually examining the assembly language produced by the underlying C compiler we

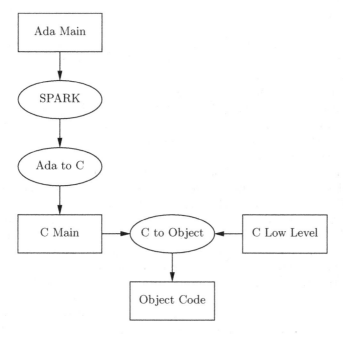

Fig. 2. Tool Chain

were able to verify that our configuration was appropriate, at least in those cases. We hoped that any remaining configuration errors would manifest themselves during testing.

Because we used SPARK to prove freedom from runtime errors we compiled our code base with runtime checks disabled. This resulted in higher execution performance in terms of both space and time.

We also made no use of the Ada runtime system. This was feasible because SPARK prohibits many Ada constructs requiring runtime support [19] and because we eliminated unnecessary runtime checks. We also imposed several additional, minor restrictions on our programming style to avoid unnecessary use of the runtime system. For example, on the MSP430 target the **mod** operator entailed a call to a runtime support function to properly handle negative arguments. Since we only used **mod** on positive values, we avoided the runtime system reference by simply using the **rem** operator instead. The **rem** operator was directly translated into C's % operator.

Removing the runtime system reduced the memory footprint of our software, which was important in our constrained environment. It also reduced the size of the trusted code base executing on the spacecraft, compensating somewhat for the added risk incurred by injecting an additional compiler into the tool chain.

Since our system consists of two largely independent programs, one running on an MSP430 micro-controller and the other on an ARM architecture processor, we used two independent instances of our tool chain, one for each target.

3.3   Design

No formal specification method nor design methodology was used in the development of our software. Instead the design was done by students, with guidance from faculty, in an informal manner.

The development of the software followed a roughly agile approach with an emphasis on pair-programming and frequent testing. Although we did not use a high integrity development process, the approach used was familiar to the students from their classwork. SPARK augmented the development process in a useful way as describe further in Section 3.4.

Our focus since the summer of 2011 has been on preparing the software for a low Earth orbiting test flight where we intend to exercise several critical subsystems. The software was divided into a main control program responsible for coordinating the general activity of the spacecraft and a navigation program responsible for interacting with the NASA provided GEONS navigation software. The control program executes on a Texas Instruments MSP430F2618 microcontroller [11] mounted on the main processor board of the CubeSat Kit [6]. The navigation program executes on an ARM architecture Intel XScale auxiliary processor on-board the Novatel OEMV-1 GPS receiver.

The control program uses several interfacing technologies to communicate with the various subsystems. Table 1 lists the subsystems used in the test flight and the interfacing method used to interact with that subsystem.

Table 1. Subsystems Used in Test Flight

Subsystem	Interfacing
Antenna	I^{2}C
Radio	RS-232
Camera	SPI
Power Supply	I^{2}C
Inertial Measurement Unit	RS-232
GPS & GEONS	SPI

Each interfacing technology has an associated package that allows SPARK programs to access that interface. Because the Ada compiler we used was unaware of certain low level details of our platform, such as how interrupts are handled, the lowest levels of the interface access code were written in platform specific C compiled directly by our underlying C compiler. However, every attempt was made to to keep the C components of the system trivial so as much application logic as possible could be exposed to SPARK's analysis.

Each subsystem includes a driver package that exposes the basic functionality of that subsystem. These packages interact with the subsystem's hardware via the appropriate interfacing package and were entirely written in SPARK. The driver packages are intended to be general and not tied to any specific application. We hope to reuse the driver packages in later flights.

On top of each driver package is a "handler" package that encodes the flight-specific logic of how that subsystem is to be used. For example the antenna handler concerns itself with deploying the antenna at a suitable time after the satellite itself is deployed. To do this it calls subprograms in the antenna driver package to query the deployment status and to start the deployment process. Those subprograms in turn use subprograms in the I^2C interfacing package to communicate with the antenna hardware.

The main program consists of a polling executive loop that periodically executes a "work unit" procedure in each handler package. This gives each subsystem an unpreemptable slice of processor time in which it can do its work. After each subsystem is polled in this way the main loop sleeps until the next cycle, putting the processor into a low power mode to conserve energy.

This design makes no use of tasks and thus does not require RavenSPARK. This reduced the runtime support needed, simplified the programming, and made the software more approachable for first time undergraduate SPARK programmers. However, our design does create potentially long delays between when a subsystem relinquishes control and then later regains control. We felt this was acceptable because our system does not have any critical timing requirements. If a subsystem wishes to perform a time sensitive operation, such as reading bulk data from the inertial measurement unit, it can simply retain control until the operation is complete.

Although it is important that the work unit procedures do not execute in an unbounded way, there is no concern of scheduling overruns since there is no particular schedule that must be kept. All the computations done by the work unit procedures are short, and potentially blocking operations are all programmed to time out after a reasonable delay.

In addition to the hardware drivers and their handlers, our system includes several supporting packages. The components of the system communicate using a message passing discipline enabled by a message queue package. Subsystems can thus send commands to each other as necessary.

Figure 3 summarizes the information flow in the system. Commands arrive from the ground station via the radio or are generated in the scheduler. These commands are processed by their respective subsystems when each subsystem is energized by the main loop. In some cases, data produced by a subsystem is saved to storage as a file on the SD card where it is later transferred to Earth.

Commands from the ground station are filtered and potentially handled by a Command Handler package. This package is also responsible for handling data file transfers from the satellite to the ground station. Commands intended for hardware subsystems are forwarded to the message queue for distribution.

Finally a scheduler, implemented as part of the message queue package, generates commands periodically to allow routine operations to be performed even in the common case when the satellite is out of communication with its ground

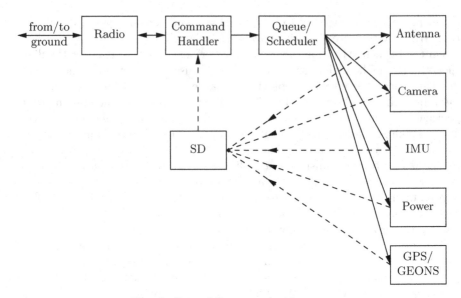

Fig. 3. Control Program Architecture

station. This design centralizes the control logic of the program to the scheduler with potential overrides from the ground station when it is available.

3.4 Testing

In addition to SPARK information flow analysis and proofs of freedom from runtime error, we also made use of traditional testing techniques. We considered this essential not only to cover correctness properties not explored by SPARK proofs, but also to help cover undischarged verification conditions and, most importantly, to verify proper interfacing with the physical hardware.

Testing was done at three levels.

At the lowest level unit testing was done for components admitting reasonable unit tests. We used the AUnit framework [2] for this purpose.

In addition a mock system was created that provided software simulations of the hardware. The interface to the mock hardware was the same as for the real hardware so that essentially all of the SPARK code was identical between the mock system and the real system. This allowed us to compile the control program as, for example, a Windows executable using the GNAT Ada compiler from AdaCore, and then observe its logged output behavior when driven with suitable test scripts.

The intent of the mock system was to allow meaning behavioral and integration testing without using any physical hardware. Since the student development team was split across two campuses, not all developers had access to the hardware for test purposes, making the mock system essential.

Finally integration and interfacing tests against the physical hardware were done using a CubeSatKit development board [6]. These tests verified proper operation of the system against the components that would be used in space. Once our spacecraft was assembled these tests were then executed again on the actual spacecraft, with some adjustments to account for the lab environment.

If SPARK had not been used our test plan would likely have been the same. SPARK was used in our project to supplement the testing and to find faults not easily explored by testing. Although we did not follow a high integrity development process, SPARK was useful in keeping our software in a reasonably self-consistent state. For example, significant refactoring was needed several times as our understanding of the hardware and system requirements changed. SPARK's analysis caught many errors during these refactorings that might have otherwise gone unnoticed.

A continuing problem for us has been limited time and personnel resources allocated to this project. Student workers turn over quickly, and by the time a student has reached a level where he or she can contribute significantly that student is often ready to graduate. We feel that the rigor imposed by SPARK on our otherwise turbulent environment has significantly enhanced the reliability of our final product.

4   Student Participation

Over the months since the project's inception several students have been involved in software development. Table 2 summarizes the number of students involved with notes about their areas of focus.

Table 2. Student Participation

Time	Students	Notes
Summer 2011	2	Design & impl. of radio and interfacing subsystems
AY 2011-2012	0	Small enhancements
Summer 2012	1	Completed impl. of most subsystems
Fall 2012	4	File transfer, integration, navigation program

A total of six students have been actively involved in software development. Of these six three had previously taken VTC's High Integrity Programming course where SPARK was introduced in a manner similar to described in [20]. The other three either learned SPARK while working on the project or, in one case, focused exclusively on the C aspects of the project.

The students involved during the summer months worked on the project full time for nine weeks. The students involved during the academic semesters worked on the project part time in addition to their other class obligations. Two of the students in the Fall 2012 semester used the project to fulfill their Senior Projects course requirements.

All students participated by invitation. Some students were self-selected in the sense that they initiated contact with the project coordinators. Other students knew nothing about the project until they were contacted.

As with many student projects, turnover was a significant problem. Most students only worked on the project for one summer or one semester. Only the student involved during the summer of 2012 continued his involvement into the following semester.

4.1   Observations

The number of students involved with the project was not large enough to obtain any meaningful statistical results. However, several informal observations can nevertheless be made.

In general the students involved in the project were able to use SPARK effectively to perform information flow analysis and to produce proofs of freedom from runtime errors. No attempt was made to formally demonstrate higher level correctness properties. Instead high level behavior was verified using traditional testing as described in Section 3.4.

As one might expect, the students who took VTC's High Integrity Programming course were much more comfortable with SPARK, and more immediately productive than those who had not taken the course. There was one notable exception: one remarkable student learned SPARK largely on his own, and yet was nevertheless able to use make good use of the tools almost right away.

Contrary to expectation the students were accepting of the rigors of SPARK programming and did not object to the restrictions imposed by the language nor to the work involved in creating and managing annotations or discharging verification conditions.

In fact several students, both in this project and in VTC's High Integrity Programming course, expressed appreciation for SPARK's restrictions saying that they were happy not to have to worry about confusing features such as access types or dynamic dispatch. The SPARK kernel language is relatively simple and allowed the students to focus on program organization and correctness rather than on finding a way to use the latest fashionable features.

There was a tendency for students to postpone SPARK examination of a package or subsystem until after that package or subsystem was "finished" and ready for testing. Although not universal, some students treated SPARK as a kind of testing tool to be used once the code was believed, via code review, to be functional.

Unfortunately the application of SPARK after the fact was more difficult than the students expected. Often the restrictions imposed by SPARK necessitated significant refactoring of the pre-SPARK implementation. As the students gained experience they came to realize the importance of using SPARK early and of at least bringing the code into an examinable state as soon as possible.

The requirements and subsequent design of the system changed several times during development. As mentioned in Section 3.4 SPARK was useful at keeping the code base organized and self-consistent even in the face of these changes.

Students were not always timely in updating design documents, but the simple requirement of keeping the software examinable at all times helped to control what might have otherwise been chaotic evolution. In this respect the discipline of SPARK helped inexperienced students produce higher quality software than they might have otherwise.

5   Conclusion

We have described the design of a CubeSat and its corresponding control program that we intend to use in our upcoming low Earth orbiting test flight. The software design and implementation in SPARK has been driven by a small collection of undergraduate students with varying abilities and backgrounds.

Although the students have been remarkably successfully at using SPARK in this project to find information flow errors and to prove freedom from runtime errors, we have also faced some challenges. In addition to educating the students about SPARK and about software engineering in general, we also experienced a high turnover rate of student workers and difficulties associated with coordinating students on two campuses. SPARK helped our development process by imposing a level of discipline on it that was easy for students to understand and accept. As a result we feel that it is feasible for motivated undergraduate students to use SPARK effectively on a realistically scaled project.

At the time of this writing we are finalizing our integration tests and proofs of freedom from runtime error. Our current spacecraft has passed thermal and vibration testing. In the longer term we intend to cultivate our team by recruiting second year students to the project who will hopefully be able to stay involved for several years. After the summer of 2013 we will start focusing on the more challenging problem of designing a CubeSat that can reach the moon.

References

1. Antcom 1.5G15A3F-XT-1 L1 GPS antenna,
   http://www.antcom.com/documents/catalogs/L1GPSAntennas.pdf
2. AUnit ada unit testing framework, http://libre.adacore.com/tools/aunit/ (accessed December 9, 2012)
3. C329-SPI-board JPEG compression VGA camera module,
   http://www.electronics123.net/amazon/datasheet/C329_SPI_data.pdf
4. Clyde space 1U electrical power system,
   http://www.clyde-space.com/documents/1819
5. Crossworks for MSP430, http://www.rowley.co.uk/msp430/ (accessed November 27, 2012)
6. Cubesat kit home, http://www.cubesatkit.com/ (accessed December 10, 2012)
7. Helium-100 radio, http://www.astrodev.com/public_html2/node/20 (accessed December 9, 2012)
8. ISIS AntS cubesat antenna system,
   http://www.isispace.nl/brochures/ISIS_AntS_Brochure_v.7.11.pdf

9. Microstrain 3DM-GX3-25 miniature attitude heading reference system, http://www.microstrain.com/inertial/3DM-GX3-25-OEM

10. Minotaur space launch vehicles, http://www.orbital.com/SpaceLaunch/Minotaur/

11. MSP430F2618, http://www.ti.com/product/msp430f2618 (accessed November 25, 2012)

12. OEMV installation and operation, http://www.novatel.com/assets/Documents/Manuals/om-20000093.pdf (accessed December 9, 2012)

13. Position and time system for the RAX small satellite mission, http://exploration.engin.umich.edu/blog/wp-content/uploads/2011/09/Spangelo_etal_2010b.pdf (accessed December 10, 2012)

14. SatPC32 satellite tracking, antenna and radio-control software, http://www.dk1tb.de/indexeng.html

15. Sofcheck compiler technology, http://www.sofcheck.com/products/adamagic.html

16. Spectrolab UTJ photovoltaic cell CICs, http://www.spectrolab.com/DataSheets/cells/PV

17. Barnes, J.: SPARK, The Proven Approach to High Integrity Software. Altran Praxis (2012)

18. Chapman, R.: Industrial experience with SPARK. Ada Lett. XX(4), 64–68 (2000), http://doi.acm.org/10.1145/369264.369270

19. Loseby, C., Chapin, P., Brandon, C.: Use of SPARK in a resource constrained embedded system. In: Proceedings of the ACM SIGAda Annual International Conference on Ada and Related Technologies, SIGAda 2009, pp. 87–90. ACM, New York (2009), http://doi.acm.org/10.1145/1647420.1647441

20. Ruocco, A.S.: Experiences using SPARK in an undergraduate CS course. In: Proceedings of the 2005 Annual ACM SIGAda International Conference on Ada: The Engineering of Correct and Reliable Software for Real-Time & Distributed Systems using Ada and Related Technologies, SigAda 2005, pp. 37–40. ACM, New York (2005), http://doi.acm.org/10.1145/1103846.1103852

Lady Ada Mediates
Peace Treaty in Endianness War

Thomas Quinot and Eric Botcazou

AdaCore
46, rue d'Amsterdam
75009 Paris, France
{botcazou,quinot}@adacore.com
http://www.adacore.com

Abstract. There is no universal agreement on the order in which the successive bytes constituting a scalar value are stored. Some machines (so-called *big-endian* architectures) store the most significant byte first, while others (*little-endian* architectures) adopt the opposite convention. When porting an application across platforms that use different conventions, programmers need to convert data to the appropriate convention, and this may cause difficulties when exact memory layouts need to be preserved (e.g. for communication with legacy systems).

This paper describes the features of the Ada language that help supporting programmers in these situations, identifies some of their shortcomings, and introduces two novel solutions: a code generation approach based on data representation modeling, and a new representation attribute *Scalar_Storage_Order*, allowing the byte order convention to be specified for a given composite data structure.

Keywords: endianness, retargeting, code generation.

1 Introduction

As Gulliver landed on Lilliput, he discovered the fierce war raging between *little endians* — whose soft boiled eggs they would always eat starting with the little end — and the *big endians* who furiously defended the exact opposite standpoint, and ended up in exile on the nearby island of Blefuscu [10].

Nowadays' software engineers, like the explorer of yore, are still finding themselves in the middle of the same battleground, where hardware interfaces, communication protocols, or other external constraints require multi-byte values to be stored and exchanged in either big-endian format (most significant digits first), or little-endian (least significant digits first). The war has been raging for decades [3], with rules imposed by standard interfaces, or stemming from the requirement of interoperability with third party or legacy applications.

All is well as long as all components of a system happen to use the same convention. Splitting any data structure into its elementary components is then just a matter of masking and shifting bits. However, as soon as different conventions must come into play, trouble arises: the order of the bytes constituting a

H.B. Keller et al. (Eds.): Ada-Europe 2013, LNCS 7896, pp. 65–80, 2013.
© Springer-Verlag Berlin Heidelberg 2013

data structure (the *endianness*) then needs to be changed at strategic conversion points, which may or may not be well identified in source code. It is up to the application developer to identify appropriate swapping points and keep track of whether or not a given value has been swapped at any given point in time. This proves a significant hassle, with a costly distributed impact.

This situation specifically arises when applications that used to rely on legacy big-endian computers, for example based on PowerPC or SPARC CPUs, are retargeted to now ubiquitous Intel-based platforms, which are little-endian. Integration with legacy components, and processing of stored data from existing systems requires that exact data representations be preserved, and software must compensate for the fact that the new platform assumes a different storage order.

Introducing explicit reordering (*byte swapping*) of scalar values throughout software may prove a costly endeavour. The mere extraction of scalars crossing byte boudaries in data structures requires extra shift and mask operations. In addition, the need for explicit code handling endianness conversions hinders maintainability as data structures themselves evolve. This paper discusses how tools can provide valuable assistance to application developers in addressing endianness conversion issues, alleviating the need for such "manual" byte swapping.

In section 2, we first give a summary of the data representation constructs provided by Ada. These allow the explicit specification of a data structure's layout according to an external constraint. They can be used to provide endianness independence to a limited extent. However, users are often disconcerted at first by the exact semantics of these features, which indeed do not provide a fully transparent and general solution to endianness conversion issues. In section 3, we focus on explicit byte swapping approaches, and we present the *Tranxgen* code generator, which affords automated support to produce endianness independent accessors. In section 4, we then describe another solution, introducing a new representation attribute providing transparent in-place access to data of arbitrary endianness.

2   Composite Layout Specifications in Ada

In this section we discuss standard features of Ada that allow the layout of a data structure to be specified according to an external constraint. We show how these features support endianness independence to a limited extent.

2.1   Record Representation Clauses

Ada record representation clauses allow developers to specify, for each component of a record:

- its starting position, i.e. the byte offset of the first underlying storage element (the one with the lowest memory address)
- a bit range indicating its specific extent over the underlying storage elements.

An elementary example is given in listing 1.

```
--- A two byte data structure
type R is record
    X : Character;
    Y : Boolean;
    Z : I7;              --- type I7 is range 0 .. 127
end record;
for R use record
    X at 0 range 0 .. 7;
    Y at 1 range 0 .. 0;
    Z at 1 range 1 .. 7;
end record;
```

Listing 1. Elementary record representation clause

These record declaration and record representation clause declare a data structure occupying two storage elements (which are assumed to be 8-bit bytes throughout this discussion) which is thus laid out:

- the first component, X, is an 8-bit character that fits exactly in the storage element at offset 0
- the second and third components, a 1-bit Boolean value Y and a 7-bit integer value Z, share space in the second storage element at offset 1. Y uses one bit numbered "0", and Z uses the remaining seven bits, numbered "1" thru "7".

It is important to note that the semantics of this very simple fragment of code in terms of data representation is different, depending on the bit numbering convention used by a particular compiler:

	Low order first	**High order first**
X	first byte of representation	
Y	Least sig. bit of 2nd byte	Most sig. bit of 2nd byte
Z	*Shift_Right* (2nd byte, 1)	2nd byte *and* 2#0111_1111#

2.2 Endianness Neutral Representation Clauses

Tricks have been proposed to express such clauses in a neutral way, so that little or no code modifications are required to obtain the same representation when porting between a big-endian and a little-endian platform [4,8]. These essentially consist in having an integer constant whose value reflects the endianness of the platform, and expressing all component positions and bit ranges as arithmetic expressions depending on this constant.

Ada 95 introduced an alternative to these tricks, in the form of the representation attribute *Bit_Order* (Ada 95 Reference Manual section 13.5.3 [5]). When this attribute is defined for some record type, a record representation clause for the type is interpreted using the specified bit numbering convention. In the above example, one can thus specify:

```
for R'Bit_Order use System.Low_Order_First;
```

The effect of this attribute definition clause is that the bit numbers in the record
representation clause will always be interpreted as on a little-endian machine.
The memory representation of objects of type R therefore becomes independent
of the machine endianness.

2.3 Crossing Byte Boundaries

The semantics of bit positions greater than the number of bits in a storage element is pretty clear when using the default (system) bit order. The situation
becomes more confused in the opposite case, and this caused a binding interpretation of the Ada 95 standard to be issued [1] to clarify the meaning of a record
representation clause in that case.

The rule as clarified in Ada 2005 (and retrospectively in Ada 95 by virtue of
this binding interpretation) is that operations on record components can only
extract information from contiguous bit ranges taken from some machine integer (what Ada 2005 calls "machine scalars"). This makes sense because this
reflects the requirement that extracting a record component is performed using
load, store, shift, and mask operations of the underlying machine architecture.
This constraint limits the spectrum of data layouts that can be specified in an
endianness independent way.

This limitation becomes clear when one considers the following data type,
together with its representation clause:

```
subtype Yr_Type is Natural range 0 .. 127;
subtype Mo_Type is Natural range 1 .. 12;
subtype Da_Type is Natural range 1 .. 31;
subtype Ho_Type is Natural range 0 .. 23;
subtype Mi_Type is Natural range 0 .. 59;

subtype S2_Type is Natural range 0 .. 29;
--  Two seconds unit

type Date_And_Time is record
   Years_Since_1980 : Yr_Type;
   --  Bits Y0 (most significannt)
   --     to Y6 (least significant)

   Month          : Mo_Type;
   --  Bits M0 (most significannt)
   --     to M3 (least significant)

   Day_Of_Month   : Da_Type;
   --  Bits D0 (most significannt)
   --     to D4 (least significant)
```

```
   Hour                 :  Ho_Type;
   Minute               :  Mi_Type;
   Two_Second           :  S2_Type;
end record;

for Date_And_Time use record
   Years_Since_1980  at 0 range  0  ..   6;
   Month             at 0 range  7  ..  10;
   Day_Of_Month      at 0 range 11  ..  15;
   Hour              at 2 range  0  ..   4;
   Minute            at 2 range  5  ..  10;
   Two_Second        at 2 range 11  ..  15;
end record;
```

Listing 2. Record with components crossing byte boudaries

The data for the first three components, as described by the above representation clause, is stored as two storage elements, as shown on figure 1.

Most sig. bit $\cdots$ Least sig. bit

	Y_0	Y_1	Y_2	Y_3	Y_4	Y_5	Y_6	M_0
Byte 0	0	1	2	3	4	5	6	7
Byte 1	M_1	M_2	M_3	D_0	D_1	D_2	D_3	D_4
	8	9	10	11	12	13	14	15

(a) Big-endian

Most sig. bit $\cdots$ Least sig. bit

	M_3	Y_0	Y_1	Y_2	Y_3	Y_4	Y_5	Y_6
Byte 0	7	6	5	4	3	2	1	0
Byte 1	D_0	D_1	D_2	D_3	D_4	M_0	M_1	M_2
	15	14	13	12	11	10	9	8

(b) Little-endian

Fig. 1. Date and time structure (first two bytes)

To extract components using shift and mask operations, this data must be considered as a single (16-bit) integer value, whose bits are numbered from 0 (MSB) to 15 (LSB) or 0 (LSB) to 15 (MSB), depending on whether Bit_Order is High_Order_First or Low_Order_First (figure 2).

Byte 0								Byte 1							
Y_0	Y_1	Y_2	Y_3	Y_4	Y_5	Y_6	M_0	M_1	M_2	M_3	D_0	D_1	D_2	D_3	D_4
0	1	2	3	4	5	6	7	8	9	10	11	12	13	14	15

Byte 1								Byte 0							
D_0	D_1	D_2	D_3	D_4	M_0	M_1	M_2	M_3	Y_0	Y_1	Y_2	Y_3	Y_4	Y_5	Y_6
15	14	13	12	11	10	9	8	7	6	5	4	3	2	1	0

Fig. 2. Date and time structure as a 16-bit scalar (BE top, LE bottom)

As an example, if the date is November 18, 2012, the values for the first three components is (Years_Since_1980 => 32, Month => 11, Day => 18), and on a High_Order_First machine the bit pattern is as shown on figure 3. The corresponding sequence of storage elements is (65, 114), and the corresponding scalar value is $65 \times 256 + 114 = 16\,754$.

MSB(byte 0) .. LSB(byte 0)								MSB(byte 1) .. LSB(byte 1)							
Y_0	Y_1	Y_2	Y_3	Y_4	Y_5	Y_6	M_0	M_1	M_2	M_3	D_0	D_1	D_2	D_3	D_4
0	1	0	0	0	0	0	1	0	1	1	1	0	0	1	0
65								114							
16 754															

Fig. 3. Bit pattern for Nov. 18, 2012 on a big-endian machine

	MSB(byte 1) .. LSB(byte 1)								MSB(byte 0) .. LSB(byte 0)							
Original data	M_1	M_2	M_3	D_0	D_1	D_2	D_3	D_4	Y_0	Y_1	Y_2	Y_3	Y_4	Y_5	Y_6	M_0
Example bits	0	1	1	1	0	0	1	0	0	1	0	0	0	0	0	1
Byte values	114								65							
Scalar value	29 249															

Fig. 4. Bits of big-endian structure from fig. 3, as seen on a little-endian machine

Now if the same memory region is accessed on a *little-endian* machine as a 16-bit integer, the binary value now is as shown on figure 4. For our example case the original bit pattern now translates to scalar value $114 \times 256 + 65 = 29\,249$. It should be noted that the Month field is not contiguous anymore in this representation: bit 0 ends up at position 0 (least significant bit), where as bits 1 to 3 end up at positions 13 to 15. More generally, on big endian machines the least significant bit of one storage element is adjacent to the most significant bit of the next one when considering a machine scalar, whereas on a little endian machine it is the most significant bit of the first byte that is adjacent with the least significant bit of the following one.

As a result, *no record component representation clause in standard Ada can describe the LE layout on a BE platform.*

The Bit_Order attribute changes the way indices are assigned to bits (i.e. in the above integer, in High_Order_First ordering the bits are denoted with indices 0 .. 15, whereas in Low_Order_First they are numbered 15 .. 0). In other words, the only effect of setting Date_And_Time' Bit_Order to Low_Order_First is to change the bit numbering from $0 \cdots 15$ to $15 \cdots 0$. This does not change the order in which a CPU load operation takes bytes from memory to build an integer value in a register, on which shift and mask operations are applied to extract an individual component.

Note that we arbitrarily chose to consider just the first three components, and the corresponding underlying *16 bit* scalar, but we could just as well have considered the complete structure and the associated 32 bit scalar: the bits of the Month component would have been separated in the same way.

This situation is encountered anytime a record component crosses a storage element boundary. In this case no standard representation clause can be written that will yield identical representations on big-endian and little-endian machines: additional work is then required to access such data structures. Several approaches are discussed in the remainder of this paper.

3   Explicit Byte Reordering

3.1   Individual Component Swapping

If each component in a record type occupies an integral number of storage elements, then the extraction of the component's bits from the enclosing data structure does not require any shifting and masking operation; the component's underlying storage itself is a machine scalar, and the only remaining issue when accessing the components is the ordering of bytes within the component itself. In other words, in this case storage elements can be reordered after extracting the component from the struture according to a record representation clause, and the reordering operation can be considered at the level of the value of a single component. (In contrast with cases such as the example discussed above, where components did not occupy integral storage elements, and reordering operations were necessary even to just gather the bits constituting a single component).

This simple situation is encountered for example when writing code that binds directly to the standard BSD sockets API, where all data structures are traditionally big-endian; byte-swapping functions htons/ntohs and htonl/ntohl are provided by the standard API to perform byte swapping (respectively for short and long integer values) when operating on little-endian platforms (these operations are nops on big-endian platforms).

The GNAT run-time library includes a set of generic procedures to perform byte swapping in package *GNAT.Byte_Swapping*. This package provides a set of generic byte swapping subprograms for 16, 32, and 64-bit objects. These take advantage of GCC builtins to perform byte swapping operations and which use dedicated, efficient CPU instructions where available.

When using explicit byte swapping at the component level, care must be taken by the programmer to identify whether a given value has been byte swapped or not at any given point in time. This means a strict isolation is desirable between the data types used for input/output (or interaction with standard library calls), which require data in the externally mandated byte order, and data structures used for internal processing (where components need to be in their correct native order). When retargeting legacy code that was not written with portability in mind in the first place, such isolation may be found wanting.

3.2   Arithmetic Component Extraction

Another alternative is for the user to extract component values from storage
elements using explicit arithmetic operations on raw storage arrays. For example,
suppose that SE (0) and SE (1) are the first and second storage elements of
the date/time structure from listing 2 as stored on a big-endian machine. The
following expressions can be used to extract the Year and Month components in
a platform independent way:

```
Year   := SE (0) / 2;
Month := (SE (0) and 1) * 8 + SE (1) / 32
--           ^^^    M0    ^^^         ^^M1 .. M3^^
```

This way of expressing data layout is independent of endianness, and as such
ensures maximum portability. However it is a cumbersome notation, reducing
the legibility, and hence the maintainability, of application code. It also hinders
optimization by the code generator, by pushing detailed representation information up to the highest levels of the intermediate representations handled by the
code generator. Moreover, in this case again there must be a strict separation
between the raw arrays of storage elements used for external operations, and the
native byte order data structures used internally by the software.

3.3   Wholesale Byte Reversal

An interesting solution has been proposed by R. Andress in [2], where he suggests
to revert the order of storage elements constituting a given data structure *as
a whole*, and to then construct a new record representation clause mapping
components on the reversed structure. He observes that when changing platform
endianness endianness, the complete reversal of byte order makes all components
that crossed byte boundaries contiguous again. One can then construct a new
representation clause that locates each component within the reversed structure.

  This approach is elegant and expressive; it has the merit of minimal intru-
siveness on existing code. On the other hand it still requires an explicit byte
reordering operation, and the storage of data structures in two copies (one in
original order, and the other in reversed order). The representation clause for the
reversed structure also needs to be carefully written and maintained up-to-date
with respect to the original one.

3.4   Data Modeling Approaches

An important drawback of the manual byte reordering approaches discussed
above is the verbosity of notations for arithmetic component extraction or record
representation clauses. One way of alleviating such a concern is to replace manually implemented code with code generated from a model.

  In the context of endianness conversions, the model is a formal description
of the bit layout of some data structure, and the operations provided by the
generated code are accessors to the components of that structure.

The idea is akin to that of the ASN.1 standard [6]. However in ASN.1 one describes a data structure in an abstract semantics perspective. This description can then be mapped to one (or more) concrete representations through some standard *encoding rules* [7].

In the case of externally mandated data representations, on the contrary, the model starts by describing the exact structure in terms of bits and bytes, and from there describes how these elementary pieces of data must be interpreted to form higher level values.

This is the approach we followed in *Tranxgen*, a code generation tool we introduced while developing a portable, certifiable TCP/IP stack. A similar path has been followed by existing tools for other languages [9].

Tranxgen accepts a data structure description description in the form of an XML document, and produces a set of Ada (more specifically, SPARK 95) accessors for the data structure.

```xml
<package name="Date_And_Time_Pkg">
 <message name="Date_And_Time">
  <field  name="Years_Since_1980"  length="7"  />
  <field  name="Month"             length="4"  />
  <field  name="Day_Of_Month"      length="5"  />
  <field  name="Hour"              length="5"  />
  <field  name="Minute"            length="6"  />
  <field  name="Two_Seconds"       length="5"  />
 </message>
</package>
```

Listing 3. Tranxgen specification for date/time record

From this specification, *Tranxgen* produces a record type declaration with representation clause, none of whose components crosses a byte boundary. Accessors decompose and reconstruct component values using arithmetic expressions, following the method outlined in section 3.2, as seen in the following generated code excerpt:

```ada
package Date_And_Time_Pkg is
   type Date_And_Time is record
      Years_Since_1980 : U7_T;    -- 7 bits
      Month_0          : Bits_1;  -- 1 bit integer
      Month_1          : Bits_3;  -- 3 bits
      Day_Of_Month     : U5_T;    -- 5 bits
      Hour             : U5_T;    --   ""
      Minute_0         : Bits_3;  -- 3 bits
      Minute_1         : Bits_3;  --   ""
      Two_Seconds      : U5_T;    -- 5 bits
   end record;

   for Date_And_Time'Alignment use 1;
```

```
for Date_And_Time ' Bit_Order
   use System . High_Order_First ;
for Date_And_Time use record
      Years_Since_1980  at 0 range 0 .. 6;
      Month_0           at 0 range 7 .. 7;
      Month_1           at 1 range 0 .. 2;
      Day_Of_Month      at 1 range 3 .. 7;
      Hour              at 2 range 0 .. 4;
      Minute_0          at 2 range 5 .. 7;
      Minute_1          at 3 range 0 .. 2;
      Two_Seconds       at 3 range 3 .. 7;
   end record ;

end Date_And_Time_Pkg ;

package body Date_And_Time_Pkg is

   -- [...]

   function Month (P : System . Address ) return U4_T is
      M : Date_And_Time ;
      for M' Address use P;
      pragma Import (Ada , M);
   begin
      return U4_T (M. Month_0) * 2**3 + U4_T (M. Month_1 );
   end Month ;

   procedure Set_Month (P : System . Address ; V : U4_T) is
      M : Date_And_Time ;
      for M' Address use P;
      pragma Import (Ada , M);
   begin
      M. Month_0 := Bits_1 (V / 2**3);
      M. Month_1 := Bits_3 (V mod 2**3);
   end Set_Month ;

   -- [...]

end Date_And_Time_Pkg ;
```

4   The *Scalar_Storage_Order* Attribute

In this section we introduce the *Scalar_Storage_Order* attribute, which allows the specification of the storage endianness for the components of a composite (record or array) type. Byte reordering is performed transparently by compiler generated code upon access to elementary (scalar) components of the data structure.

4.1 Formal Definition

Scalar_Storage_Order is an implementation-defined attribute specified as follows by the GNAT Reference Manual.

> For every array or record type S, the representation attribute
> Scalar_Storage_Order denotes the order in which storage elements that
> make up scalar components are ordered within S. Other properties are
> as for standard representation attribute Bit_Order, as defined by Ada
> RM 13.5.3(4). The default is System.Default_Bit_Order.
> For a record type S, if S'Scalar_Storage_Order is specified explicitly,
> it shall be equal to S'Bit_Order.

This means that if a Scalar_Storage_Order attribute definition clause is not confirming (that is, it specifies the opposite value to the default one, System. Default_Bit_Order), then the type's Bit_Order shall be specified explicitly and set to the same value. Also note that a scalar storage order clause can apply not only to a record type (like the standard Bit_Order attribute), but also to an array type (of scalar elements, or of other composite elements).

> If a component of S has itself a record or array type, then it shall also
> have a Scalar_Storage_Order attribute definition clause. In addition,
> if the component does not start on a byte boundary, then the scalar
> storage order specified for S and for the nested component type shall be
> identical.
> No component of a type that has a Scalar_Storage_Order attribute
> definition may be aliased.

These clauses ensure that endianness does not change except on a storage element boundary, and that components of a composite with a *Scalar_Storage_Order* attribute are never accessed indirectly through an access dereference (instead all accesses are always through an indexed or selected component).

> A confirming Scalar_Storage_Order attribute definition clause (i.e. with
> a value equal to System.Default_Bit_Order) has no effect.
> If the opposite storage order is specified, then whenever the value of a
> scalar component of an object of type S is read, the storage elements
> of the enclosing machine scalar are first reversed (before retrieving the
> component value, possibly applying some shift and mask operatings on
> the enclosing machine scalar), and the opposite operation is done for
> writes.

This is where the new attribute introduces the byte reordering.

The following clause generalizes the notion of *machine scalar* to cover some useful cases not taken into account by the original wording of the standard in the definition of the underlying machine scalar of a given (scalar) component.

In that case, the restrictions set forth in 13.5.1(10.3/2) for scalar components are relaxed. Instead, the following rules apply:

- the underlying storage elements are those at
  (position + first_bit / SE_size) .. (position + (last_bit +
  SE_size - 1) / SE_size)
- the sequence of underlying storage elements shall have a size no greater than the largest machine scalar
- the enclosing machine scalar is defined as the smallest machine scalar starting at a position no greater than
  position + first_bit / SE_size and covering storage elements at least up to position + (last_bit + SE_size - 1) / SE_size
- the position of the component is interpreted relative to that machine scalar.

4.2   Example Usage and Effect

Let us assume that the type declaration for the Date_And_Time structure in listing 2 is from a legacy big-endian application, a component of which is now being retargeted to a new little-endian board. Of course the underlying memory representation must not be changed, as this board exchanges messages with a legacy black-box module whose source code is unavailable. We will therefore apply attribute definition clauses as follows as shown in listing 4.

```
for Date_And_Time'Scalar_Storage_Order
  use System.High_Order_First;

for Date_And_Time'Bit_Order use System.High_Order_First;
--   Bit order and scalar storage order must be consistent.
```

Listing 4. Attribute definition clauses for scalar storage order and bit order

The memory representation of an object of type Date_And_Time as created on a big-endian machine is shown on figure 1. If we read the Month component of an object of that type, we first load the underlying machine scalar. As noted above, the storage elements have values 65 followed by 114, and on a little-endian machine this represents the 16-bit scalar value 29 249.

But now by virtue of the *Scalar_Storage_Order* that has been defined for the type as High_Order_First, since we are on a little-endian machine we reverse the order of bytes within this machine scalar, which gives us back the original value 16 754. The bit pattern of this scalar is now identical to the original one from the big-endian specification, and thus shifting and masking operations will yield the original component value.

The reverse byte swapping is performed upon write operations, after the component value has been installed into a machine scalar, and prior to this machine scalar being stored back to memory. This transformation is applied only for scalar components, so that nested records are handled correctly (i.e. no extra swapping is introduced when accessing a subcomponent of a nested record).

4.3   Implementation

The implementation of the *Scalar_Storage_Order* attribute has been done in the version of the GNAT compiler using the GCC back-end as the code generator.

Even if a growing number of processors have the capability to run either in big-endian or in little-endian mode, the mode is generally selected once for all at startup and cannot be changed afterwards. The compiler therefore needs to generate explicit byte swapping operations.

The primary design decision to be considered is the level at which these byte swapping operations are made explicit in the hierarchy of intermediate representations of the compiler. The GCC-based GNAT compiler has a 4-tiered hierarchy of representations (the framed boxes):

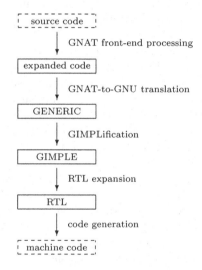

The higher in the hierachy the byte swapping operations are made explicit, the simpler the implementation is, but the less efficient the machine code will be when run on the target. This is because the bulk of the compiler is parameterized for the endianness of the target, and so explicit byte swapping operations act as optimization barriers in the various intermediate representations.

The choice has been made to generate the byte swapping operations during RTL expansion: the first intermediate representation in which they are explicitly present is RTL (Register Transfer Language), which is a very low-level representation. All high-level GIMPLE optimizations, which are the most powerful ones, work without change on code requiring endianness conversions; only the low-level RTL optimizations are affected.

```
movzwl    (%ecx), %eax
rolw      $8, %ax
shrw      $5, %ax
andl      $15, %eax
```

Listing 5. x86 assembly code generated for load of Month

The other major design decision pertains to the representation and the manipulation of the storage order in the GIMPLE representation (the expanded code and the GENERIC representation being essentially extremely verbose versions of the source code, they do not need substantial adjustments; at these levels, the scalar storage order is just another property of composite types, like packedness or atomicity). Storage order could conceivably be tracked on a scalar-by-scalar basis, i.e. with the finest possible granularity. With this approach, every scalar gets a new property, the endianness, in addition to the usual properties, for example the size and the bounds. However this would have required major surgery in the high-level part of the code generator, and would have introduced an undesirable additional layer of complexity.

We therefore chose instead to consider storage order only as a property of memory stored scalars (and specifically, only those scalars stored as part of an enclosing composite object); all other scalars always have the default storage order. Moreover, scalar *values* (considered outside of any *object*) are always in the default endianness. This makes the implementation far simpler, because the various transformations and optimizations applied to the intermediate representation need not take the endianness into account. They only have to preserve the invariant that some particular scalars in memory must be accessed in a special way.

It is also worth noting that, in a few specific cases, the GNAT front-end needs to apply low-level transformations to the source code before passing it to the code generator, which may depend on the storage order. In these cases, the front-end may need to generate explicit byte swapping operations (for example to initialize bit-packed arrays). The code generator therefore exposes its internal byte swapping primitives as builtins that can be directly invoked by the front-end. These are ultimately translated into explicit byte swapping operations during RTL expansion.

The implementation is fully generic: it imposes no additional requirement on the target architecture, such as availability of specific byte swapping or byte manipulation instructions. However, the code generator will take advantage of them if present, for example on the Intel x86 and IBM PowerPC architectures, with a measurable performance gain in these cases.

Going back to the example of the `Month` component of an object of type `Date_And_Time`, the assembly code generated on x86 to read the component is shown on listing 5.

The first instruction `movzwl` loads the underlying machine scalar, i.e. the 16-bit integer value at offset 0 in the record. The second instruction `rolw $8` swaps the bytes in this scalar. The remaining instructions extract the component.

4.4 Performance Discussion

The introduction of the *Scalar_Storage_Order* attribute represents a significant gain in terms of application development cost, in that in relieves developers from the need to implement data conversions from one endianness to the other.

However the execution time cost of such conversions does not disappear: they are still present, and if opposite-endianness data structures are frequently used, they are liable to cause an unavoidable degradation in application performance (compared to the same application using data structures in native endianness). This is less likely when explicit data conversions are used, because in the latter case conversion points are well identified, and internal processing in the application is done efficiently on data structures that have native endianness.

It may therefore be advisable, even when relying on *Scalar_Storage_Order* to perform data conversions, to apply this attribute to a derived type used for external interfaces. Ada type conversions from the derived type to the ancestor type (which has no representation attributes, and hence has the standard native representation) can then be used to convert data from the external representation (possibly using a different endianness than the native one) to the internal (native endianness) representation, as show on listing 6.

```ada
type Date_And_Time is record
   . . .
end record;
--  Native, efficient representation

type External_Date_And_Time is new Date_And_Time;
for External_Date_And_Time use record
   . . .
end record;
for External_Date_And_Time'Scalar_Storage_Order
   use External_Bit_Order;
for External_Date_And_Time'Bit_Storage_Order
   use External_Bit_Order;

function To_Internal
   (DT : External_Date_And_Time) return Date_And_Time
is
begin
   return Date_And_Time (DT);
   --  Type conversion with change of representation
end To_Internal;
```

Listing 6. Setting scalar storage order on a derived type

In this manner, developers retain the advantage of automated, transparent generation of the code effecting the required representation change, while at the same time avoiding the distributed overhead of pervasive byte swapping throughout the application.

5   Conclusion and Future Directions

We have presented the issues posed by data representations with different endianness in Ada applications. We have discussed the current Ada features supporting record layout specification, and identified some of their limitations in conjunction with support for endianness conversions. We have introduced two separate approaches to overcoming these limitations: a code generation tool *Tranxgen* producing accessors from a data representation model, and a new representation *Scalar_Storage_Order* allowing transparent access to data structures of arbitrary endianness. These tools allow application code to be written in a portable way, guaranteeing consistent data representations between little-endian and big-endian platforms without the need for explicit conversion operations.

Possible improvements to *Tranxgen* include support for a wider variety of data structures, and using the *Scalar_Storage_Order* attribute in generated code. The specification for the attribute will be proposed to the Ada Rapporteur Group for inclusion in the next revision of the Ada language.

References

1. Ada Rapporteur Group: Controlling bit ordering. Ada Issue AI95-00133, ISO/IEC JTC1/SC22/WG9 (2004),
   http://www.ada-auth.org/cgi-bin/cvsweb.cgi/ais/ai-00133.txt?rev=1.17,
   adopted amendment to the Ada 95 standard [5]
2. Andress, R.P.: Wholesale byte reversal of the outermost Ada record object to achieve endian independence for communicated data types. Ada Letters XXV(3), 19–27 (2005)
3. Cohen, D.: On Holy Wars and a Plea for Peace. IEEE Computer 14(10), 48–54 (1981)
4. Cohen, N.H.: Endian-independent record representation clauses. Ada Letters XIV(1), 27–29 (1994)
5. ISO: Information Technology – Programming Languages – Ada. ISO (February 1995), ISO/IEC/ANSI 8652:1995
6. ITU-T: Information technology — Abstract Syntax Notation One (ASN.1): Specification of basic notation. Recommendation X.680 (November 2008)
7. ITU-T: Information technology — ASN.1 encoding rules: Specification of Basic Encoding Rules (BER), Canonical Encoding Rules (CER) and Distinguished Encoding Rules (DER). Recommendation X.690 (November 2008)
8. Mardis, M.: Endian-safe record representation clauses for Ada programs. Ada Letters XIX(4), 13–18 (1999)
9. Protomatics: Transfer Syntax Notation One (TSN.1). Tech. rep.,
   http://www.protomatics.com/tsn1.html
10. Swift, J.: Travels into Several Remote Nations of the World. By Lemuel Gulliver (1726)

Provably Secure DNS:
A Case Study in Reliable Software[*]

Barry Fagin and Martin Carlisle

Department of Computer Science
US Air Force Academy
Colorado Springs, CO 80840 USA
{barry.fagin,martin.carlisle}@usafa.edu

Abstract. We describe the use of formal methods in the development of IRONSIDES, an implementation of DNS with superior performance to both BIND and Windows, the two most common DNS servers on the Internet. More importantly, unlike BIND and Windows, IRONSIDES is impervious to all single-packet denial of service attacks and all forms of remote code execution.

Keywords: domain name server, formal methods, software systems, DNS, Ada, internet security, computer security, network security, buffer overflows, domain name system, denial of service.

(Distribution A, Approved for public release, distribution unlimited.)

1   Introduction

DNS is a protocol essential to the proper functioning of the Internet. The two most common implementations of DNS are the free software version BIND and the implementations that come bundled with various versions of Windows. Unfortunately, despite their ubiquity and importance, these implementations suffer from security vulnerabilities and require frequent patching. As of this writing, according to the Internet Systems Consortium's web site, there are 51 known vulnerabilities in various versions of BIND [1]. Over the past five years, Microsoft has released at least 8 security bulletins relating to vulnerabilities in Windows DNS. Since neither of these products have ever been, to our knowledge, formally validated, it is likely that further flaws remain for hackers to discover and exploit.

The existence of security flaws in such a vital component of the Internet software suite is troubling, to say the least. These vulnerabilities permit not only bad-packet denial of service attacks to crash a DNS server, but in the worst case can actually lead to remote code execution exploits, giving the adversary control over the host machine.

To address this problem, the authors have used formal methods and the SPARK tool set from Praxis Systems [2] to develop a high-performance version of DNS

---

[*] The rights of this work are transferred to the extent transferable according to title 17 U.S.C. 105.

H.B. Keller et al. (Eds.): Ada-Europe 2013, LNCS 7896, pp. 81–93, 2013.
© Springer-Verlag Berlin Heidelberg 2013

that is provably exception-free. We first give a brief overview of DNS, and our implementation of it using the SPARK tools. We then describe our experimental test bed and the results we obtained. We conclude with lessons learned and directions for future work.

2   Overview of DNS

DNS is an abbreviation for the Internet's Domain Name System. Theoretically it is a naming system for any resource connected to the Internet, but in practice it associates host names (www.cnn.com) with IP addresses (157.166.226.26). The DNS protocol was developed by Paul Mockapetris, first codified in IETF documents RFC 882 and RFC 883 and later superseded by RFC's 1034 and 1035. Clients of a DNS server interact with it supplying queries of various types, with the server providing the answers. Communication between a DNS client and server takes place at either the UDP or TCP layers of the Internet protocol stack.

The distinguishing feature of DNS is its hierarchical and distributed nature. Because it is hierarchical, a single DNS server may not and need not know the answer to a client query. If it does not, it can query another DNS server at a higher level in the Internet domain name space for further information. This process may be repeated up to the root server, with further information then propagating back down to the original querying server.

The system's distributed nature means that there is no central DNS server. Hundreds of thousands of implementations of DNS are all running at once, and because they all use the same protocols to communicate they all function correctly.

Simple implementations of DNS may perform solely as authoritative name servers, responsible only for managing the IP addresses associated with a particular zone. To reduce the load on the root zone servers and to improve performance of applications that rely on nearby DNS servers, more complex implementations of DNS may cache query answers as well as fully implement the recursive query protocol described previously.

The most popular implementation of DNS is the Berkeley Internet Name Domain server, or BIND. Originally written in 1984, it has been ported to a number of systems and compilers, and has been distributed as free software since its inception. According to the Wikipedia entry on DNS, it is the dominant name service software on the Internet. However, numerous alternatives remain available, including implementations bundled with Microsoft Windows.

3   SPARK: A Tool For Creating Provably Correct Programs

The SPARK language and toolset from Altran Praxis is used in the creation of software systems with provable correctness and security properties. SPARK is a subset of Ada, augmented with special annotations. These annotations appear as ordinary comments to Ada compilers, but are parsed by SPARK's pre-processing tools used to validate the software. SPARK is a fairly mature technology and has been used on several projects [3-5]. Accordingly, given our prior institutional experience with Ada (see for example [6]), we chose SPARK and Ada as the platform for constructing DNS software that would not be subject to most of the vulnerabilites of BIND and Windows versions currently deployed around the globe.

4   Overview of IRONSIDES

IRONSIDES is an Ada/SPARK implementation of the DNS protocols. The IRONSIDES authoritative DNS server was described previously in [7]. Since that publication, off-line signed DNS records have been added to IRONSIDES using DNSSEC, the protocol that adds encryption to DNS transactions to further reduce vulnerability to spoofing and other attacks [8]. Below we describe the architecture of the IRONSIDES recursive service. In actual operation, both versions would be run-ning concurrently.

The high level structure of the IRONSIDES recursive service is shown in Figure 1:

RECURSIVE QUERIES

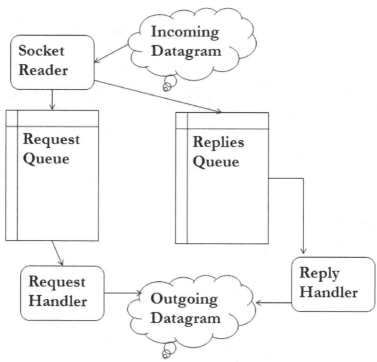

Fig. 1. High-level structure of IRONSIDES recursive service

Incoming DNS messages are either queries from a "downstream" client, in which case they are placed in a request queue, or responses from an "upstream" server, which are placed in a reply queue. Queries are checked against a DNS record cache (not shown). If appropriate matching records are found, a response DNS message is constructed and sent out on the wire back to the requesting server. Otherwise, the query is forwarded to one or more upstream servers. Responses are sent back to the original requesting server and stored in the DNS record cache. The modules that implement the above structure and their data dependency relationships are shown below. Lines indicate a data dependency from the module above on the module below. Transitive dependencies are implied.

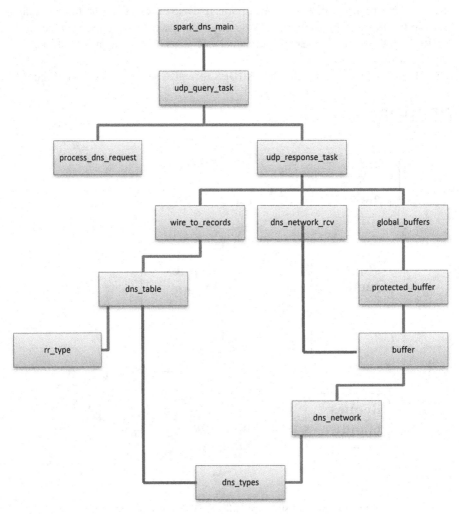

Fig. 2. Module and data dependency representation of IRONSIDES

The functions of these modules are as follows:

- spark_dns_main: Top-level executable
- udp_query_task: Concurrently executing task responsible for all incoming DNS traffic
- udp_response_task: Concurrently executing task responsible for managing all responses from upstream servers
- process_dns_request: Interprets incoming packet, queries DNS table, queues query if answer not found
- wire_to_records: Builds DNS resource records from DNS packets on the wire
- dns_network_rcv: SPARK wrapper for network traffic to guarantee no over-flows
- global_buffers: Query and response queues
- protected_buffer: ADT for the query and response queues
- buffer_pkg: ADT for a queue
- dns_table: Cache of DNS resource records
- rr_type: Top-level package for all DNS resource record types
- dns_network: Handles low-level network IO
- dns_types: Data types for working with DNS packets

As a result of the software validation process, IRONSIDES code is known to be free of uninitialized values, data flow errors (e.g. writes that are never read or values derived from incorrect sources), array bounds errors, and all runtime exceptions. This renders it invulnerable to single-packet denial of service attacks and all remote execution exploits. If IRONSIDES is properly compiled and configured, it cannot be taken over as a result of any external input, no matter when the input arrives and no matter how it is formatted. Also, it cannot be crashed and all its loops are guaranteed to terminate, which renders it invulnerable to denial of service attacks that rely on badly formatted packets.

Current statistics on the proof requirements and code size of IRONSIDES authoritative are shown in Tables 1 and 2.

Table 1. Proof requirements of IRONSIDES authoritative

	Total	Examiner	Simplifier	Victor
Assert/Post	3106	2209	884	13
Precondition	561	0	532	29
Check stmt.	12	0	12	0
Runtime check	3750	0	3704	46
Refinement. VC s	44	42	2	0
Inherit. VCs	0	0	0	0
Totals:	7473	2251	5134	88
%Totals:		30%	69%	1%

Table 2. IRONSIDES source lines

Total Lines:	11598
Blank Lines:	871
Non-blank non-comment lines:	7543
Lines of SPARK annotations:	133
Semicolons:	5403

A "Verification Condition", or VC, is a theorem that must be proved in order for SPARK to consider the program as validated. Typical VC's include assertions that integers do not overflow or wraparound, that array bounds are not exceeded, and so forth. Simpler VC's are proved by the Spark Examiner. More complicated ones are proved by the Verifier. According to AdaCore Technologies [9], over 95% of VCs are proven automatically by the SPARK toolset. In our case, this was 99%. We were unwilling to allow any VCs to remain unproven, lest they be false and lead to a security vulnerability. Consequently, we used Victor, a wrapper for the advanced Satisfiability Modulo Theories (SMT) solver Alt-Ergo, developed at the University of Paris-Sud [10], to prove the final 1%. Readers interested in learning more about the SPARK tool set are referred to [2].

We see from Table 2 that the overhead of SPARK annotations in terms of code size and typing time is negligible, approximately ten percent of the total number of lines in the program.

5   Experimental Results

Having software that is crash-proof is valuable, but unless its performance is comparable to existing implementations it is not likely to be accepted by the user community. System administrators, if faced with the choice, might regard software vulnerabilities as acceptable risks if fixing them significantly impacts performance. Furthermore, from a computer security research perspective, it would be useful to understand the nature of the tradeoff between security and performance, or even better to discover that in at least some cases no such tradeoff is required. We present here the results of a case study performed to better understand these questions.

Previous work [7] compared the performance of the IRONSIDES authoritative server to BIND running on a Linux system (Ubuntu 11.0). We now present results comparing the performance of IRONSIDES authoritative with BIND and Windows DNS on Windows Server 2008. As in [7], we use the DNS stress testing tool 'dnsperf' [11]. Because IRONSIDES is still in development, it does not yet have the feature range of BIND or Window DNS (though we are continually adding more features and the gap is rapidly closing). Any comparison should take these differences into account. Following the style of [12], we show a comparison of these three DNS packages below. Footnotes and parenthetical comments for BIND and Windows are omitted to save space.

Table 3a/3b. Comparison of BIND, Windows and IRONSIDES functionality

Server	Authoritative	Recursive	Recursion ACL	Slave mode	Caching
BIND	Y	Y	Y	Y	Y
Windows DNS	Y	Y	N	Y	Y
IRONSIDES	Y*	in progress	N	N	in progress

DNSSEC	Server	TSIG	IPv6	Wildcard	Free Software	split horizon
Y	**BIND**	Y	Y	Y	Y	Y
Y	**Windows DNS**	Y	Y	Y	N	N
offline-signed	**IRONSIDES**	N	Y	N	Y	N

*The following resource record types are currently supported: A, AAAA, CNAME, DNSKEY, MX, NS, NSEC, PTR, RRSIG, SOA.

Our experimental test bed is shown in Figure 3:

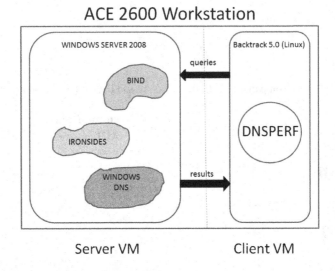

Fig. 3. Experimental test bed for performance comparisons of DNS software

'dnsperf' runs on a Backtrack 5.0 client virtual machine. A Windows Server 2008 virtual machine is loaded as a server. Testing is done by starting up the DNS server to be tested under the server virtual machine, and then running dnsperf. Only one DNS server is active at a time.

Since the purpose of the experiment is to measure the computational performance of the server, both VMs are loaded on the same computer, in this case an ACE 2600 Workstation with 8GB of RAM. Using the same computer for client and server eliminates the effect of network latency. 'dnsperf' issues queries over the standard DNS port to whichever server is listening. The server in turn responds as appropriate. At the end of a run, the tool generates a performance report.

We performed three test runs for three DNS implementations and then averaged the results, scaling them to queries per millisecond. The raw data are shown in Table 4. Averaged results are shown in Figure 4:

Table 4. Comparison of DNS software (queries per second for three test runs)

BIND		
16478.3	16667.9	17020.0
IRONSIDES		
37329.1	37814.6	37024.4
Win DNS		
34188.0	35676.1	35089.3

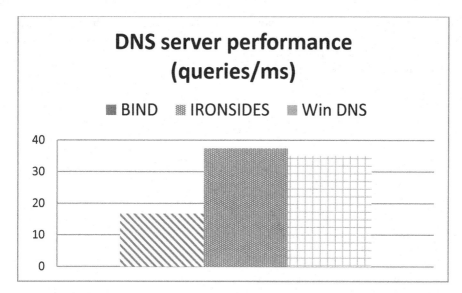

Fig. 4. Comparison of DNS software (queries per millisecond, averaged)

The most important result of our experiment is that IRONSIDES not only has better security properties than the two most popular DNS servers, but outperforms them as well. On a Windows machine, IRONSIDES is 7% faster than Windows DNS and more than twice as fast as BIND. Given IRONSIDES superior security posture, we find these results significant. They show that one need not sacrifice security for performance in software design.

In fact, it should not be that surprising that there are at least some instances in which the use of formal methods can improve performance. Data flow analysis, for example, can identify redundant or ineffective statements that generate unnecessary code. Code that has been proven exception-free no longer needs run-time bounds checking, so that code can be eliminated as well.

On the other hand, there are also cases where total reliance on formal methods negatively impacts performance. Allowing users to override formal proof requirements when appropriate is an important feature that we believe formal methods tools should continue to support.   In one case, performing this type of optimization in IRONSIDES led to a 14% improvement in performance on a Windows VM. Since such overriding is optional, users in environments where manual verification of source code is deemed too risky can revert to the original, formally verified source code at some cost in performance.

IRONSIDES is invulnerable to denial of service attacks caused by badly formatted packets that raise exceptions. But terminating a server is not the only way to deny service. If the server can be thrown into an infinite loop, service is just as effectively denied. IRONSIDES is invulnerable to this form of service denial as well, because the tools employed help prove that all of its 85 loops terminate. This is accomplished by using loop invariant assertions to show that loop variables monotonically increase and have an upper bound. This is not accomplished automatically by SPARK, but with appropriate loop assertion annotations added by the programmer SPARK can assist in showing these properties to be true.

For example, consider the code below:

```
-- Amount_Trimmed prevents infinite loop
while Answer_Count=0 and Amount_Trimmed < RR_Type.WireStringType'Last
and Natural(Character'Pos(Current_Name (Current_Name'First)))/=0 and
Current_Qname_Location <= DNS_Types.QNAME_PTR_RANGE(Output_Bytes)loop
--# assert Answer_Count=0 and Amount_Trimmed>=0 and
--# Amount_Trimmed<RR_Type.WireStringType'Last
--# and Output_Bytes <= DNS_Types.Packet_Length_Range'Last and
--# Current_Qname_Location <=DNS_Types.QNAME_PTR_RANGE(Output_Bytes);
     Trim_Name(Domainname => Current_Name,
      Trimmed_Name     => Trimmed_Name,
      Qname_Location   => Current_Qname_Location,
      New_Qname_Location => New_Qname_Location);
     Create_Response_SOA(Start_Byte => Start_Byte,
      Domainname     => Trimmed_name,
      Qname_Location => New_Qname_Location,
      Output_Packet  => Output_Packet,
      Answer_Count   => Answer_Count,
      Output_Bytes   => Output_Bytes);
     Current_Name := Trimmed_Name;
     Current_Qname_Location := New_Qname_Location;
     Amount_Trimmed := Amount_Trimmed +
              Natural(Character'Pos(Domainname(Domainname'First))+1);
   end loop;
```

Fig. 5. Using loop invariants to prove termination

SPARK annotations begin with "--#". Here the annotations are loop invariants that serve as both a postcondition for one part of the loop and as preconditions for the next. In this case the tools prove that Amount_Trimmed is at all times both non-negative and below a constant upper bound. Data flow analysis shows that Amount_Trimmed is not modified elsewhere in the loop. Given these properties and the last line of the loop, we can conclude that Amount_Trimmed is monotonically increasing, therefore the loop terminates.

Note that without the use of this variable and the proof annotations, we could not prove loop termination. This would leave open the possibility for the other termination conditions to never be reached, something that could be exploited under the right circumstances to deny service through an infinite loop.

6   Lessons in Humility

The use of formal methods and the SPARK tools in particular produced results that were both impressive and humbling. Both the authors are experienced software engineers, having written compilers, introductory programming environments, circuit emulators, and other non-trivial software systems. In addition to over 40 years combined computer science teaching experience, we have consulted for both industry and government. Nonetheless, the formal methods tools we employed caught boundary conditions and potential problems. Some examples are shown below:

1) The use in a zone file of a domain name consisting of a single character:

```
--SPARK caught possible exception if length=1, modified
--by adding "length > 1 and then"
if Name(1) = '.' or Name(1) = '-' or (length > 1 and then
(Name(Length-1) = '.' or Name(Length-1) = '-')) then
  RetVal := False;
```

2) A resource record of length equal to the maximum line length allowed:

```
--endIdx might be the maximum value possible, so must
catch last character here. Caught by SPARK.
  if Ctr = EndIdx and numSeparators <= REQ_NUM_SEPARATORS
then
```

3) Failure to account for erroneous input:

```
if Query_Class /= IN_CLASS then  …
elsif Query_Type = A then  …
end if;
--Forgot else to handle erroneous input! Caught by SPARK.
```

4) Failure to check for subscript overflow:

```
--copy name from packet to Domainname (null terminated)
while Integer(Byte) < Integer(Input_Bytes) and then In-
put_Packet.Bytes(
  Byte)/=0 loop
--this could overflow Domainname array! Caught by SPARK.
  Domainname(I) := Input_Packet.Bytes(Byte);
  I := I + 1;
  Byte := Byte + 1;
end loop;
Domainname(I) := ASCII.NUL;
```

These are all problems we should and could have detected on our own, but did not. Had they gone undetected, they could have led to security holes exploitable by hackers, particularly if they had access to source code. Our experience suggests the use of formal methods and tools is an essential part of improving the security properties of software. Using experienced, security-conscious programmers is not enough.

7   Hitting the Sweet Spot

Much of the emphasis on applying formal reasoning to computer programs has focused on proofs program correctness. This has proven to be quite difficult. Correctness properties for all but the most trivial programs are extremely complex, requiring elaborate formal models and axiomatic formulations that may be more difficult to construct than the original program.

While we anticipate continued progress in the use of formal methods to prove program correctness, our results suggest that an exclusive focus on proofs of correctness may be causing researchers to miss a"sweet spot" of opportunity: Proofs of security.

On one end of the spectrum, correctness properties are useful to prove but very hard for most interesting programs: Existing tools and technology are not yet sufficiently sophisticated to complete them. On the other hand, there are properties of programs that are easy to prove (correctness of mathematical functions, small subroutines, and so forth), but are not particularly interesting or important. Security properties fall into that middle ground of things that are both important to prove and provable with existing technology.

With the help of SPARK and the use of Ada, for example, we can formally prove the following security properties of the IRONSIDES DNS server:

1) No classic buffer overflow
2) No incorrect calculation of buffer size
3) No improper initialization
4) No ineffective statements
5) No integer overflow/wraparound
6) No information leakage
7) All input validated
8) No allocation w/o limits (no resource exhaustion)
9) No improper array indexing
10) No null pointer dereferencing
11) No expired pointer dereferencing (use after free)
12) No type confusion
13) No race conditions
14) No incorrect conversions
15) No uncontrolled format strings
16) All loops guaranteed to terminate

Problems with all of the above have so vexed BIND that the US Defense Advanced Research Projects Agency is funding a program to crowd source it and other important software to achieve formal verification of security properties [13]. By contrast, because IRONSIDES is written in Ada, a language designed from the beginning with software engineering principles in mind, and because a commercially backed tool is available for formal analysis of Ada programs, we are able to achieve provably exception-free code despite being only two academic researchers employed at an undergraduate university.

8   Conclusions and Future Work

Our work indicates that the theory and practice of formal methods has progressed considerably in the past few years, to the point where formal verification of certain desirable properties of software is now achievable at relatively little additional cost. Within less than a year, two academics whose primary duties are teaching were nonetheless able to produce a verifiably exception-free version of DNS. We did this despite having no prior familiarity with SPARK or indeed any formal language tools from industry.

While overriding the requirements for explicit storage initialization does indeed permit software engineers to trade security for performance, our results show that in general no such tradeoff is required. The IRONSIDES authoritative server runs significantly faster than either BIND or Windows DNS, and does so on a Windows "home court" VM running Windows Server 2008.

IRONSIDES is in the public domain, and is distributed free of charge at http://ironsides.martincarlisle.com. Currently development focuses on the IRONSIDES recursive service. Future work could include testing under other operating systems, testing under actual network loading, online zone signing, GUI and web interfaces, and other more advanced features. Other implementations of Internet protocols that suffer from security flaws could also benefit from the approach described here.

This work was funded by the US Defense Advanced Research Projects Agency, whose support is gratefully acknowledged. We thank AdaCore Technologies and Altran Praxis for providing technical support on using their tools. We also wish to thank the USAFA Department of Computer Science, the Academy's Director of Research, and the Academy Center for Cyberspace Research.

References

1. Internet Systems Consortium, `http://www.isc.org`
2. Barnes, J.: High Integrity Software: The SPARK Approach to Safety and Security. Addison-Wesley Publishing (2003) 0-321-13616-0
3. `http://www.adacore.com/2010/08/16/spark-skein/`
4. Barnes, J., et al.: Engineering the Tokeneer Enclave Protection Software. In: 1st IEEE Symposium on Secure Software Engineering (2006)
5. Woodcock, J., et al.: Formal methods: Practice and experience. ACM Comput. Surv. 41(4), Article 19, 36 (2009)
6. Sward, R.E., Carlisle, M.C., Fagin, B.S., Gibson, D.S.: The case for Ada at the USAF Academy. In: ACM SIGAda International Conference on Ada, pp. 68–70 (2003)
7. Carlisle, M., Fagin, B.: IRONSIDES: DNS With No Single-Packet Denial of Service or Remote Code Execution Vulnerabilities. In: Proceedings of IEEE GLOBECOM 2012, Anaheim CA (2012)
8. DNSSEC – The DNS Security Extensions, `http://www.dnssec.net/`
9. `http://www.adacore.com/sparkpro/language-toolsuite/`
10. `http://alt-ergo.lri.fr`
11. Nominum, Inc. DNS measurement tools,
    `http://www.nominum.com/support/measurement-tools/`
12. Comparison of DNS Server Software, `http://en.wikipedia.org/wiki/Comparison_of_DNS_server_software`
13. `http://www.darpa.mil/Our_Work/I2O/Programs/Crowd_Sourced_Formal_Verification_(CSFV).aspx`

Using Ontologies in the Integration of Structural, Functional, and Process Perspectives in the Development of Safety Critical Systems

Irene Bicchierai, Giacomo Bucci, Carlo Nocentini, and Enrico Vicario

Dipartimento di Ingegneria dell'Informazione - Università di Firenze
{irene.bicchierai,giacomo.bucci,carlo.nocentini,enrico.vicario}@unifi.it

Abstract. We present a systematic approach for the efficient management of the data involved in the development process of safety critical systems, illustrating how the activities performed during the life-cycle can be integrated in a common framework. Information needed in these activities reflects concepts that pertain to three different perspectives: i) structural elements of design and implementation; ii) functional requirements and quality attributes; iii) organization of the overall process. The integration of these concepts may considerably improve the trade-off between reward and effort spent in verification and quality-driven activities.

We address the exploitation of ontological modeling and semantic technologies so as to support cohesion across different stages of the development life-cycle, attaching a machine-readable semantics to concepts belonging to structural, functional and process perspectives. The formalized conceptualization enables the implementation of a tool leveraging on well established technologies aiding the accomplishment of crucial and effort-expensive activities such as the identification of the associations between requirements and the SW components implementing them.

Keywords: Ontologies, automated reasoning, Traceability Requirements, SW Engineering, Reliability Availability Maintainability and Safety, certification standards.

1 Introduction

In the development of safety-critical systems, verification and documentation activities comprise a major component of the overall effort. While intended to support quality assessment along the entire development process, they become crucial in a more evident manner at the time of certification. In industrial environments the development life-cycle is generally tailored to the V-Model [4] while Military Standard 498 (MIL-STD-498) [24] rules the documental process. Furthermore, specific standards exist for different class of products, such as CENELEC EN 50128 [5] for railways signalling, RTCA DO 178B [19] for airborne SW, ISO IEC 62304 [12] for medical devices.

H.B. Keller et al. (Eds.): Ada-Europe 2013, LNCS 7896, pp. 95–108, 2013.

The inherent complexity of prescribed activities is largely exacerbated by their dependency on information relative to the different stages of development. Furthermore, these data are formalized in different documental artifacts, often contributed by different parties or units, and pertaining to three different perspectives: structural elements of design and implementation, functional and quality requirements, and organization of the overall process. Systematization of the integration of these three perspectives may largely improve the trade-off between reward and effort spent in verification and quality-oriented activities, and it may open the way to agile tailoring of the process model to the specific characteristics of each project and organization. Ontological modeling and semantic technologies provide a relatively recent yet mature basis that may support this systematization aim. Ontologies are defined as an explicit specification of a conceptualization [10], this means that they are used to formalize concepts involved in any domain of interest. In [9], three ontological models are proposed to characterize relations among components, functions and quality attributes in complex embedded systems. In [26], a method and a system aiming at facilitating reuse of knowledge, supporting complete and precise description of processes and products, is proposed. The semantic knowledge is hierarchically organized in form of taxonomies, containing typical recurring technical knowledge about systems, functions, failure modes and actions. In [15], an ontology-based model-driven engineering process for compositional safety-analysis is introduced. The authors elaborate a domain ontology allowing the integration of a reasoner and inference rules to detect lack of model elements and inconsistent parts. In [6], an ontology for the formalization of Fault Trees is proposed. In [3], we proposed an ontological approach to support the automation of activities and the management of information related to the SW Failure Modes and Effects Analysis (SW-FMEA) process, showing the effectiveness of the methodology in the context of a space project. In [2], we showed how the ontological model of the SW-FMEA process can be integrated with SW metrics.

We further develop this approach, with a major advancement on the management of the overall process so as to enable the verification of required development activities and to integrate them with the documental process. To this end, we show how the conceptual model concerning with the structural and functional perspectives is integrated with a third orthogonal process model. The model provides a self-consistent representation of available information and artifacts required by applicable regulatory standards, so as to guarantee consistency with the industrial practice. Furthermore, we add a practical technique based on black box testing and aspect oriented code instrumentation, that supports automated extraction of dependencies between structural components and requirements. This allows the semi-automatic production of the data needed in required documents and the validation of their completeness and consistency. The proposed approach permits to preserve the coherence of the model across the maintenance and the refactoring occurring during development.

This paper is organized as follows. In Sect. 2 we introduce three fragments of the ontological model, each representing concepts of a different perspective.

In Sect. 3 we describe the connections among the three perspectives, explaining how the instances of concepts and associations establish the connections. In Sect. 4 we introduce a tool integrating the ontological model and a pluggable module implementing the Aspect Oriented Programming. Finally, in Sect. 5, we draw conclusions about the proposed approach.

2 Applying Ontologies in Systematizing the Development Process

The fundamental elements of an ontological model are *classes* and *properties*: classes represent categories or sets of elements; properties specify the internal structure of a class or the relations among classes. Classes and properties represent the *intensional* part of the ontology, while their instances represent the *extensional* part: *individuals* are realizations of concepts described by classes and *attributes* are realizations of properties. Ontological technologies comprise a rich framework of integrating components, including *ontological languages* such as OWL [14], *query languages*, such as SPARQL [17], and *rule languages*, such as SWRL [11]; in addition, off-the-shelf reasoners are available [22]. In order to provide a visual representation of the ontology elements, we use UML notation enriched with stereotypes for RDF and OWL concepts as standardized in the Ontology Definition Metamodel (ODM) [16]. Ontological entities are represented as classes, datatype properties are represented as their attributes, and object properties are represented as relations among classes.

In this section we describe how the formal characterization of concepts involved in the development process and the automatic manipulation of their data instances are supported by the ontological abstraction. These concepts belong to three different perspectives: i) the structural perspective concerned with the structural decomposition; ii) the functional perspective concerned with functional requirements and quality attributes; iii) the process perspective concerned with the phases of the development and the documents produced.

2.1 Structural Perspective

The structural perspective, shown in Fig. 1, comprises ontological concepts which model structural SW elements. A generic structural element is represented by the *Item* class. An item can be the entire *Computer SW Configuration Item (CSCI)* (i.e. an aggregation of SW with an individual configuration), a *SW Component*, a *SW Module*, or a *Method*. The model is hierarchically organized from the entire CSCI to the method (i.e. the smallest SW part with precise functionalities). The CSCI is made of SW components, which are physically organized in SW modules, containing methods written in some programming language (e.g. C, Assembly). Each *Method* is associated with *Code Metrics* which represent structural metrics of the code. Examples of code metrics are number of Lines Of Code (LOC), level of nesting, and cyclomatic complexity. Instances of code metrics are associated with a method through an instance of the *Code Metric Accountability* association

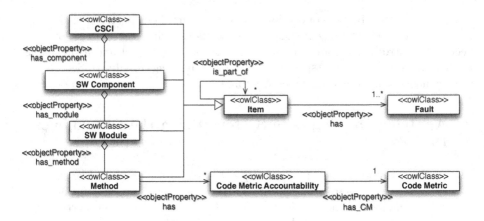

Fig. 1. The ontological concepts belonging to the structural perspective

class representing the value of the specific metric for that method. A structural item is associated with the *Faults* that represent the structural defects of the item itself.

2.2   Functional Perspective

The functional perspective comprises ontological concepts concerned with functional and quality requirements. Fig. 2 shows the involved ontological concepts. A *Requirement* can be either a *Functional Requirement*, if it refers to the functionalities implemented by the CSCI or a *RAMS Requirement*, if it refers to RAMS attributes (Reliability, Availability, Maintainability, and Safety). A *Test*, associated with a requirement, verifies the correct implementation of it. A requirement is associated also with *Failure Events*, that are the different ways in which the delivered service deviates from the correct implementation of the system function [1]. A failure event can be a *Testing Failure* or an *Operational Failure*, whether the failure is discovered during the testing phase or during the operational phase, respectively. A requirement is associated with the *Assurance Level* which is defined depending on the risk associated with the implementation of the requirement itself. The assurance level must be satisfied in the development of SW elements implementing the requirement. Regulatory standards as [5,19] recommend to allocate assurance levels to requirements according to consequences of failures in relation to dependability attributes (e.g. reliability, availability, safety) relevant for the considered application [21].

2.3   Process Perspective

The process perspective comprises the ontological concepts concerned with the development process such as activities and documents. Fig. 3 shows the involved

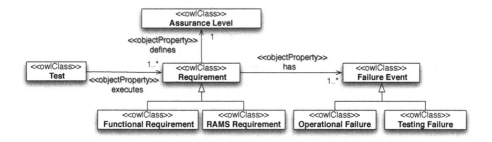

Fig. 2. The ontological concepts belonging to the functional perspective

ontological concepts. Standards and regulation adopted in the specific context (e.g. CENELEC EN 50128 [5], ISO IEC 62304 [12], RTCA DO 178B [19]) are represented by the *Applicable Regulation* class. They prescribe to perform activities represented by *Development and Verification Activity* class, and guide the production of documents, represented by *Document* class, along the development life-cycle. Examples of development and verification activities are testing, Hazard Analysis, and FMEA.

We assume the adoption of the MIL-STD-498 [24] which defines several type of documents fully describing their content. Each subclass of the *Document* class models a different document: the Software Requirements Specification (*SRS*), the Software Design Description (*SDD*), and the Software Testing Description (*STD*). Each of them contains information needed for the development. Following the common practice, an SRS can be divided into two parts, one listing the functional requirements, the other summing up the quality attributes. The former part is modeled by a class labelled *CSCI Capabilities Reqs. Section*, the latter is modeled by a class labelled *Other Reqs. Section*.

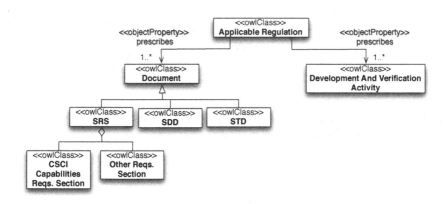

Fig. 3. The ontological concepts belonging to the process perspective

3   Connecting Different Perspectives

The proposed ontological formalization provides a systematic ground for the integration of concepts concerned with the structural, functional and process perspectives. In this section, we describe the connections between the three perspectives showing how instances of associations between concepts of different perspectives can be obtained.

3.1   Finding Instances in Documents

The specific instances of some concepts are reported in documents produced along the development life-cycle [24]. This enables the population of the extensional part of the ontological model while maintaining consistency with the industrial practice and improves cohesion among the activities of the life-cycle and the documents, enabling their automatic production.

Fig. 4 shows (in bold) the connections among the classes representing documents and the classes corresponding to the concepts reported in the documents. Concepts belonging to the structural perspective addressing the SW structure (i.e. *Item* class) are reported in the *SDD*. Concepts belonging to the functional perspective addressing requirements (i.e. *Requirement* class) are contained in the *SRS*. In particular, the former part of the SRS contains *Functional Requirements* while the latter reports *RAMS Requirements*. Concepts representing tests (i.e. *Test* class) are reported in the *STD*.

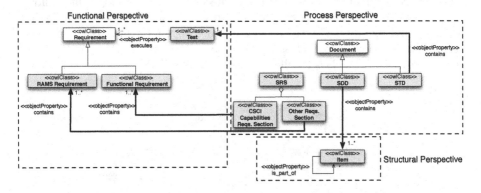

Fig. 4. The connections among the three perspectives, established through the documents produced along the development life-cycle

3.2   Tracing Requirements

The association among structural and functional elements is important with respect to maintainability, since it impacts on the ability of the system in isolating or correcting a defect as well as on satisfaction of new requirements. In addition, the identification of SW components that implement a requirement is also relevant to verify that the implementation is compliant with design specification. As a matter of fact, the regulatory standards expressly require that documents, such as SRS and SDD, contain the *traceability matrix*.

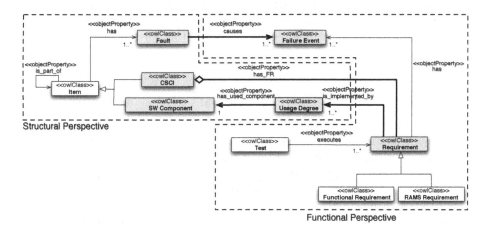

Fig. 5. The connections among the structural and the functional perspectives, established through the associations between a SW component and the implemented requirements and between a failure event and the faults causing it

Traceability of requirements has been addressed in various works [8,27]. In [8], the identification of required computational units is performed through a technique that combines the extraction of the static dependency graph and the dynamic execution of some features. In [27], three metrics are introduced to quantitatively evaluate the association of a component with a feature: the *concentration* of a feature in a SW component, the *dedication* of a component to a feature, and the *disparity* which measures the closeness between a feature and a component.

In our case the objective of the analysis is the identification of instances of the association between *Requirement* and *SW Component*(s) which is indirect through the *Usage Degree* class, as shown in Fig. 5. The association between *Test* and *Requirement*(s) exercised in the test is also shown.

Formally, let r_i be a generic requirement and c_j a generic SW component, we look for the relation $\mathcal{T} \subseteq 2^{FR} \times 2^C$ where FR is the set of requirements and C is the set of SW components. We define the generic element $T \in \mathcal{T}$ as $< T_r, T_c >$ where $T_r \in 2^{FR}$ and $T_c \in 2^C$. In doing so, $< T_r, T_c >\in \mathcal{T}$ means that a set of SW components T_c are related to a set of requirements T_r. Abusing of terms, we call a component c_i *necessary* for a requirement r_j if

$$\forall T \in \mathcal{T} : r_j \in T_r \Rightarrow c_i \in T_c,$$

we call a component c_i *potential* for a requirement r_j if

$$\exists T', T'' \in \mathcal{T} : r_j \in T'_r \wedge r_j \in T''_r \Rightarrow c_i \in T'_c \wedge c_i \notin T''_c.$$

Instances of the association between a requirement and SW components are obtained for each requirement extracting the components *necessary* for its implementation. As in [7], we express a usage degree (UG) of a SW component c_i in the implementation of a requirement r_j, accounting for how many methods M of c_i are executed in realizing r_j:

$$UG(c_i, r_j) = \frac{M(c_i, r_j)}{M(c_i)}.$$

To identify the relation $\mathcal{T}$ we perform a set of tests aimed at exercising one or more requirements tracing the SW components implementing them. This has been done resorting to Aspect Oriented Programming [13,23]. The associations of each requirement with the SW components *necessary* for its implementation (mediated by *Usage Degree* class in Fig. 5) are imported in the ontology, so as to add the extensional part.

The connection between the functional and the structural perspectives is realized also with the association between a *Failure Event*, which represents a failure of the associated *Requirement*, and the *Faults* that model the causes of the failure. The association between an *Item* and its *Fault*(s) cannot be completely automated. However, given a failure, thanks to the association of the requirement with SW components implementing it, the analyst is led to find those items that more likely contain a fault causing the failure.

3.3   Extracting Code Metrics for Assurance Verification

The three perspectives are connected also through the verification of the level of assurance obtained in the development process. A requirement defines a required level of assurance depending on the risk associated with the implementation of

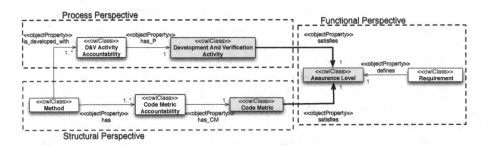

Fig. 6. The connections among the structural, functional and process perspectives, established through the verification of the level of assurance

the requirement itself. The development of SW components implementing the requirement must satisfy the required level of assurance. For each level of assurance, standards prescribe to execute activities and to develop SW with specific values of code metrics. Therefore each level of assurance is associated with a set of required predicates about code metrics and development and verification activities [3,2].

A set of predicates for a requirement r has the form

$$\mathcal{P}_r = \left\{ X_1 \lesseqgtr k_1, \ldots, X_n \lesseqgtr k_n, Y_1 = s_1, \ldots, Y_m = s_m \right\} \text{ with } n, m \in \mathbb{N}$$

where, referring to the fragment of the ontological model shown in Fig. 6, X_i and Y_j, with $i = 1 \ldots n$ and $j = 1 \ldots m$, are instances of *Code Metric* and *Development and Verification Activity* classes, respectively, while k_i and s_j are instances of *Code Metrics Accountability* and *D&V Activity Accountability* classes, respectively. If all the SW components contributing to the realization of r are implemented with values of X_i lower (greater) than k_i and Y_j equal to s_j, then r is considered rigorously implemented.

Predicates can be operatively verified by collecting values of code metrics and information about executed activities. Several tools supporting static analysis can be used to extract values of code metrics [25,18], while data regarding activities can be extracted directly from the documentation. Once data relative to metrics are available, the validation process for a requirement implementation consists in checking whether each SW component implementing it satisfies the predicates. This will be shown in Section 4.1.

4   Practical Experience

The ontological abstraction of the proposed methodology can be directly converted into an advanced SW architecture incorporating the ontological model. This has been done by implementing a web application, called *RAMSES* (Reliability Availability Maintainability and Safety Engineering Semantics), built on top of a stack of semantic web technologies and standards.

The web application architecture is shortly sketched in Fig. 7. The *Object-to-Ontology Mapping (OOM) Layer* bridges the gap between the *Domain Layer* and the *Data Layer* solving the *impedance mismatch*, i.e. the conceptual distance between the object model and the ontological model. In so doing, the domain logic is captured by the ontological model, enabling the generalization of the application logic in order to adapt it to the evolution of concepts.

4.1   Tool Capabilities

The tool's ontological architecture brings about a number of benefits in terms of reusability, interoperability, and extensibility. First, since the extensional part of the ontology that is built for any given development is represented in OWL, it can be exported so as to be used in different developments, thus avoiding the

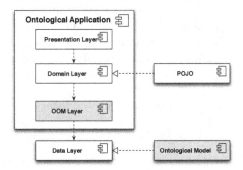

Fig. 7. Three-tier ontological architecture of a web application incorporating layers interfacing to users (*Presentation Layer*), managing application logic (*Domain Layer*), mapping between object model and data model (*Object to Ontology Mapping Layer*), and realizing data representation and conceptualization (*Data Layer*). The *Domain Layer* is implemented using *Plain Old Java Object* (*POJO*) and the *Data Layer* is realized through an *Ontological Model*.

effort for its (re)construction. Second, the ontological model can be modified at little cost in order to adapt the tool to different industrial contexts and specific regulatory standards.

The tool exploits the inference capabilities of an ontological reasoner by means of SPARQL query or predefined SWRL rules. The reasoning capability is crucial for the verification of the level of assurance. As reported in Section 3.3, a requirement is rigorously implemented if the related SW components satisfy a predefined set of predicates. For instance, the SWRL rule of Listing 1.1 can be used to verify a predicate (an instance of the general form shown at the end of that section). Thanks to this kind of rules, RAMSES is able to recommend appropriate actions to the analyst, taking advantage of the ontology.

```
ramses:FunctionalRequirement(?r) ∧
∧ ramses:isImplementedBy(?r,?ud) ∧
∧ ramses:hasUsedComponent(?ud,?swc) ∧
∧ ramses:hasSWModule(?swc,?swm) ∧
∧ ramses:hasMethod(?swm,?m) ∧
∧ ramses:hasParamAcc(?m,?spa) ∧
∧ ramses:hasLinkedParameter(?spa, ?sp) ∧
∧ ramses:hasName(?sp,''cyclomatic complexity'') ∧
∧ ramses:hasParamValue(?spa, ?pv) ∧
∧ swrlb:greaterThan(?pv, 5) ⇒
⇒ ramses:NotRigorous(?f)
```

Listing 1.1. SWRL rule verifying the satisfaction of a predicate: if there exists a SW component ?swc which is implemented by a SW module ?swm containing a method ?m having a McCabe's cyclomatic complexity ?sp greater than 5 the predicate is violated and the functional requirement is considered not rigorously implemented.

RAMSES aids the analyst in the identification of failure events and supports the accomplishment of testing activities. If a failure event is discovered during the operational phase, the associations between failures, requirements and tests permit to identify the tests that should have covered the failure. Once the analyst has identified the faults that cause the failure and associated them with structural items (i.e. SW components), other requirements that could be not satisfied are identified by means of the association between SW components and requirements.

The tool can also ease and improve the process of recertification. This can be useful when some changes happen in the development process. These changes may refer to the implementation of SW (i.e. the structural perspective), the requirements (i.e. the functional perspective), or the adopted standard/regulation (i.e. the process perspective). The ontological model reacts to these changes giving evidence of possible inconsistencies arisen among the data inserted in the ontology. The tool also recommends the re-execution of tests or the accomplishment of specific activities so as to conform with a specific standard.

Furthermore, pluggable modules, supporting specific activities, can be devised to produce concepts and associations that, leveraging on OWL, can be integrated in the ontology, assuring consistency and coherence with data already present. For instance, appropriate plug-ins allow the automatic import of requirements from specification documents.

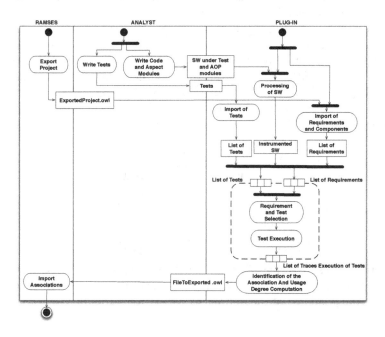

Fig. 8. UML Activity Diagram showing actions performed by RAMSES and the plug-in module during the tracing of functional requirements

4.2   Experimentation on a Scheduler of an Electromechanical System

The major application of the tool has been in a space project for a star tracker with more than 250 requirements, developed at the FinMeccanica site of Selex Galileo in Florence. In the following we report on the application of the tool to a smaller project concerning a scheduler of an electromechanical system for immunoenzymatic analysis, manufactured by BioMérieux, a worldwide group specialized in the field of in vitro diagnostics for medical and industrial applications. The scheduler [20] has been developed in the Software Technologies Laboratory (University of Florence). The system executes multiple concurrent analyses, the aim of the scheduler is to minimize the completion time for the overall set of analyses, avoiding conflicts in the shared hardware. The scheduler is composed of a single CSCI and has to satisfy 7 functional requirements; one of them, called "Constraints loading", imposes timing constraints to analyses execution. The CSCI is made up of 10 SW components, 10 SW modules, and 76 methods.

In order to test our approach, a plug-in module implementing the process of tracing requirements, described in Section 3.2, has been integrated in the tool RAMSES. Fig. 8 shows an UML Activity Diagram describing actions performed by the plug-in module and by RAMSES to obtain instances of the association between requirements and SW components. This is used to verify information contained in the traceability matrix reported in the SDD document. The plug-in is implemented as a Java application which uses AspectC to instrument the scheduler code so as to extract information about SW components executed. The process follows the activities shown in Fig. 8; the result is an OWL file which is imported in RAMSES to add to the ontology the instances of the association between Requirements and SW Components (Fig. 5). Application of the plug-in to the scheduler has shown that the functional requirement "Constraints loading" is implemented by 5 SW components whose usage degrees are as follows:

SW Component	Usage Degree (%)
block	100.00
matrix	42.86
problem	60.00
problem_solver	10.00
startingjitter_strategies	16.67

This particular result verifies that the actual implementation is compliant with the traceability matrix reported in the documentation of the scheduler, thus witnessing the goodness of the approach.

5   Conclusions

We proposed an ontological model formalizing concepts and data involved in the development process of safety-critical systems, giving them a precise semantics, so as to integrate in a common framework the activities performed and the outcomes produced during the whole life-cycle. We enhanced the work presented in previous papers by adding the process perspective to the structural and functional ones, capturing concepts involved in the regulation of industrial processes. In this manner, we obtained a framework general enough to be adapted to any given context. The framework can be tailored to different regulatory standards leveraging on the extensibility and the manageability provided by the ontological architecture.

The formalized model was integrated in a web application, called RAMSES, built on top of well-established semantic-web technologies. We discussed the use of plug-ins to supplement the ontology with concepts derived from specific activities. We have experimented the tool in a satellite star tracker and in a scheduler of an electromechanical system performing biological analysis; we reported some results from the latter. A specific plug-in was devised and the information generated by its execution has been integrated in the ontology to verify the consistency of documents produced along the development life-cycle. The experimentation has proved feasibility and effectiveness of both the ontological approach and the tool, showing improvements over current practices.

References

1. Avizienis, A., Laprie, J., Randell, B., Landwehr, C.: Basic Concepts and Taxonomy of Dependable and Secure Computing. IEEE Transactions on Dependable and Secure Computing 1(1), 11–33 (2004)
2. Bicchierai, I., Bucci, G., Nocentini, C., Vicario, E.: Integrating metrics in an ontological framework supporting sw-fmea. In: 2012 3rd International Workshop on Emerging Trends in Software Metrics, WETSoM, pp. 35–41 (2012)
3. Bicchierai, I., Bucci, G., Nocentini, C., Vicario, E.: An ontological approach to systematization of SW-FMEA. In: Ortmeier, F., Lipaczewski, M. (eds.) SAFECOMP 2012. LNCS, vol. 7612, pp. 173–184. Springer, Heidelberg (2012)
4. BWB - Federal Office for Military Technology and Procurement of Germany. V-Model 97, Lifecycle Process Model-Developing Standard for IT Systems of the Federal Republic of Germany. General Directive No. 250 (June 1997)
5. CENELEC European Committee for Electrotechnical Standardization. CENELEC EN 50128 Railway applications - Communications, signalling and processing systems - Software for railway control and protection systems (March 2001)
6. Dokas, I.M., Ireland, C.: Ontology to support knowledge representation and risk analysis for the development of early warning system in solid waste management operations. In: Int. Symp. on Environmental Software Systems, ISESS 2007 (2007)
7. Eaddy, M., Aho, A., Murphy, G.C.: Identifying, assigning, and quantifying crosscutting concerns. In: Proc. of the First International Workshop on Assessment of Contemporary Modularization Techniques, ACoM 2007, Washington, USA (2007)
8. Eisenbarth, T., Koschke, R., Simon, D.: Locating features in source code. IEEE Trans. Softw. Eng. 29, 210–224 (2003)
9. Fiaschetti, A., Lavorato, F., Suraci, V., Palo, A., Taglialatela, A., Morgagni, A., Baldelli, R., Flammini, F.: On the Use of Semantic Technologies to Model and Control Security, Privacy and Dependability in Complex Systems. In: Flammini, F., Bologna, S., Vittorini, V. (eds.) SAFECOMP 2011. LNCS, vol. 6894, pp. 467–479. Springer, Heidelberg (2011)

10. Gruber, T.R.: A Translation Approach to Portable Ontology Specifications. Knowledge Acquisition 5(2), 199–220 (1993)
11. Horrocks, I., Patel-Schneider, P.F., Boley, H., Tabet, S., Grosof, B., Dean, M.: SWRL: A Semantic Web Rule Language Combining OWL and RuleML (May 2004), http://www.w3.org/Submission/SWRL/
12. Jordan, P.: IEC 62304 International Standard Edition 1.0 Medical device software - Software life cycle processes. The Institution of Engineering and Technology Seminar on Software for Medical Devices (2006)
13. Kiczales, G., Lamping, J., Mehdhekar, A., Maeda, C., Lopes, C.V., Loingtier, J., Irwin, J.: Aspect-Oriented Programming. In: Akşit, M., Matsuoka, S. (eds.) ECOOP 1997. LNCS, vol. 1241, pp. 220–242. Springer, Heidelberg (1997)
14. McGuinness, D.L., van Harmelen, F.: OWL Web Ontology Language (February 2004), http://www.w3.org/TR/owl-features/
15. Mokos, K., Meditskos, G., Katsaros, P., Bassiliades, N., Vasiliades, V.: Ontology-based model driven engineering for safety verification. In: 2010 36th EUROMICRO Conference on Softw. Eng. and Advanced Applications, SEAA, pp. 47–54 (2010)
16. Object Management Group. Ontology Definition Metamodel v1.0 (2009)
17. Prud'hommeaux, E., Seaborne, A.: SPARQL query language for RDF (January 2008), http://www.w3.org/TR/rdf-sparql-query/
18. QA Systems - The Software Quality Company. Cantata++, http://www.qa-systems.com/cantata.html
19. Radio Technical Commission for Aeronautics. DO-178B, Software Considerations in Airborne Systems and Equipment Certification (1992)
20. Ridi, L., Torrini, J., Vicario, E.: Developing a scheduler with difference-bound matrices and the floyd-warshall algorithm. IEEE Software 29, 76–83 (2012)
21. Sahner, R.A., Trivedi, K.S., Puliafito, A.: Performance and reliability analysis of computer systems: an example-based approach using the SHARPE software package. Kluwer Academic Publishers, Norwell (1996)
22. Sirin, E., Parsia, B., Grau, B.C., Kalyanpur, A., Katz, Y.: Pellet: A practical OWL-DL reasoner. J. Web Sem. 5(2), 51–53 (2007)
23. Spinczyk, O., Gal, A., Schröder-Preikschat, W.: AspectC++: An Aspect-Oriented Extension to C++. In: Proc. of the 40th Int. Conf. on Technology of Object-Oriented Languages and Systems, TOOLS, pp. 53–60 (2002)
24. United States Department of Defense. MIL-STD-498, Military Standard For Software Development And Documentation. Technical report, USDoD (1994)
25. USC Center for Software Engineering. UCC: Unified Code Count, http://sunset.usc.edu/research/CODECOUNT/
26. Wirth, R., Berthold, B., Krämer, A., Peter: Knowledge-Based Support of System Analysis for Failure Mode and Effects Analysis. Engineering Applications of Artificial Intelligence 9, 219–229 (1996)
27. Wong, W.E., Gokhale, S.S., Horgan, J.R.: Quantifying the closeness between program components and features. J. Syst. Softw. 54, 87–98 (2000)

Measuring the Odds of Statements Being Faulty

Xiaozhen Xue and Akbar Siami Namin

Department of Computer Science
Texas Tech University
Lubbock, TX, USA
{xiaozhen.xue,akbar.namin}@ttu.edu

Abstract. The statistics captured during testing a faulty program are the primary source of information for effective fault localization. A typical ranking metric estimates suspiciousness of executable statements and ranks them according to the estimated scores. The coverage-based ranking schemes, such as the metric used in Tarantula and Ochiai score, utilize the execution profile of each test case, including code coverage and the statistics associated with the number of failing and passing test cases. Although the coverage-based fault localization metrics could be extended to hypothesis testing and in particular to the chi-square test associated with crosstab or known as contingency tables, not all contingency table association metrics are explored and studied.

We introduce the odds ratio metric and its application to the fault localization problem. The odds-ratio metric has been used extensively in categorical data analysis and in measuring the association of dependency between dichotomous variables. However, its application to fault localization metric is new. Furthermore, we investigate the effectiveness of conditional odds ratio metric for fault localization when there are multiple faults in the programs. Our experimental results show that the odds ratio metric performs better than the other ranking metrics studied for single faults, whereas, the conditional odds ratio ranking scheme is competitive when there are multiple faults in the software under test.

Keywords: testing, fault localization.

1 Introduction

Fault localization techniques use the information captured during program analysis to rank a program's statements in decreasing order of suspiciousness. The suspiciousness score is an uncertainty measure associated with the hypothesis that the underlying statement is faulty. The information required to estimate the suspiciousness is obtained through the execution profiles captured when running a set of test cases.

Several fault localization metrics have been proposed based on the number of passing and failing test cases and capturing the code coverage obtained by the execution profiles. The most discussed fault localization metrics are the one used in the Tarantula [1] tool and the Ochiai metric[2]. The Tarantula fault localization tool and Ochiai metric estimate suspiciousness of statements based on

H.B. Keller et al. (Eds.): Ada-Europe 2013, LNCS 7896, pp. 109–126, 2013.

the number of passing or failing test cases exercising the underlying statements. A statement is likely to be ranked as highly suspicious if more failing test cases exercise the statement. Similarly, a statement is unlikely to be suspicious if more failing test cases cover statements other than the underlying one.

Empirical studies show the effectiveness of the Tarantula fault localization tool and the Ochiai metric [3] in estimating the suspiciousness of statements. Naish et al. [4] report several ranking metrics in most of which the suspiciousness of a statement has a direct relationship to the number of failing test cases that exercise the underlying statements. Though the set of ranking metrics reported in [4] is diverse enough, the performance of statistical-based ranking scores to the fault localization problem still remains an open question.

The statistics required for estimating the suspiciousness of statements form a 2×2 matrix or table, often called a *contingency table*, in which each cell represents the frequency of events observed for two variables. A contingency table is a type of matrix or table that displays the joint and marginal distributions of two categorical variables. The main advantage of contingency table analysis is to measure the association between the variables.

The measures developed by contingency table analysis have already been adapted in many areas including machine learning and in particular feature selection research. Wong et al. [5] have explored the statistically-driven ranking metrics based on contingency tables and reported that these metrics were competitive to the existing and traditional fault localization ranking metrics. More specifically, Wong et al. discussed two statistical-based ranking metrics known as Chi-square and Fisher score, both based on statistics used for analyzing contingency tables. However, one of the most important statistically-driven association metric known as odds-ratio has less or never been addressed in the software testing literature.

This paper investigates the performance of the *odds ratio* scoring metric and its variation the *conditional odds ratio* for the fault localization problem. The odds ratio metric is a measure of effect size describing the strength of association or dependency between two data values. The odds ratio ranking metric is extensively used in many classification problems, including bioinformatics [6] and text mining [7].

The case studies conducted in this paper show that the odds ratio ranking metric outperforms the fault localization metrics based on Tarantula tool and Ochiai as well as the other statistically-driven metrics such as Chi-square. Moreover, we report that in the case of multiple faults, the conditional odds ratio is competitive to the existing ranking metrics.

The main contributions of this paper are as follows:

- Investigate the performance of the odds ratio metric as a new statistical-based ranking metric for the fault localization problem;
- Introduce conditional odds ratio as a new statistical-based ranking metric for the fault localization problem when multiple faults exist in the program;
- Report the outperformance of proposed ranking metrics compared to the technique based on Tarantula, Ochiai, and chi-square metrics.

The paper is organized as follows: Section 2 introduces the odds ratio and explores its concept. An illustrative example is presented in Section 3. Section 4 reports the results of case studies and evaluates the performance of odds-ratio metric in the context of the fault localization problem. The conditional odds ratio and an analysis on multiple faults are reported in Section 5. The threats to validities are discussed in Section 6. We review the literature in Section 7. Section 8 concludes the new metrics we proposed.

2   Odds Ratio: A Metric for Associations

The odds ratio is a measure of effect size, describing the strength of association between two binary (yes or no) data values. It is used as a measure to compare the probability of a certain event for two groups. The odds ratio offers an idea of how strongly a given variable is associated with other variables. The odds ratio metric plays an important role in logistic regression where the goal is to measure the strength of association between a predictor and the response variable.

There are numbers of ways to measure the association between two binary variables in the contingency table. However, most of the measures focus on different aspects of associations. The concept of the odds ratio is better understood by analyzing contingency tables. The contingency tables whose entries are the frequencies or counts of some events display the frequency distribution of the variables and are often used to analyze the relationship between categorical variables. The general form of a 2×2 contingency table is given in Table 1(a), in which a sample of N ($N=a+b+c+d$) observations is classified with respect to two qualitative variables X and Y. The categorical variable X has 2 categories, i.e. $X-$ and $X+$, whereas, the variable Y has 2 categories, i.e. $Y-$ and $Y+$. The notations are adapted from the categorical data analysis where "-" and "+" represent the "low" and "high" values. There is a lot of information that a contingency table can provide. One of the primary interests is investigating the relationship between two variables X and Y and the contingency table can identify how strong the relationship shown in the contingency table is. Wong et al. [5] discuss the use of contingency table analysis or crosstab-based statistical method for the fault localization problem. The categorical-based ranking metrics based on contingency tables, as shown by Wong et al. [5], were χ^2 and Fisher score ranking metrics. However, the odds-ratio as one of the most important metrics for analyzing contingency tables have not been taken into consideration in [5].

Odds are the ratio of the probability or frequency that an event will occur versus the event will not occur. For example, given a random variable X whose probability distribution is known, written as $P(X = x) = p(x)$, the odds for x occurring is $\frac{p(x)}{1-p(x)}$. In fact, the odds ratio refers to the ratio of the odds of an event occurring in the one control group versus its treatment group. In a typical 2×2 contingency table as illustrated in Table 1, the odds for row $Y-$ are $\frac{a}{b}$, whereas, the odds for row $Y+$ are $\frac{c}{d}$. The odds ratio (OR) is then simply the ratio of the two odds and is expressed by Expression 1:

Table 1. 2×2 contingency tables

(a) Frequentist

	$X-$	$X+$
$Y-$	a	b
$Y+$	c	d

(b) Probabilistic

	$X-$	$X+$
$Y-$	$\frac{a}{a+b}$	$\frac{b}{a+b}$
$Y+$	$\frac{c}{c+d}$	$\frac{d}{c+d}$

$$Odds\ Ratio = \frac{\frac{a}{b}}{\frac{c}{d}} = \frac{a \times d}{c \times b} \tag{1}$$

The odds ratio can also be defined in terms of the conditional probability distribution. We still utilize the two binary random variables X and Y as shown in Table 1(a). The conditional probability distribution of variables X under the condition of Y is shown in Table 1(b), which can be deducted from the following expression:

$$P(X - |Y-) = \frac{P(X-, Y-)}{P(Y-)} = \frac{\frac{a}{a+b+c+d}}{\frac{a+b}{a+b+c+d}} = \frac{a}{a+b}$$

where $P(X-, Y-)$ is the joint probability distribution of the two variables X and Y. Therefore, the odds for $X-$ within the two sub-populations, i.e. $Y-$ and $Y+$, can be written as $\frac{a/(a+b)}{b/(a+b)}$. Similarly the odds for $X+$ is $\frac{c/(c+d)}{d/(c+d)}$. Hence, the odds ratio is defined in terms of the conditional probabilities, as shown in the following expression:

$$Odds\ Ratio = \frac{\frac{\frac{a}{a+b}}{\frac{b}{a+b}}}{\frac{\frac{c}{c+d}}{\frac{d}{c+d}}} = \frac{a \times d}{c \times b}$$

Since the odds ratio is a measure of effect size, then the question is about the relationship between the odds ratio scores to statistical independence. To illustrate the relationship between the odds ratio and statistical independence, we assume X and Y are independent as shown in in Table 1(a), and the marginal probabilities of $X-$ and $Y-$ are $p(x)$ and $p(y)$. Thus the joint probabilities can be expressed in terms of the product of their marginal probabilities as shown in Table 2. Through simple calculation based on Expression 1, we conclude that the odds ratio is equal to one in this case. The odds ratio can only be equal to 1 if the joint probabilities can be factored in this way. Thus the odds ratio equals 1 if and only if X and Y are independent. Furthermore, we can easily conclude that an odds ratio of 1 implies that the event $X-$ is equally likely in the both treatment and control groups, i.e. $Y-$ and $Y+$. Accordingly, an odds ratio greater than one implies that the event $X-$ is more likely to occur in the first group, i.e. $Y-$. In an analogous way, an odds ratio less than one implies that

Table 2. Joint probability distribution of two variables

	$X-$	$X+$	Total
$Y-$	$p(x)p(y)$	$(1-p(x))p(y)$	$p(y)$
$Y+$	$p(x)(1-p(y))$	$(1-p(x))(1-p(y))$	$1-p(y)$
Total	$p(x)$	$1-p(x)$	

the event $X-$ is less likely to occur in the first group $Y-$. In other words, an odds ratio greater than 1 implies that there exists a strong dependence between $X-$ and $Y-$. The greater odds ratio score is, the stronger the dependence is. Conversely, the odds ratio less than 1 is an indication of a strong dependence between $X-$ and $Y+$.

We use the conceptualization of the fault localization problem and ranking metrics based on contingency table analysis as introduced by Wong et al. [5]. We develop a set of notations for the fault localization problem. Table 3 represents an adapted 2×2 contingency table that we make for each statement in a given program. The problem of fault localization is then expressed in terms of analysis of the contingency tables made for statements and computing a ranking based on these tables. We investigate the performance of the odds ratio as a fault localization metric compared to those discussed by Wong et al. [5]. More specifically, we define:

- n_{ef}: The number of test cases exercising the underlying statement and failed;
- $n_{e\bar{f}}$: The number of test cases exercising the underlying statement and not failed;
- $n_{\bar{e}f}$: The number of test cases not exercising the underlying statement but failed;
- $n_{\bar{e}\bar{f}}$: The number of test cases not exercising the underlying statement and not failed;
- n_e: The total number of test cases exercising the underlying statement;
- $n_{\bar{e}}$: The total number of test cases not exercising the underlying statement;
- n_f: The total number of failing test cases;
- $n_{\bar{f}}$: The total number of passing test cases;
- N: The total number of test cases.

In terms of notations developed for fault localization, the odds ratio measures the odds of a block (statement) i executed by the failing test cases divided by the odds of a block (statement) not exercised by the passing test cases; the odds ratio is then measured by Expression 2:

$$Odds\ Ratio(s) = \frac{\frac{n_{ef}+0.1}{n_e+0.1} / \frac{n_{e\bar{f}}+0.1}{n_e+0.1}}{\frac{n_{\bar{e}f}+0.1}{n_{\bar{e}}+0.1} / \frac{n_{\bar{e}\bar{f}}+0.1}{n_{\bar{e}}+0.1}} \tag{2}$$

where the constant 0.1 is added to avoid division by zero and computational problems as suggested by in the book written by Liu and Motoda [7]. Similarly,

Table 3. A two-way contingency table for each statement in a given program

	e	$\bar{e}$	Total
f	n_{ef}	$n_{\bar{e}f}$	n_f
$\bar{f}$	$n_{e\bar{f}}$	$n_{\bar{e}\bar{f}}$	$n_{\bar{f}}$
Total	n_e	$n_{\bar{e}}$	N

an odds ratio of 1 implies that the event is equally likely to happen in the both treatment and control groups. In other words, the odds ratio is equal to 1 if and only if the two variables are independent in the table. In terms of the fault localization context, the greater odds ratio scores are the indications of statements being more suspicious. We use Expression 2 for further computations in the experimentations reported in this paper.

3   An Illustrative Example

To have better insights of the mechanism of computing the odds ratio and the other metrics, we present an example. The program listed in Figure 1 presents an illustrative example, a bonus program, where the sum of three input numbers is calculated. A negative input value causes the program to add one, as bonus, to the sum computed. The code is composed of 10 lines with a fault on the line three. The program is exercised with eight test cases of which two have failed. Figure 1 also demonstrates the statement coverage achieved by each test case.

Table 4 shows the suspiciousness score calculated using the given ranking metrics, including existing metrics such as the metric used in Tarantula [1], Ochiai [2], and χ^2 [5], in addition to the odds ratio metric. These metrics are computable as following where s represents the underlying statement for which the statistics are collected:

$$Tarantula(s) = \frac{\frac{n_{ef}}{n_{ef}+n_{\bar{e}f}}}{\frac{n_{ef}}{n_{ef}+n_{\bar{e}f}} + \frac{n_{e\bar{f}}}{n_{e\bar{f}}+n_{\bar{e}f}}}$$

$$Ochiai(s) = \frac{n_{ef}}{\sqrt{(n_{ef}+n_{\bar{e}f})(n_{ef}+n_{e\bar{f}})}}$$

$$\chi^2(s) = \frac{N \times (n_{ef} \times n_{\bar{e}\bar{f}} - n_{\bar{e}f} \times n_{e\bar{f}})^2}{n_e \times n_f \times n_{\bar{e}} \times n_{\bar{f}}}$$

Similar to the other researchers [8], we compute the fault localization cost by measuring the percentage of statements in the program that must be examined before reaching the first faulty statement in the code. More precisely, we define

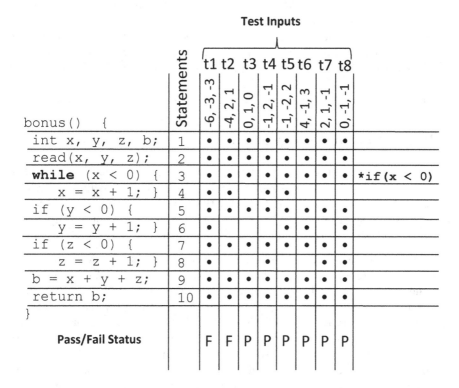

Fig. 1. An illustrative example

Table 4. The suspiciousness of statements for the illustrative example

Statement	n_{ef}	$n_{\bar{e}f}$	$n_{e\bar{f}}$	$n_{\bar{e}\bar{f}}$	Tarantula	Ochiai	Chi-Square	Odds Ratio
	Statistics				Metrics			
1	2	0	6	0	0.5	0.5	0	0.3
2	2	0	6	0	0.5	0.5	0	0.3
3	2	0	6	0	0.5	0.5	0	0.3
4	2	0	2	4	0.8	0.7	2.7	4
5	2	0	6	0	0.5	0.5	0	0.3
6	1	1	3	3	0.5	0.4	0	1
7	2	0	6	0	0.5	0.5	0	0.3
8	1	1	3	3	0.5	0.4	0	1
9	2	0	6	0	0.5	0.5	0	0.3
10	2	0	6	0	0.5	0.5	0	0.3

cost for localizing faults as the total number of statements exercised before reaching (examining) the first statement containing faults over the total number of statements in the program under test. More specifically, the cost is defined as the proportion of the program to be inspected before inspecting a faulty statement.

It may be possible that some statements rank equally, i.e. tie ranking scores. In calculating the overall fault localization cost when some non–faulty statements are ranked tie with a faulty statement, we took into computation exercising all those statements that were ranked tie with the faulty statement, i.e. the worst case where the debugger inspects all non-faulty and faulty statements with equal ranks.

4   Evaluation and Case Studies

This section evaluates the fault localization ranking metrics based on the odds ratio introduced in the paper through a number of case studies including versions with single fault and synthesized versions with multiple faults where single faults are incorporated simultaneously. First, we describe the experimental setup. Then we report the results of the analysis.

Subject Programs. Table 5 lists the subject programs used for experimentations. We obtained these Java programs from two sources. First, We studied some extensively used Java programs, including two releases of NanoXML, two releases of XMLsec, two releases of Jmeter, and three releases of Jtopas, from the Software Infrastructure Repository (SIR) [9]. The faults for these programs are hand-seeded by the other researchers. Second, we selected some other Java programs from Java standard libraries, including Bitset, RE, Math and FilteredRowSetImpl. We then used MuJava tool [10] to generate some mutants and randomly selected 10 mutants from the pool of mutants generated by all mutation operators implemented by MuJava. The test cases for these programs were generated by some graduate students, majoring in computer sciences and software engineering, using JUnit framework based on the specifications provided for each program. We excluded the faults or mutants for which no available test cases failed.

Experimental Setup. In order to obtain the required statistics for each fault, we instrumented the code manually by adding print command into each block of statements, i.e. a series of statements with only one entry point and one exit point, and capturing the statement coverage and the other statistics. We ran each test case for each single fault, recorded the test status (i.e. passing/failing) and computed the required statistics for each block in the source code including (i.e. n_{ef}, $n_{\overline{ef}}$, $n_{\overline{e}f}$ and $n_{e\overline{f}}$). We then calculated the suspiciousness score for each block and ranked it according to the odds ratio calculated. As we pointed out earlier in Section 3, we measured the fault localization cost as the percentage of statement in the program that must be examined before reaching the first faulty statement [8].

Data Analysis and Results. Table 6 reports the performance of the fault localization metrics including the odds ratio. The average cost of fault localization

Table 5. Subject programs

Program (version)	Description	LOC	Class	Tests	Faults
NanoXML(v1)	XML parser	7646	24	214	7
NanoXML(v2)	XML parser	7646	24	214	7
XMLsec(v1)	XML encryption	21,613	143	92	1
XMLsec(v2)	XML encryption	21,613	143	92	2
Jmeter (v1)	Load tester	43,400	389	78	1
Jmeter (v3)	Load tester	43,400	389	78	5
Jtopas (v1)	Text parser	5400	50	54	10
Jtopas (v2)	Text parser	5400	50	126	1
Jtopas (v3)	Text parser	5400	50	140	1
Bitset (v1)	Bits vector	565	1	24	10
FilteredRowSetImpl (v1)	Row set filter	615	1	28	10
Math (v1)	Basic numeric operations	384	1	116	10
RE (v1)	Expression evaluator	974	1	27	10

using metric introduced by Tarantula, Ochiai, and χ^2 metrics is 14.32%, 14.05%, and 12.69%, respectively. The average cost of debugging as required by the odds ratio is 11.92%, outperforming the other fault localization metrics. In most cases, the cost associated with fault localization is similar for the four metrics. However, for Jemeter, NanoXML, Bitset and FilteredRowSetImpl programs, the odds ratio metric performs significantly better.

5 Discussion

In practice, there exist many faults in a program under test. The existence of multiple faults in a given code may introduce some interactions among multiple faults. The presence of multiple faults and their interactions in a given code raise the concerns of whether the coverage-based fault localization technique is still effective in debugging programs. This section first introduces and discusses the significance of the application of the conditional odds ratio to the fault localization problem in the presence of multiple faults in the given code. Second, it provides further analyses related to the performance of the conditional odds ratio for debugging programs with multiple faults.

5.1 Conditional Odds Ratio

We introduce the concept of probabilistic odds ratio known as the conditional odds ratio and demonstrate that conditional odds ratio better formulate the fault localization problem when multiple faults exist in a given program.

The traditional odds ratio follows that each sample can be classified according to the values of the binary responses from two parameters or factors. For instance, under the context of fault localization whether: a) a statement is exercised, b) the test cases failed. The results of N samples can be expressed in a

Table 6. Fault localization costs

Program	Version	Cost%			
		Tarantula	Ochiai	Chi-Square	Odds Ratio
Jemeter	v1	17.00	17.00	17.00	17.00
Jemeter	v3	4.44	4.44	4.44	4.44
XMLSec	v1	6.90	6.90	6.90	6.90
XMLSec	v2	7.85	5.88	5.88	5.88
NanoXML	v1	21.88	21.88	18.49	16.93
NanoXML	v2	41.95	43.39	41.75	37.31
Jtopas	v1	2.00	1.33	1.33	1.33
Jtopas	v2	8.82	8.82	8.82	8.82
Jtopas	v3	17.24	17.24	17.24	17.24
Bitset	v1	6.33	6.83	5.83	4.50
FilteredRowSetImpl	v1	26.13	26.13	25.25	22.13
math	v1	3.50	3.50	3.50	3.50
RE	v1	17.50	15.33	10.00	12.67
Average		14.32	14.05	12.69	11.92

2×2 table as shown in Table 3 where N is the number of observations. However, if more than two factors are received at the same time, we would extend the concept of odds ratio to multi-dimensional contingency tables where the third dimension accounts for the third factor added to the analysis and so forth. A possible way to analyze multi-dimensional contingency tables is to exploit the notion of conditional odds ratio. Consider a 3-way contingency table with three variables (X, Y, Z). It is possible to utilize the odds ratio in order to measure the association between X and Y conditioned on the fixed categories of $Z = z$. This is the conditional odds ratio of X and Y conditioned on $Z = z$ and is denoted as $COR(X, Y|Z = z)$.

The concept of conditional odds ratio can be expressed in terms of higher dimensional contingency tables. For instance, the associations among three factors can be represented by a 3-way (three dimensional) contingency table. Figure 2(a) illustrates a 3-way contingency table $X \times Y \times Z$ where the association among three variables X, Y and Z is of interest. The conditional odds ratio for measuring the associations among these three variables is defined by fixing the level of one variable and computing the ordinary (traditional) odds ratio between the other two variables. More precisely, the conditional odds ratio is the odds ratio between two variables for fixed level l of the third variable [11, 12].

The procedure results in making a series of 2-way contingency tables and computing ordinary odds ratio for these tables. The 2-way contingency tables are called *"partial tables."* The conditional odds ratio are thus computable using the partial tables, and sometimes are referred to as measures of partial associations [11, 12]. The computation of conditional odds ratio then yields:

- K frontal planes or XY for each level of Z.
- J Vertical planes or XZ for each level of Y.
- I Horizontal planes or YZ for each level of X.

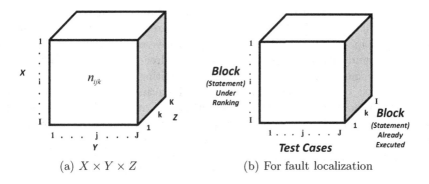

(a) $X \times Y \times Z$ (b) For fault localization

Fig. 2. Three-dimensional contingency tables

For the fixed level of Z, the conditional XY association with binary responses where the given k–th level of Z is measurable through Expression 3 which is quite similar to Expression 1:

$$Conditional\ Odds\ Ratio_{XY(k)} = \theta_{XY(k)} = \frac{n_{11k}n_{22k}}{n_{12k}n_{21k}} \tag{3}$$

where n_{ijk} is the observed frequency in the (i, j, k)th cell. There might be some cases where the exact number of observations in a given cell is unknown and therefore the expected frequency needs to be estimated. The estimation of the expected frequency is then possible through utilization of marginal values in the tables as expressed in the following expression [11, 12]:

$$Conditional\ Odds\ Ratio_{XY(k)} = \theta_{XY(k)} = \frac{\mu_{11k}\mu_{22k}}{\mu_{12k}\mu_{21k}}$$

where μ_{ijk} is the expected frequency in the (i, j, k)th cell and it is defined as:

$$\mu_{ijk} = N.\pi_{ijk} = N.\frac{Grand\ total\ for\ the\ (i, j, k)th\ cell}{Sample\ Size}$$

where N is the total number of observations and π_{ijk} is the sample proportion of the (i, j, k)th cell. If $\theta_{XY(k)} \neq 1$, then variables X and Y are conditionally associated. In other words, conditional independence means that $\theta_{XY(k)} = 1$ for all $k = 1, ..., K$, whereas, the conditional dependence means that $\theta_{XY(k)} \neq 1$ for at least one $k = 1, ..., K$.

The conditional odds ratio can formulate the causality and association between program statements or blocks, i.e. a series of statements with only one entry and one exit point. It is a common practice that test practitioners often debug their programs through inspecting whether exercising two blocks of statements together would cause the exposition of failures.

Assume that a test practitioner is interested in inspecting whether exercising two blocks of statements might cause exhibition of faulty behavior. In terms of the fault localization domain, we make a 3-dimensional contingency table with three factors i.e. X, Y, Z where factor X represents the current block i of the program, factor Y represents the test cases and their status (i.e. failing or passing), and factor Z represents the other already executed block j of the program. We can formulate the problem by exploiting the conditional odds ratio where the first variable is the current block of execution, the second variable is the test cases and their status, i.e. failed or passed, and the third variable is the already exercised block of code. More specifically, as Figure 2(b) demonstrates, for the fault localization context the three dimensions are defined as:

$$Current\ Block \times Test\ Cases \times Already\ Executed\ Block$$

The purpose of exploiting the conditional odds ratio is to study the relationship between an executed block i and failing test cases under the condition that other block j is also exercised. We believe that this definition addressed the causality between blocks i and j.

In our experiments, we computed all possible odds ratios by fixing the "Already Executed Block" and calculating the ordinary odds ratio for each level of the other two variables, i.e. current block and test cases. For instance, assuming that there are 100 blocks of statements, we considered all $100 * 99$ possible cases for each block then made $100 * 99$ partial contingency tables and calculated the odds ratio for each table.

5.2   Experiments on Multiple Faults

Similar to the fault localization problem with single fault, the cost of debugging a program with multiple faults is defined as the percentage of statements in the program that must be examined before reaching the first faulty statement. In this section, we investigate the effectiveness of coverage-based fault localization when the program under test contains multiple faults.

We reused the same subject programs we studied in the first experiment. We generated faulty versions of each program containing multiple faults by re–introducing (re–injecting) the existing single faults from different faulty versions. We generated faulty instances of 1 up to 10 faults for each program when number of faults allowed, i.e. some of the programs studied have only a few number of hand-seeded faults. We ran each test case for each newly generated faulty version with multiple faults, recorded the test status, and collected the statistics for each block of the program in the source code including n_{ef}, $n_{\overline{ef}}$, $n_{\overline{e}f}$, and $n_{e\overline{f}}$. Finally, we calculated the fault localization cost as defined inspecting the proportion of programs inspected before reaching the first faulty block in the faulty version containing multiple faults.

Table 7 reports the average of the fault localization cost for the metrics studied including the conditional odds ratio for multiple faults. On average, the cost of fault localization based on the conditional odds ratio metric is 4.65%; whereas, the cost of debugging for the Tarantula, Ochiai, Chi-square, odds ratio metrics are 10.31%, 5.24%, 5.20% and 5.11%, respectively.

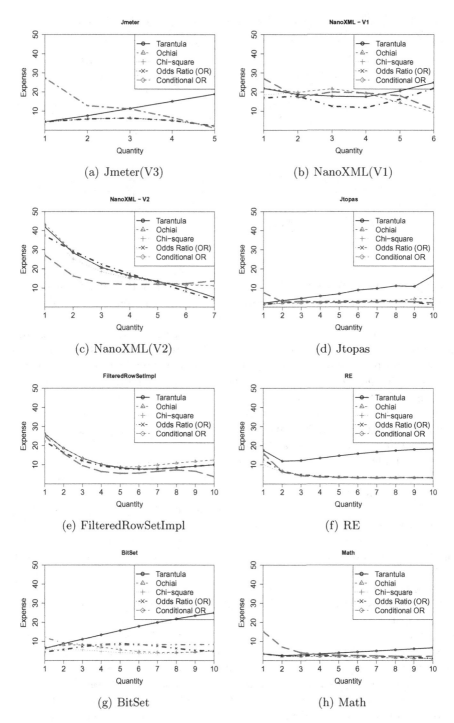

(a) Jmeter(V3)

(b) NanoXML(V1)

(c) NanoXML(V2)

(d) Jtopas

(e) FilteredRowSetImpl

(f) RE

(g) BitSet

(h) Math

Fig. 3. The average cost of localizing each fault quantity per subject

Table 7. The average computed fault localization cost for all programs

| #Faults | Cost% | | | | |
	Tarantula	Ochiai	Chi-Square	Odds Ratio	Conditional Odds Ratio
1	14.32	14.05	12.69	11.92	17.85
2	11.48	9.60	9.06	9.13	9.08
3	10.56	7.25	7.15	6.91	6.30
4	9.58	4.96	4.98	5.01	4.30
5	9.81	4.18	4.27	4.35	3.69
6	10.54	4.03	4.03	3.97	3.56
7	11.63	4.11	4.11	3.98	3.64
8	8.13	7.34	7.28	6.06	5.25
9	12.45	4.79	4.44	4.01	3.66
10	14.00	4.94	4.28	3.78	2.97
Average	10.31	5.24	5.20	5.11	4.65

The results indicate that on average the odds ratio and the conditional odds ratio outperform the other fault localization metrics. The conditional odds ratio underperforms for programs with single fault (17.85%) compared to the Tarantula, Ochiai, chi-square, and the traditional odds-ratios (14.32%, 14.05%, 12.96% and 11.92%, respectively). However, the results for multiple faults strongly indicate the outperformance of the conditional odds ratio when more than three faults exist in the program. Our controlled experiments indicate that when the program under testing contains more than three faults, the conditional odds ratio offers better estimation of location of faults. Furthermore, the improvement obtained through the conditional odds ratio seems to be significant compared to the other ranking metrics, i.e. approximately 0.5%.

For the faulty versions with two faults, the conditional odds ratio metric is still competitive compared to the other metrics and the difference is small. For the programs with two faults, the most accurate metric is the chi-square metric (9.06%), whereas the cost based on the condition odds ratio metric is 9.08%. However, for programs with greater number of faults, the odds ratio and its conditional variation performs better than Tarantula and Ochiai metrics (11.48% and 9.60%). We also noticed that the condition odds ratio metric performs worst for programs with single fault and its effectiveness increases with the increase of the number of faults.

A notable observation is that the results vary for different subject programs. Figures 3(a)–3(h) provide detailed views of the fault localization cost calculated for each program. Figure 3(a) illustrates the reduction in cost for the conditional odds ratio metric when the quantity of fault increases for the Jmeter-V3 program. The cost calculated through the conditional odds ratio is the lowest value when program contains five faults and it is the most effective compared to the other metrics. However, when the quantity of faults is between 1 and 4, the odds ratio, chi-square and Ochiai metrics perform better than the conditional odds ratio metric and localization effort requires less cost.

The NanoXML-V1 program (Figure 3(b)) exhibits a consistent result compared to the Jemeter-V3 program in that the cost decreases when the quantity of faults increases with a minor exception that the cost increases slightly when the quantity of faults is three. For the NanoXML-V2 program (Figure 3(c)), the conditional odds ratio metric demonstrates the best performance regardless of the number of faults. A slight increase in the cost based on the conditional odds ratio is observable when the number of faults increases to five.

For the Jtopas-V1 program (Figure 3(d)), except the metric used in the Tarantula fault localization, the other metrics perform similarly. The metric used in Tarantula exhibits very poor performance compared to the other metrics. The poor performance is more noticeable for programs with greater number of faults. For the FilterRowSetImpl program (Figure 3(e)), we observed the effectiveness of all 5 metrics increase with the increase of number of faults with minor exception, and the conditional odds ratio metric provides better performance.

The remaining subject programs Bitset-V1, Math-V1, and RE-V1 exhibit similar results indicating the better performance obtained through the conditional odds ratio metric. They are all consistent with FilterRowSetImpl except the metric used in Tarantula, whose effectiveness decreases with the increase of the number of faults.

6   Threats to Validity

Similar to any empirical studies in software engineering, the quasi experimentations reported in this paper are also controlled [13] and thus prone to possible experimental threats. By quasi-experiments we mean experiments that lack random assignments to conditions and the selection is performed by means of self-selection and employing certain methods of control. The quasi-experimentations usually are designed for measuring causal inferences between dependent and independent variables where the conditions are controlled for.

The subject programs used in this paper are Java applications with hand-seeded faults and mutants. Other programs written in various programming languages may behave differently and thus the results may not carry over to other similar cases. In particular, As pointed out by Andrews et al. [14] hand-seeded faults may not exhibit the characteristics of real faults and thus the metrics discussed may exhibit varying performances.

The purpose of code instrumentation is to capture the execution flow of the programs under different test cases. Since the location and the number of code instrumentations has been chosen randomly, no systematic bias has been introduced in the experimental procedure as reported in this paper.

We utilized and computed fault localization cost as introduced and used by other researchers. Different fault localization cost metrics may yield different results. Additionally, we implemented the Tarantula, Ochiai, and chi-square metrics by developing our own Java scripts. We double checked the accuracy of our implementation on different programs as reported in literature.

7   Related Work

Debugging is one of the most time consuming parts of software development activities. Many fault localization techniques and metrics have been developed to localize the cause of failures and accelerate the debugging activities. Delta-debugging [15, 16], dynamic program slicing [17–19], interactive fault localization [20], machine learning approaches [21], and probabilistic reasoning [22–24] are some of the techniques introduced in the literature.

In a typical machine learning technique a learning model is developed which provides a means to define proper ranking or classification schemes. Briand et al. [25, 21] discuss the RUBAR method, a rule-based statement ranking mechanism to identify suspicious statements, using decision trees to learn various failure conditions with respect to execution profiles.

Statistical learning and probabilistic reasoning are the other approaches for ranking statements [22–24]. A common practice is to develop a probabilistic model capable of learning from execution profiles of test cases. Baah et al. [23] discuss the application of causal inference for statistical fault localization. The causal graphs are probabilistic representations of structural causal models. The causal graphs are based on program dependency graphs, an intermediate representation that explicitly identifies data and control dependencies for each operation in a program. Zimmermann and Nagappan [26] report an application of dependency graph for predicting defects in code. Similarly, the statistical debugging method discussed by Liblit et al. [22], the universal probability model [24] and the causal dependency-based fault localization methods learn a probabilistic model to rank the suspiciousness of statements.

The most widely discussed fault localization approach is the use of proper metrics to rank statements in terms of their suspiciousness also known as coverage-based fault localization. A common practice for localizing faults is to execute the test suite on the faulty program and calculate some statistics similar to those discussed in Section 2 about each statement. The computed statistics for each statement are then combined to estimate the suspiciousness of the underlying statement. Hence, the effectiveness of the fault localization techniques relies on the ranking metric employed to combine the statistics computed. Metrics such as the one used in Tarantula fault localization tool [1] and Ochiai [2] are two predominant ranking metrics. Similarly a crosstab-based statistical method based on Chi-Square was proposed by [5].

Empirical studies show that these ranking metrics outperform other fault localization metrics in reducing the debugging cost [3, 2] where cost is defined as the percentage of statements in the program that must be examined before reaching the first faulty statement [8]. DiGiuseppe and Jones report that the fault localization metrics such as Ochiai are still effective even in the presence of multiple faults [27].

Lucia et al. [28] report an empirical study in which the performance of the association metrics including the odds ratio is compared to the metric used in Tarantula and Ochiai. The small scale experiment conducted by Lucia et al. on the Siemens C program shows that both Ochiai metric and the metric used in Tarantula are more effective than the association metrics and even the odds ratio metric. However, our experiment on larger programs developed in the Java programing language show that the odds ratio metric outperforms the metric used in Tarantula as well as the Ochiai metric significantly.

8   Concluding Remarks

The Odds ratio metric is the most widely used association metric by which the strength of the association between categorical variables is measured. We introduced the odds ratio metric and its variation the conditional odds ratio to be exploited and used for localizing faults based on the contingency table analysis.

In this paper, we showed that the ranking metrics offered by contingency table analysis and in particular the odds ratio could be effectively apply to the fault localization problem. We discussed the odds ratio metric as a new ranking metrics and investigated its effectiveness compared to the existing ranking metrics. The results of our empirical studies showed that the odds ratio ranking metric outperformed the other ranking metrics studied in this paper including the metric used in the Tarantula tool, Ochiai, and even statistically-driven ranking metrics such as Chi-square.

We also introduced the conditional odds ratio ranking metric as a probabilistic-based ranking metric and showed its effectivenessin the presence of multiple faults in a given program. In particular, we observed that the conditional ranking metric outperformed the other metrics when the number of faults in a given program under test was greater than two. As we discussed in this paper, the conditional odds ratio metric can be exploited as a fault localization technique to identify the causality or interaction of faults.

References

1. Jones, J.A.: Fault localization using visualization of test information. In: ICSE, pp. 54–56 (2004)
2. Abreu, R., Zoeteweij, P., van Gemund, J.: On the accuracy of spectrum-based fault localization. In: Proceedings of the Testing: Academic and Industrial Conference Practice and Research Techniques, pp. 89–98 (2007)
3. Jones, J.A., Harrold, M.J.: Empirical evaluation of the tarantula automatic fault-localization technique. In: ASE, pp. 273–282 (2005)
4. Naish, L., Lee, H.J., Ramamohanarao, K.: A model for spectra-based software diagnosis. ACM Transactions on Software Engineering and Methodology 20 (August 2011)
5. Wong, W.E., Wei, T., Qi, Y., Zhao, L.: A crosstab-based statistical method for effective fault localization. In: ICST, pp. 42–51 (2008)
6. Jin, X., Xu, A., Bie, R., Guo, P.: Machine learning techniques and chi-square feature selection for cancer classification using SAGE gene expression profiles. In: Li, J., Yang, Q., Tan, A.-H. (eds.) BioDM 2006. LNCS (LNBI), vol. 3916, pp. 106–115. Springer, Heidelberg (2006)

7. Liu, H., Motoda, H.: Computational Methods of Feature Selection. Chapman and Hall/CRC (2008)
8. Santelices, R.A., Jones, J.A., Yu, Y., Harrold, M.J.: Lightweight fault-localization using multiple coverage types. In: ICSE, pp. 56–66 (2009)
9. Do, H., Elbaum, S.G., Rothermel, G.: Supporting controlled experimentation with testing techniques: An infrastructure and its potential impact. Empirical Software Engineering: An International Journal 10(4), 405–435 (2005)
10. Ma, Y.-S., Offutt, J., Kwon, Y.R.: MuJava: a mutation system for Java. In: ICSE, pp. 827–830 (2006)
11. Agresti, A.: An Introduction to Categorical Data Analyis, 2nd edn. Wiley, NY (2007)
12. Anderson, C.J.: Applied categorical data analysis - a graduate course (February 2013), http://courses.education.illinois.edu/EdPsy589/#general
13. Shadish, W., Cook, T., Campbell, D.: Experimental and Quasi-Experimental Designs for Generalized Causal Inference. Houghton Mifflin Company, New York (2002)
14. Andrews, J.H., Briand, L.C., Labiche, Y.: Is mutation an appropriate tool for testing experiments? In: ICSE, pp. 402–411 (2005)
15. Zeller, A., Hildebrandt, R.: Simplifying and isolating failure-inducing input. IEEE Transactions on Software Engineering 28(2), 183–200 (2002)
16. Cleve, H., Zeller, A.: Locating causes of program failures. In: ICSE, pp. 342–351 (2005)
17. Buse, R.P.L., Weimer, W.: The road not taken: Estimating path execution frequency statically. In: ICSE, pp. 144–154 (2009)
18. Zhang, X., Gupta, N., Gupta, R.: A study of effectiveness of dynamic slicing in locating real faults. Empirical Software Engineering 12(2), 143–160 (2007)
19. Agrawal, H., Horgan, J.R., London, S., Wong, W.E.: Fault localization using execution slices and dataflow tests. In: Proceedings of IEEE Software Reliability Engineering, pp. 143–151 (1995)
20. Hao, D., Zhang, L., Xie, T., Mei, H., Sun, J.: Interactive fault localization using test information. Journal of Computer Science Technology 24(5), 962–974 (2009)
21. Briand, L.C.: Novel applications of machine learning in software testing. In: QSIC, pp. 3–10 (2008)
22. Liblit, B., Naik, M., Zheng, A.X., Aiken, A., Jordan, M.I.: Scalable statistical bug isolation. In: PLDI, pp. 15–26 (2005)
23. Baah, G.K., Podgurski, A., Harrold, M.J.: Causal inference for statistical fault localization. In: ISSTA, Trento, Italy (July 2010)
24. Feng, M., Gupta, R.: Learning universal probabilistic models for fault localization. In: ACM SIGPLAN-SIGSOFT Workshop on Program Analysis for Software Tools and Engineering, Toronto, Canada (June 2010)
25. Briand, L.C., Labiche, Y., Liu, X.: Using machine learning to support debugging with tarantula. In: International Symposium on Software Reliability Engineering, pp. 137–146 (2007)
26. Zimmermann, T., Nagappan, N.: Predicting defects using network analysis on dependency graphs. In: ICSE, pp. 531–540 (2008)
27. DiGiuseppe, N., Jones, J.A.: On the influence of multiple faults on coverage-based fault localization. In: ISSTA, pp. 210–220 (2011)
28. Lucia, Lo, D., Jiang, L., Budi, A.: Comprehensive evaluation of association measures for fault localization. In: ICSM, pp. 1–10 (2010)

A Model-Based Framework for Developing Real-Time Safety Ada Systems*

Emilio Salazar, Alejandro Alonso, Miguel A. de Miguel,
and Juan A. de la Puente

Universidad Politécnica de Madrid (UPM)
{esalazar,aalonso,mmiguel,jpuente}@dit.upm.es

Abstract. This paper describes an MDE framework for real-time systems with safety requirements. The framework is based on industry standards, such as UML 2.2, MARTE, and the Ada Ravenscar profile. It integrates pre-existing technology with newly developed tools. Special care has been taken to ensure consistency between models and final code. Temporal analysis is integrated in the framework in order to ensure that the real-time behaviour of the models and the final code is consistent and according to the specification.

Automatic code generation from high-level models is performed based on the Ravenscar computational model. The tools generate Ravenscar-compliant Ada code using a reduced set of code stereotypes.

A case study is described for a subsystem of the on-board software of UPMSat2, a university micro-satellite project.

Keywords: Real-time systems, high-integrity systems, model-driven engineering, Ada, Ravenscar profile.

1   Introduction

Model-driven engineering (MDE) is a software development approach that allows engineers to raise the abstraction level of the languages and tools used in the development process [17]. It also helps designers isolate the information and processing logic from implementation and platform aspects. A basic objective of MDE is to put the model concept on the critical path of software development. This notion changes the previous situation, turning the role of models from contemplative to productive.

Models provide support for different types of problems: i) description of concepts, ii) validation of these concepts based on checking and analysis techniques, iii) transformation of models and generation of code, configurations, and documentation. Separation of concerns avoids confusion raised by the combination of different types of concepts. Model-driven approaches introduce solutions for the specialization of the models for specific concerns, as well as the interconnection

---

* This work has been partially funded by the Spanish Government, project HI-PARTES (TIN2011-28567-C03-01).

H.B. Keller et al. (Eds.): Ada-Europe 2013, LNCS 7896, pp. 127–142, 2013.

of concerns based on models transformations. It improves communication between stakeholders using the models to support the interchange of information. But the separation of concerns often requires specialized modelling languages for the description of specific concerns.

This paper describes an MDE framework for the development of real-time high-integrity systems. The functional part of the system is modelled using the Unified Modeling Language (UML2) [12]). Real-time and platform properties are added to functional models by means of annotations, using the UML profile for Modelling and Analysis of Real-Time and Embedded Systems (MARTE) [13]). An analysis model for verifying the temporal behaviour of the system using MAST[1] [6] is automatically generated from the MARTE model. Finally, Ada code skeletons are generated, based on the system model and the results of response time analysis. Code generation is based on the Ravenscar computational model [3], and generates Ravenscar-compliant code [18, D.13.1].

Related work includes the Ada code generator in IBM Rhapsody[2] [5], which generates complex Ada code but does not support MARTE or the Ravenscar profile. Papyrus[3] [9], on the other hand, supports functional Ada code generation from UML models, but cannot generate Ravenscar code and does not fully integrate temporal analysis with system models.

The tools developed in ASSERT[4] follow a closer approach. Two sets of tools were developed in this project, one based on HRT-UML [10,14,2], and the other one on AADL[5] [7,8], which later evolved to the current TASTE[6] toolset [15]. Both can generate Ravenscar Ada code and include timing analysis with MAST.

The main differences between these toolsets and the framework presented here are: i) This framework uses up-to date industrial standards such as UML2 and MARTE, instead of ad-hoc adaptions of UML; ii) the transformation tools in this framework have been built with standard languages; iii) the extensive use of standards in this framework makes it possible to use it with different design environments, without being tied to a specific development platform.

The rest of the paper is organised as follows: Section 2 reviews the use of MARTE stereotypes in the framework. Section 3 describes the logical architecture of the framework and the different models that are used in it. Section 4 describes the techniques that are used to generate Ravenscar Ada code. It also includes as a case study some examples from UPMSat2, an experimental microsatellite project which is being carried out at Universidad Politécnica de Madrid (UPM). Finally, some conclusions of the work are drawn in section 5.

---

[1] Modelling an Analysis Suite for Real-Time Applications, mast.unican.es

[2] www.ibm.com/developerworks/rational/products/rhapsody

[3] www.papyrusuml.org

[4] Automated proof-based System and Software Engineering for Real-Time systems, www.assert-project.net/

[5] Architecture Analysis Description Language, http://www.aadl.info

[6] The ASSERT Set of Tools for Engineering, www.assert-project.net/-TASTE-

2   Modelling Real-Time Systems with MARTE

MARTE is a UML2 profile aimed at providing support for modelling and analysis of real-time and embedded systems [13]. It includes several packages for describing non-functional properties of embedded systems, as well as some secondary profiles for different kinds of systems. This makes MARTE a rather big standard. However, since the framework is aimed at real-time high-integrity systems, only those parts of the MARTE specification that are relevant for this kind of systems are used. The main requirement is to be able to model systems with a predictable behaviour that can be analysed against their specified temporal properties. Such models must be transformed into implementations running on a predictable platform. The Ravenscar computational model [4] is a suitable basis for this purpose.

The modelling elements to be considered are:

- *Input events* describing the patterns for the activation of computations (sequences of actions) in the system, e.g. periodic or sporadic activation patterns.
- *Actions* that have to be executed in response to input events.
- *Precedence constraints and deadlines* for the actions to be executed as a response to an event. Precedence constraints define end-to-end flows of computation that have to be executed within the interval defined by the activation event and the deadline.
- *Resources* needed to execute the actions of the system. Resources can be grouped into *active resources* (e.g. CPUs and networks), and *passive resources* (e.g. shared data). Access to shared resources has to be scheduled in order to guarantee the required temporal properties of the system.

These elements can be described in MARTE using some of its specialized subprofiles. The GQAM (Generic Quantitative Analysis Modelling) profile, which is part of the MARTE analysis model, defines common modelling abstractions for real-time systems. For example, the GaWorkloadEvent stereotype can be used to model input events and the associated timing constraints, and the GaScenario and GaStep stereotypes can be used to specify the response to an event in terms of flows and actions. The SAM (Scheduling Analysis Modelling) profile defines additional abstractions and constraints to build analysable models, including a refined notion of an end-to-end flow.

The resources available for execution can be described using the GQAM:: GaResourcesPlatform stereotype, together with other stereotypes in the GQAM and SAM profiles. Examples of the latter are SaExecHost, SaComm Host, and SharedResource. Scheduling resources are defined with the Scheduler and SecondaryScheduler stereotypes.

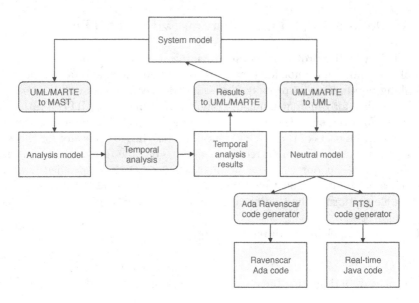

Fig. 1. Architecture of the real-time safety systems development framework

3   A Model-Based Framework

3.1   Overview

A model-based framework has been designed in order to provide support for the
development of high-integrity real-time systems based on the MDE principles
and using UML/MARTE as the main modelling formalism. The overall architecture of the framework is shown in figure 1. Its main elements are four kinds
of models:

- **System Model**: This is the model that the developer creates using UML
  and the MARTE profile. It starts as a Platform Independent Model (PIM)
  that uses MARTE stereotypes to represent the load of the system and the associated real-time attributes (activation patterns, deadlines, etc.). Resources
  are then incorporated using the appropriate stereotypes to get a platform-
  specific model (PSM). The model is initially populated with estimates of
  time attributes, such as blocking times or worst case execution times. Later
  on, when the actual code is available, these values can be replaced with real
  measurements, and accurate temporal analysis can be carried out. If the estimates of time attributes are used as requirements for the implementation
  phase, the results of preliminary analysis based on them should still be valid.
- **Analysis Model**: This model is aimed at performing temporal analysis on
  the system. MAST [6] has been selected as the analysis tool to be used in
  the framework, as it covers many different situations and analysis methods.
  The tool can check if the specified time requirements are met, and thus
  can be used to validate the temporal behaviour of the system early in the

development cycle. Since more accurate execution time measurements are available as the system development advances, the analysis can be repeated as many times as needed.

The analysis model is described using the MAST notation. It is automatically generated from the system model using a transformation tool. The results of the analysis are fed back to the system model by means of another tool, so that the developer can modify the model as needed if the temporal requirements are not met.

– **Neutral Model**: This model is intended to simplify code generation for different platforms and programming languages. The model is automatically generated from the system model by transformation tools that have been developed to this purpose, and it is not intended to be read or modified by the user.

The neutral model is described in plain UML, and has a lower abstraction level than the system model.

– **Implementation Model**: The source code for the system is automatically generated from the neutral model. Generator tools for Ada 2005 with the Ravenscar profile and Real-Time Java (RTSJ) have been developed. The Ada generator is further described in section 4. The work on RTSJ is explained in reference [11].

The transformation tools between the above models have been developed by the research team using QVT[7] and MTL.[8]

A more detailed description of the models follows.

3.2   System Model

The system model is incrementally built by the developer using UML classes and relations to model the system architecture and its components. MARTE stereotypes are used to define the real-time properties of the relevant classes. Depending on how a class is stereotyped, it can be categorized as a particular real time archetype. The framework recognizes four class archetypes, based on the Ravenscar computational model:

– **Periodic**. Instances of a periodic class execute an action cyclically, with a given period. An offset may be specified for the first execution. Each execution has a fixed deadline with respect to its activation time.
– **Sporadic**. Sporadic objects execute an activity on each occurrence of some activation event. As above, a deadline is defined relative to the activation time.

  Periodic and sporadic classes are *active* classes. Their activation patterns and deadlines are defined using the GQAM::GaWorkloadEvent stereotype with a periodic/sporadic arrival pattern and a deadline. Scheduling details are

---

[7] Query/View/Transformation, www.omg.org/spec/QVT/
[8] Model to Text Transformation Language, http://www.omg.org/spec/MOFM2T/1.0/

defined when appropriate in the design process using the GRM::Schedulable-Resource stereotype. A fixed-priority preemptive scheduling policy is assumed by default.

- **Protected**. Protected objects encapsulate shared data that is accessed in mutual exclusion. A protected class is defined with the GRM::MutualExclusion Resource stereotype.
- **Passive**. Passive objects have no real-time properties and are not used by more than one active object. Classes without any MARTE stereotypes are characterized as passive.

3.3   Analysis Model

The GRM, GQAM and SAM MARTE profiles are designed for the automatic generation of schedulability analysis models. These models can be generated and analysed at early modelling phases, so that design decisions can be made depending on the temporal behaviour of the system.

The MARTE analysis annotations are represented with UML extensions. In practice, the analysis model only depends on the UML specification of sequence behaviours. These extensions include references between them, and all together define an analysis model. A UML model may include as many analysis scenarios as SAM::SaAnalysisContext stereotype applications.

Figure 2 shows some relations between analysis stereotypes that summarize the general structure of the models. The root is the analysis context (typically a package or a model; alternative solutions can include several analysis contexts). It identifies the set of workload behaviours and platform resources.

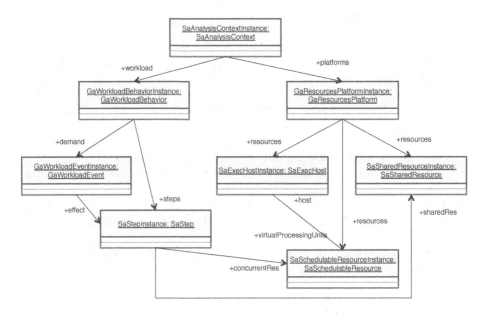

Fig. 2. General structure of an analysis model

A workload behaviour is associated to a workload event and to the sequence of steps and scenarios that are executed when the event occurs. Notice that sub-scenarios can also be specified as an effect of a workload event. Steps are associated to schedulable resources.

Platform resources include schedulable resources, executable resources, and mutual exclusion resources. Schedulable resources define a flow of execution of steps. They are associated with a processor and a scheduler.

In summary, the analysis model is based on four basic concepts:

- *Specification of load events in the system.* These are the sources of load in the system. The arrival pattern of events must be specified in order to analyse the temporal behaviour of the system.
- *Event responses.* A sequence of steps defining behaviour associated to event occurrences. The required information includes the precedence relations between events and the resources needed to execute them, including timing data (e.g. execution time budgets).
- *Resources.* Steps are executed in the context of schedulable resources (e.g. threads, processes or tasks). Scheduling parameters, such as priorities, must be also defined.
  Some additional resources may also be required. Examples of different kinds of resources include computing resources (e.g. processors), communication resources, synchronisation resources, and mutual exclusion resources. All of them require some parameters to be defined for temporal analysis (e.g. ceiling priorities for mutual exclusion resources).
- *Schedulers.* Schedulers define the rules for sharing resources among schedulable resources. For example, fixed-priority is a well-known scheduling method for computing resources.

All of these analysis elements can be modelled in MARTE, using the stereotypes mentioned in section 2 above. The MARTE model is translated into the input language of the MAST analysis toolset[9] by means of a transformation tool. The tools make use of different schedulability analysis methods to compute temporal data such as worst case response time for events and steps, occupation of resources, and optimal protocol and scheduling parameters for resources.

The code generated in Ada generator must be consistent with the results of the scheduling analysis results. To this purpose, the results are fed back to the system model in order to fix any inconsistencies and provide a feasible description of the system to the neutral model.

3.4   Neutral Model

In order to implement code generation in a flexible and efficient way, a neutral model is used as an intermediate step between the system model and the final code. Since the framework is focused on high-integrity systems, the code has to be restricted according to appropriate profiles in order to ensure that it runs

---

[9] See mast.unican.es for details on the analysis tools.

in a predictable way and its timing behaviour complies with the specification. The use of profiles simplifies code generation, which can be based on a common notation independent of the programming language to be used.

The neutral model is defined in plain UML, without using any MARTE stereotypes. Only information that is relevant for code generation is included in this model. Language-dependent elements are avoided, in order to enable code generation for different implementation languages.

The driving principles in the generation of the neutral model are:

- *Include only data that is needed for code generation*, e.g. period, phase, priority. The system model may include other kinds of information, which are not needed for this purpose. This rule simplifies the implementation of the code generator, and increases its efficiency.
- *Keep data types as simple as possible*, in order to reduce the semantic gap between UML and the implementation languages. The neutral model uses mostly simple data types (e.g. natural, integer, string), and tries to avoid the use of complex data types. In particular, custom MARTE data types, which would be difficult to translate into a specific programming language, are excluded.
- *Keep the model independent of the target programming language*. Indeed, the main goal of using an intermediate model is to be able to generate code for different programming languages.
- *Support traceability between the system model and the final code and vice versa*, in order to make it possible to indicate which part of code corresponds to which part of the system model at any time in the development process. This also includes the temporal analysis results, which should also be traceable in order to identify the source of scheduling-related constructs in the code. In this way, if a problem arises in the final code, the original model element that causes the error can be quickly identified and corrected as needed.

The neutral model is built from a small number of common real-time patterns matching the archetypes described in section 3.2 These patterns are represented by UML plain classes with additional annotations including all the required data coming from the original system model that cannot be expressed in UML.

The most relevant kinds of annotations include:

- WCET, for the worst-case execution time of an activity.
- Deadline error handler. Defines the user code to be executed when a deadline overrun occurs.
- General exception handler. Defines the code to be executed when an exception is raised.
- Last chance exception handler. Defines the user code to be executed as "last wishes routine", before terminating a program.
- Task initialization. Defines some code to be executed at system start time by a periodic or sporadic object.

4   Ravenscar Ada Code Generation

4.1   Ada Generation Overview

This section describes the generation of Ada source code from the neutral model, which only includes the necessary information for this purpose, in a language-independent way. The neutral model can be used for generating code in Ada, RTSJ, or any other language suitable for real-time systems.

The Ada code generator relies on international industrial standards. It has been developed using QVT and MTL, as mentioned in 3.1 above. The neutral model is described with plain standard UML 2.2, and the output is Ada 2005 with the Ravenscar Profile restrictions [18]. The generator produces Ada code skeletons with a temporal behaviour consistent with the system model, including the results of temporal analysis as previously described in section 3.3. This approach facilitates the link with functional code.

Some aspects of the code generation process are illustrated with fragments of the Attitude Determination and Control Subsystem (ADCS) subsystem of the UPMSat2 on-board software system[1].

4.2   Code Generation for Components

The top level description of the system is based on UML components, which are composed of a set of classes. UML components include an interface, and a set of classes that implement the public operations and the component functionality. The interface defines the component contract with the client, which specifies its public functionality. It is mapped into an Ada package. Its specification includes the signature of the operations that are exported from the interface of the UML component. The corresponding body simply redirects the exported operation to the corresponding internal package operation. This approach follows software engineering principles, such as information hiding, loose coupling, and facilitates code generation and maintenance for different execution platforms. Figure 3 shows the external view of the ADCS component, as well as its internal structure.

The internal classes of the component are mapped into private packages, as described below, according to their real-time archetypes: periodic, sporadic, protected or passive activities. Hierarchical packages are used for representing the structure modelled with the UML components.

The Ada code generated for the interface is shown in figure 4. This component exports three methods that are mapped into Ada operations in the package specification. In the body, these operations call the corresponding internal implementation method.

Figure 5 shows a detailed view of the internal classes belonging to the ADCS subsystem. It can be noticed that the MARTE stereotypes are printed in the upper part of the corresponding classes.

The *ADCS.AttitudeControl* class implements the control algorithm for keeping a given attitude for the satellite. It is a periodic entity, and its graphical representation shows the annotations GRM::SchedulableResource and GQAM:: WorkloadEvent.

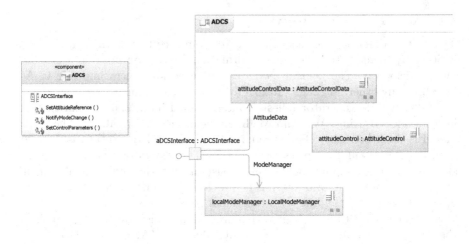

Fig. 3. Attitude Determination and Control Subsystem UML component

```
with ADCS.BasicTypes; use ADCS.BasicTypes;
package ADCS.Interfaces is
   procedure NotifyModeChange      (mode : in Mode_Type);
   procedure SetAttitudeReference (ref  : in Reference_Type);
   procedure SetControlParameters (conf : in Configuration_Type);
end ADCS.Interfaces;
```

```
with ADCS.LocalModeManager;
with ADCS.AttitudeControlData;
package body ADCS.Interfaces is

  procedure NotifyModeChange (mode : in Mode_Type) is
  begin
    ADCS.LocalModeManager.LocalModeManager.SetMode (mode);
  end NotifyModeChange;

  procedure SetAttitudeReference (ref : in Reference_Type) is
  begin
    ADCS.AttitudeControlData.AttitudeControl.SetActitudeReferece(ref);
  end SetAttitudeReference;

  procedure SetControlParameters (conf : in Configuration_Type) is
  begin
    ADCS.AttitudeControlData.AttitudeControl.SetControlParameters(conf);
  end SetControlParameters;

end ADCS.Interfaces;
```

Fig. 4. Generated package for an UML component interface

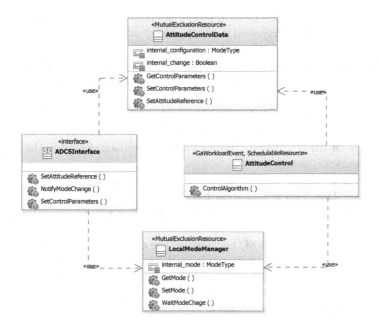

Fig. 5. Design view of the ADCS classes

There are two protected entities, which are stereotyped with the GRM::Mutual ExclusionResource annotation: *ADCS.AttitudeControlData* and *ADCS.LocalMode Manager*. One is in charge of keeping information for the control algorithm. The other one is used for managing the operational mode of the component.

4.3   Code Generation for Classes

Code generation is based on a set of code templates, which are directly related with the archetypes in the neutral model. As mentioned above, classes in this model are annotated with its related archetype. Currently, four archetypes are supported: Periodic, Sporadic, Protected, and Passive.

There are several suitable implementations of these archetypes in the literature. This work is based on the Ravenscar Ada generic packages defined in [16]. Some additional features have been added, for including issues such as deadline overrun handling, WCET overrun handling, Ada standard exceptions handling, user defined task initialization, or user-defined stack size. These features were included in order to enable dealing with more general tasking models. In the context of this work, some of them are disabled by default, as they are not Ravenscar-compliant.

Each class in the neutral model is represented by an Ada package. The package includes in its private part an instance of a generic package where the class archetype is defined. All the required dependencies are included in the package description.

Class dependencies in the neutral model are converted into Ada with clauses. There are three different types of dependencies:

- Explicit user-defined dependencies. These dependencies are explicitly defined in the system model, and they are directly translated, without any additional processing.
- Implicit dependencies due to attributes or parameter types. If an attribute or a parameter is defined as a non-primitive type (e.g. attributes which are instances of other classes), the generator automatically adds the required dependencies.
- Implicit dependencies due to automatically generated code. Several Ada features (e.g. last chance exception handler, etc.) have dependencies on other Ada packages. They are also automatically added when they are required.

With respect to the internals of the package, the main action is the instantiation of the generic package that corresponds to the class archetype, which is carried out in the private part of the package. The parameters needed for the generic instantiation depend on the type of the archetype. In the case of active classes, the following parameters are required:

- Real-time parameters: priority, period or minimal inter-arrival time, and initial offset.
- Functional code parameters: periodic or sporadic activity, and initialization procedure.
- Error handling parameters: procedures for dealing with timing related exceptions and with Ada standard exceptions.

The code listed in figure 6 shows an example of a specification file generated for a periodic activity. The instantiation call is located at the end of the private part.

Protected classes, annotated as mutual exclusion resources, are translated into a package that includes a protected object. The stereotype allows to define the ceiling priority for the object, which is directly translated into the corresponding parameter in Ada. The code generated for the *ADCS.AttitudeControlData* class is shown in figure 7

Finally, the framework supports two types of passive classes, in order to provide additional flexibility to the developer:

- *Singleton class:* If the developer annotates an UML class as singleton, there may only be one instance of it in the system. In this case, the code generator produces a package with a public interface that is composed by a set of operations.
- *Standard passive class:* Multiple instances of this classes are allowed. The Ada code generator produces a package that implements an abstract data type. The public interface includes the type definition and its primitive operations.

```
with Ada.Real_Time.Timing_Events;
use  Ada.Real_Time.Timing_Events;
with GNAT.IO;                        use GNAT.IO;
with Ada.Exceptions;                 use Ada.Exceptions;
with uml2ada.exceptions;            use uml2ada.exceptions;
with uml2ada.periodic_tasks;

package example.examplePlatform.subsystem1.OBDH.ADCS.PeriodicADCS is

   PeriodicADCS_priority : constant := 8;
   PeriodicADCS_period   : constant := 9854;
   PeriodicADCS_offset   : constant := 234000000;
private

   procedure Activity;

   procedure Activity_Initialization;

   protected DeadlineHandler is
      procedure DeadlineErrorHandler (Event : in out Timing_Event);
   end DeadlineHandler;

   procedure ConstraintErrorHandler (e : in Exception_Occurrence);

   package PeriodicADCS_periodic_task is new
     uml2ada.periodic_tasks (
      Priority                => PeriodicADCS_priority,
      Period                  => PeriodicADCS_period,
      Offset                  => PeriodicADCS_offset,
      Periodic_Activity       => Activity,
      Initialization          => Activity_Initialization,
      Deadline_Ovr_Handler    => DeadlineHandler.DeadlineErrorHandler'Access,
      Constraint_Error_Handler => ConstraintErrorHandler'Access,
      Program_Error_Handler   => Default_Exception_Handler,
      Storage_Error_Handler   => Default_Exception_Handler,
      Tasking_Error_Handler   => Default_Exception_Handler,
      Other_Error_Handler     => Default_Exception_Handler);

end example.examplePlatform.subsystem1.OBDH.ADCS.PeriodicADCS;
```

Fig. 6. Specification of a generic periodic archetype

```
with ADCS.BasicTypes; use ADCS.BasicTypes;
private package ADCS.AttitudeControlData is

   protected AttitudeControl is
      pragma Priority (10);

      procedure SetActitudeReferece (reference : in Reference_Type);
      procedure SetControlParameters (config : in Configuration_Type);
      function GetControlParameters return Configuration_Type;

   private
      internal_configuration : Configuration_Type;
      internal_reference     : Reference_Type;
   end AttitudeControl;
end ADCS.AttitudeControlData;
```

Fig. 7. Specification of a generated protected object

4.4 Code Generation for Methods

The methods specified in classes of the neutral model are translated into Ada subprograms according to the following rules:

a) Each UML method is translated into an Ada procedure or function:
   - Methods with a return parameter are translated as functions.
   - Methods without a return parameter are implemented as procedures.
   - Parameters specified as in, out, and inout are translated into their Ada equivalents.
   - Methods that are declared as private in the *neutral* model are generated in the private part of the Ada specification. Otherwise, they are placed in the public part.
b) UML attributes and method parameter types are implemented as Ada types.
   - Integer, Positive and Boolean primitive types are directly implemented by the corresponding Ada types.
   - The implementation of the String primitive type is a little more difficult since Ada strings must be constrained at compilation time. Unconstrained string parameter types are thus translated into the library Unbounded_String type instead of the Ada String type. Consequently, a dependence on the package Ada.Strings.Unbounded has to be added.
   - Enumerations are translated into Ada enumeration types.

   Parameters can also be defined as types of model-defined classes or as constrained arrays.
c) Initialization of primitive or enumeration type attributes is also supported. An initialized string attribute results in an Ada String, since its length is known at compilation time.
d) Standard Ada exceptions raised in the functional code are, by default, propagated. Nevertheless, is possible to provide user-defined handlers for such exceptions. A handler for user-defined exceptions can also be provided.
e) It is also possible to provide a user-defined last-chance exception handler in order to execute a "last wishes" routine if the system unexpectedly terminates.
f) By default, periodic activities raise a Program_Error exception in case of a deadline overrun. However, a user-defined routine can be specified to be executed instead.

5 Conclusions

Model-driven Engineering allows developers to raise the abstraction level of software design, so making the development process safer and faster. At the implementation side, Ada and the Ravenscar profile provide excellent support for building predictable real-time systems that can be statically analysed for a specified temporal behaviour. The work described in this paper has been directed at combining the best of both worlds through the use of a specialised framework covering the design and implementation development phases of high-integrity real-time systems.

The main contributions of the framework are its alignment with industrial standards, specifically OMG standards and Ada, and the tight integration of the system model with the analysis model. Moreover, the strict adherence to UM2/MARTE standards and the use of standard tools make it possible to implement the framework on a variety of tools, without depending on a particular toolset. Most of the transformation tools described in the paper have been implemented and tested on IBM RSA (Rational Software Architect), but migrating to other environments (e.g. Eclipse) can be done with comparatively little effort. The transformation tools are freely available at `www.dit.upm.es/str`.

The use of neutral model facilitates generating code for different programming languages. Generators for Ada and Real-Time Java have been implemented and can be found at the same location as the transformation tools.

Future work includes enhancing the transformations between the system model and the analysis model, which are now at an early stage of development, and adding support to include functional code generated from other tools (e.g. Simulink) into the real-time skeletons generated by the framework.

Acknowledgments. The framework described in this paper was originally developed within the European project CHESS,and has been completed and extended in the HIPARTESproject. We would like to acknowledge the financial support of the European Commission FP7 program and the Spanish national R+D+i plan as well as the collaboration with the partners in both projects.

References

1. Alonso, A., Salazar, E., de la Puente, J.A.: Design of on-board software for an experimental satellite (2103), `www.dit.upm.es/~str/papers/pdf/alonso&13a.pdf`
2. Bordin, M., Vardanega, T.: Correctness by construction for high-integrity real-time systems: A metamodel-driven approach. In: Abdennadher, N., Kordon, F. (eds.) Ada-Europe 2007. LNCS, vol. 4498, pp. 114–127. Springer, Heidelberg (2007)
3. Burns, A., Dobbing, B., Romanski, G.: The Ravenscar tasking profile for high integrity real-time programs. In: Asplund, L. (ed.) Ada-Europe 1998. LNCS, vol. 1411, pp. 263–275. Springer, Heidelberg (1998)
4. Burns, A., Dobbing, B., Vardanega, T.: Guide for the use of the Ada Ravenscar profile in high integrity systems. Ada Letters XXIV, 1–74 (2004)
5. Gery, E., Harel, D., Palachi, E.: Rhapsody: A complete life-cycle model-based development system. In: Butler, M., Petre, L., Sere, K. (eds.) IFM 2002. LNCS, vol. 2335, pp. 1–10. Springer, Heidelberg (2002)
6. González Harbour, M., Gutiérrez, J.J., Palencia, J.C., Drake, J.M.: MAST modeling and analysis suite for real time applications. In: Proceedings of 13th Euromicro Conference on Real-Time Systems, pp. 125–134. IEEE Computer Society Press, Delft (2001)
7. Hamid, I., Najm, E.: Operational semantics of Ada Ravenscar. In: Kordon, F., Vardanega, T. (eds.) Ada-Europe 2008. LNCS, vol. 5026, pp. 44–58. Springer, Heidelberg (2008)

8. Hugues, J., Zalila, B., Pautet, L., Kordon, F.: From the prototype to the final embedded system using the Ocarina AADL tool suite. ACM Tr. Embedded Computer Systems 7(4), 1–25 (2008)

9. Lanusse, A., Tanguy, Y., Espinoza, H., Mraidha, C., Gerard, S., Tessier, P., Schnekenburger, R., Dubois, H., Terrier, F.: Papyrus UML: an open source toolset for MDA. In: Proc. of the Fifth European Conference on Model-Driven Architecture Foundations and Applications (ECMDA-FA 2009), pp. 1–4 (2009)

10. Mazzini, S., Puri, S., Vardanega, T.: An MDE methodology for the development of high-integrity real-time systems. In: Design, Automation and Test in Europe, DATE 2009, pp. 1154–1159. IEEE (2009)

11. de Miguel, M.A., Salazar, E.: Model-based development for RTSJ platforms. In: Proceedings of the 10th International Workshop on Java Technologies for Real-time and Embedded Systems, JTRES 2012, pp. 175–184. ACM, New York (2012)

12. OMG Unified Modeling Language (UML), version 2.4.1 (2011), http://www.omg.org/spec/UML/2.4.1/

13. OMG UML Profile for MARTE: Modeling and Analysis of Real-Time Embedded Systems, version 1.1 (2011), http://www.omg.org/spec/MARTE/

14. Panunzio, M., Vardanega, T.: A metamodel-driven process featuring advanced model-based timing analysis. In: Abdennadher, N., Kordon, F. (eds.) Ada-Europe 2007. LNCS, vol. 4498, pp. 128–141. Springer, Heidelberg (2007)

15. Perrotin, M., Conquet, E., Dissaux, P., Tsiodras, T., Hugues, J.: The TASTE toolset: Turning human designed heterogeneous systems into computer built homogeneous software. In: 5th Int. Congress on Embedded Real-Time Software and Systems, ERTS2 2010 (May 2010)

16. Pulido, J., de la Puente, J.A., Bordin, M., Vardanega, T., Hugues, J.: Ada 2005 code patterns for metamodel-based code generation. Ada Letters XXVII(2), 53–58 (2007), Proceedings of the 13th International Ada Real-Time Workshop (IRTAW13)

17. Schmidt, D.C.: Model-driven engineering. IEEE Computer 39(2) (2006)

18. Tucker Taft, S., Duff, R.A., Brukardt, R.L., Plödereder, E., Leroy, P. (eds.): Ada 2005 Reference Manual. LNCS, vol. 4348. Springer, Heidelberg (2006)

Towards a Time-Composable Operating System

Andrea Baldovin, Enrico Mezzetti, and Tullio Vardanega

Department of Mathematics, University of Padua,
via Trieste, 63 - 35121 Padua, Italy
{baldovin,emezzett,tullio.vardanega}@math.unipd.it

Abstract. Compositional approaches to the qualification of hard real-time systems rest on the premise that the individual units of development can be incrementally composed preserving the timing behaviour they had in isolation. In practice, however, the assumption of time composability is often wavering due to the inter-dependences stemming from inherent nature of hardware and software. The operating system, mediator between the applications and the underlying hardware, plays a critical role in enabling time composability. This paper discusses the challenges faced in the implementation of a truly time-composable operating system based on ORK+, a Ravenscar-compliant real-time kernel.

Keywords: Time composability, Real-time operating system.

1 Introduction

The timing dimension plays a critical role in the development and qualification of hard real-time systems: the correctness of such systems does not only rely on the functional correctness but also on timely delivery of the results. Scheduling analysis techniques are increasingly adopted by system engineers to attain trustworthy guarantees on the timing behaviour of a system. State-of-the-art analysis frameworks rely on the assumption that the timing behaviour of a system can be determined *compositionally*, as a combination of the worst-case execution time (WCET) bounds of all the system activities [26]. Analogous assumptions of composition stand at the base of incremental software development, where at the top-down decomposition of the system design eventually corresponds a bottom-up integration of the corresponding implementation artefacts.

The timing behaviour of the individual software units to which timing analysis is applied is generally assumed to be fully composable. In other words, every individual software unit is expected to exhibit exactly the same timing behaviour regardless of the nature, the activity and the interference caused by other software units in the system. Unfortunately, time composability is not an innate characteristic for a system and it is generally not guaranteed to hold. The importance of time composability as a fundamental enabler to trustworthy timing analysis has been only recently acknowledged in the literature [17, 18]. The authors of the cited works highlight the negative effects on time composability caused by complex hardware features, with consequent serious threats to the

H.B. Keller et al. (Eds.): Ada-Europe 2013, LNCS 7896, pp. 143–160, 2013.

soundness of schedulability analysis. Some issues along what we call hardware-to-software axis of composition have been discussed for both single-processor [1,14] and multi-processor [10] platforms.

Time composability, however, is not solely a hardware-level issue. It in fact carries an equally important, albeit less studied, software-to-software dimension of interest. The effect of the real-time operating system (RTOS) on time composability should be studied on two accounts: the RTOS is a separate unit of analysis itself, which must therefore be proven to comply with the premises of time composability; moreover, a non-composable RTOS service would transitively compromise the composability of each program that invokes it.

The provision of a time-composable RTOS is highly desirable in those contexts where firm guarantees on the timing behaviour of a system should be provided. In a recent work [4], we singled out those properties that a RTOS should exhibit to be time-composable and to enable time composability vertically across the execution stack. We also provided a concrete implementation of our approach on a simple ARINC-653 compliant RTOS for use in avionics applications [3,4]. The implementation therein provided, however, took much benefit from the simplifying assumptions that could be derived from the essentially cyclic nature of the underlying software architecture and ARINC-653 task model. Even though the fundamentals of time composability should hold true regardless of the underlying software architecture, it appeared to us that the actual implementation of a time-composable RTOS is largely dependent on the task model of choice. Those solutions that we proved to be effective on a restrictive ARINC-compliant kernel are therefore not likely to allow an equally straightforward application in less restrictive hence favourable task models.

We selected ORK+ [8,23], a Ravenscar-compliant RTOS, as a more general real-time reference kernel to study how far time composability could be attained on a more general task model. Acknowledging that the base principles of timing analysability that inspired ORK+ seem to naturally conform to the same objectives of time composability [24], we still identified a few modifications that would help improve the degree of time composability in ORK+. The results presented in this paper should be understood as a step toward the final objective of the implementation of a time-composable real-time operating system that supports a general sporadic task model, restricted in accord with the Ravenscar Profile [6].

The remainder of this paper is organised as follows: in Section 2 we introduce the concept and role of time composability in RTOS; in Section 3 we present how we envision a time-composable RTOS, and then present ORK+, identifying the set of kernel services that we looked at; in Section 4 we report on the experiments we performed to assess the degree of time composability we attained with our modifications of ORK+; in Section 5 we draw our conclusions.

2   Time-Composable RTOS

The idea of time composability, while being a fundamental assumption behind common compositional schedulability analysis approaches, has only recently gained interest in the real-time community. A formalization attempt to define the very concept of composability in the timing dimension has been in fact studied in few recent works [10, 12, 14, 17, 18, 21].

Time composability is the property of a generic software component or task to exhibit a timing behaviour that is independent of its actual context of execution [21]. In particular [17, 18] jointly provide a valuable insight on the obstacles that current hardware and software development approaches pose to time composability and compositionality. Analogous observations on the difficulties in guaranteeing time composability and predictability in cutting-edge platforms motivates the adoption of simpler specialized hardware in [14]; a specular approach in [12] proposes a probabilistic method as a means to enable composability by reducing dependence on execution history. Similar concerns apply, even more significantly, to multicore systems, as suggested out by the work in [10].

All cited works mainly focused on the hardware-to-software axis of composition, thereby failing to account for the role of the underlying operating system and its effects on time composability. This is not very surprising, as the contribution of RTOS in the determination of the end-to-end timing behaviour of a system has been traditionally dispensed with by classic timing analysis. This simplifying assumption was justified by the optimistic claim that the incidence of the RTOS on the granularity of interest to timing analysis is negligible and, where necessary, could be easily treated as a simple additive factor. The fact is, instead, that actual RTOS implementations fail this assumption quite badly.

The more services a RTOS is required to provide to a running application, the larger its potential influence on the overall execution time. Although not explicitly labelling it as lack of time composability, it has been observed in [22] that the potentially tight interdependence between the RTOS and the application implies that their respective timing analysis cannot be performed in reciprocal isolation. This is even more true in the presence of advanced hardware acceleration features – like caches, complex pipelines, translation look-aside buffers, etc. – as the execution of RTOS services may pollute their execution-history dependent inner state, which their timing behaviour depends on. Interdependence between user applications and operating system has obvious potential for wrecking the very essence of time composability.

Moreover, from the timing analysis point of view, providing a clear separation between RTOS services and user application can be still unsatisfactory. In fact, the results of timing analysis are easily impaired by the existence of a large extent of jitter in the execution time. An interesting study, reporting on an attempt of analysing the timing behaviour of a complex real-time kernel [5], has shown massive gaps between the observed execution time and the statically computed WCET bounds for a set of operating system services. As suggested by the authors, part of those gaps originates from the overestimation brought in by the conservative assumptions of static WCET analysis; the remaining part, however, is likely to stem from large execution time jitter, a typical side-effect of the optimization-oriented way of programming. Jittery execution has detrimental effects on timing analysis and composition as we are conservatively forced to always assume the worst case, no matter how much larger than the average case.

When it comes to operating systems, the definition of time composability certainly includes the fact that the OS should exhibit the same timing behaviour independently of the number and nature of other run-time entities in the system: for example, the execution of the thread selection primitive should not vary with the number of tasks in the system. In addition, as the operating system interacts and consequently interferes with the user application, it should also avoid to negatively concur to their execution time jitter: in the presence of hardware features that exhibit history-dependent timing behaviour, the execution of an OS service should not have disturbing effects on the application.

The multifaceted role of RTOS in determining the time composability of a system is confirmed by the classic layered decomposition of the execution stack, as in Figure 1, that clearly shows how the RTOS is deeply engaged in both the hardware-to-software and software-to-software axes of composition. An application program is in fact time-composable with the RTOS only if the WCET estimate computed for that program is not affected by the underlying presence and execution of the RTOS, and those RTOS services that are explicitly invoked by the application are known to contribute compositionally to the overall WCET, without incurring any hardware- or software-related jitter.

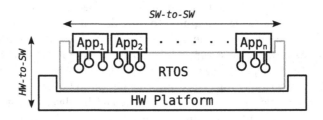

Fig. 1. Layered decomposition of the execution stack

As we already observed in [4], in order for the RTOS to be time-composable with respect to the application, it must pursuit the following principles.

Steady timing behaviour. RTOS services with jittery behaviour impair time composition with the application: the larger the jitter the greater the pessimism in the WCET bound for the service itself and transitively for the caller. RTOS whose services exhibit a constant (or at least near-constant) timing behaviour will thus reduce the jitter to be accounted for in their response time. Timing variability in the RTOS execution depends on the interaction of software and hardware factors: the RTOS data structures and the algorithms used to access them, as well as the hardware state retained by stateful hardware resources. On the software side, timing variability can be only coped with by a re-engineering of the RTOS internals without compromising the functional behaviour, in a similar fashion as it was done with the $O(1)$ Linux scheduler [15]. On the hardware side, the variability stemming from hardware resources, though much more difficult to attenuate, is somehow overclouded by the symmetrical issue of hardware state pollution, which is addressed by the next property.

Zero-disturbance. The RTOS may variably affect the response time of an application because it may either interrupt or interleave with the user code. A time composable RTOS should avoid or minimize both the frequency and the effects of such disturbing events. This is even more evident in the presence of history-sensitive hardware as the interference on the application timing is exacerbated by the pollution (by the RTOS code) of the inner state of such resources. In this case it is important to guarantee that the execution of any RTOS service cannot cause hardware-related disturbance on application timing upon return from the RTOS. This prescription requires isolating the application-related part of the hardware state from any possible perturbation caused by the RTOS: techniques analogous to cache partitioning [16] may serve that purpose, while at the same time preserving the RTOS performance.

Finding the most effective implementation of the RTOS features that meet the above goals is of course largely dependent on the target processor architecture as well as the adopted task model. A periodic task model suffers less preemption overheads than a sporadic one because periods can be made harmonic whereas sporadic arrivals cannot. Analogously, tick scheduling is a very intrusive style of servicing dispatching needs. It should be noted that in any case these properties should not be pursued at the cost of performance loss: the overall performance, although not the primary concern in hard real-time systems, should not be penalised.

2.1   Characterization of a Time-Composable RTOS

Whereas steadiness and zero-disturbance are universally valid principles, the practical means and the degree to which they are exhibited by a RTOS is dependent on the underlying hardware platform, the architectural specification and the task model assumed for the application. An extremely restrictive software architecture resting on a simple periodic task model represents the most favourable precondition for the implementation of a time-composable RTOS.

This clearly emerged during the RTOS refactoring on which we reported in [3,4]. In that case, we took a rather simplified implementation of an ARINC-653 [2] compliant operating system and evaluated the services it provided from the standpoint of time composability, that is with respect to the steady timing behaviour and zero disturbance properties. The ARINC-653 architectural specification allowed us to introduce several simplifying assumptions: the reduction to a strictly periodic task model was probably the most important one. Those assumptions, in turn, gave us the opportunity to reimplement a number of RTOS services at both kernel and ARINC-653 API level with time composability in mind. In that work we succeeded redesigning a real-time partitioned kernel and provided experimental evidence that the degree of time composability may greatly benefit from proper design choices in the implementation of the operating system, without giving up performance.

Unfortunately the favourable assumptions on which we built that particular solution do not hold in general: they are instead of scarce utility outside of the restrictive domain of application of partitioned operating systems. We consider the partitioned RTOS in [3,4] to be a first attempt to inject time composability in a RTOS and the starting point towards the definition of a time-composable RTOS that is more flexible and lends itself to a wider application.

From a more general standpoint, we identify a minimal set of desirable properties, hence potential areas of intervention, that cannot be disregarded in any serious attempt to inject steadiness and zero-disturbance – hence time composability – on a full-fledge RTOS:

1. *Non-intrusive time management:* The way the progression of time is managed by the operating system should have no side effects on the timing behaviour of the applications running on top of it. Intuitively tick-based time management should be avoided in so far as it subjects the user applications to unnecessary periodic interruptions. Moreover the tick-based approach usually implies an intrusive approach to task management where many activities are performed at each tick to keep the ready queue updated.

2. *Constant-time scheduling primitives:* Most of the RTOS execution time is typically spent on scheduling activities: either task state updates (activation, suspension, resumption) or actual dispatching. Reducing the variability stemming from scheduling primitives is intuitively an essential enabler of composable RTOS. In particular, those primitives whose execution time is linearly dependent on the number of tasks in a system should be revised.

3. *Flexible task model:* Leaving aside exceptionally favourable circumstances (e.g., the ARINC model), a realistic RTOS cannot limit itself to support periodic run-time entities only. Sporadic activations, low-level interrupts and programmable timers (e.g., Ada timing events) make the quest for time composability much more complicated. The introduction of more flexible run-time entities breaks the fairly-predictable cyclic pattern of task interleaving, otherwise exhibited by a system with periodic tasks only. Mechanisms to reduce the jittery interference introduced by the incurred task preemptions are required to protect time composability.

4. *Composable inter-task communication:* We intend the area of inter-task communication to cover all kinds of interactions with bearing on hardware or software resources, including I/O, communication and synchronization. From this wider perspective, the problem of providing a time-composable communication subsystems largely intersects with the problem of providing controlled access to shared resources. Uncontrolled forms of synchronization and unbounded priority inversion manifestly clash with the steadiness and zero-disturbance principles.

5. *Selective hardware isolation:* The very concept of zero-disturbance insists on the opportunity of some form of isolation of the history-dependent hardware state as a means to preventing RTOS-induced perturbations: the provided

support may vary from partitioning approaches to plain disabling of hardware resources. Clearly this is more a system-level or hardware issue than a software one as not many solutions can be devised when the underlying hardware platform does not support any form of isolation. When necessary, however, the RTOS should be able to exploit the available features by means of ad-hoc low-level interfaces (e.g., for advance cache management).

Although we would want our ideal time-composable RTOS to exhibit all the above properties, we are also aware that implementing such a comprehensive operating system from scratch is a challenging task. We therefore considered it worthwhile to cast composability upon an existing RTOS, that would preferably already exhibit nice properties from the analysability standpoint.

In this respect, the Open Ravenscar Kernel (ORK+ [23]), developed by the Technical University of Madrid, represented the perfect candidate as reference OS on which we can try to inject time composability. ORK+ is an open-source real-time kernel of reduced size and complexity, especially suited for mission-critical space applications, providing an environment which supports both Ada 2005 [11] and C applications.

As the namesake suggests, ORK+ also complies with the Ravenscar profile [6,24], a standard subset of the Ada language that specifies a reduced tasking model where all language constructs that are exposed to non-determinism or unbounded execution cost are strictly excluded[1]. As additional distinctive features, the Ravenscar profile prescribes the use of a static memory model and forces task communication and synchronization via protected objects under the ceiling locking protocol. Ravenscar-compliant systems are expected to be amenable to static analysis by construction.

The design and implementation of a time-composable operating system of the scale and completeness of ORK+ is not an easy target. Its extent and complexity require to approach the final solution by successive approximations. In the following sections we describe the first steps we took towards the definition of a time composable RTOS: we describe and assess some preliminary modifications we have made to the ORK+ in order to improve its behaviour with respect to time composability.

3   Time-Composable ORK+

In the previous section we observed how injecting time composability within an RTOS kernel is easier in the condition where the system architecture and the supported task model restrict the allowable run-time entities and their interactions. On the particularly favourable conditions in [4] time composability can be greatly improved with modest effort. Unfortunately those conditions may prove untenable for most applications. For this reason we now focus on understanding how and to what extent time composability understood in terms of zero

---

[1] ORK+ is therefore meant to support the restricted subset of the Ada 2005 standard, as determined by the Ravenscar profile.

disturbance and steady timing behaviour, can be achieved in a RTOS that supports a more general sporadic task model. The immediate challenge that leaving the simpler periodic task model brings about is the absence of a-priori knowledge on the release times of all tasks in the system.

We limited our scope of investigation to a more deterministic scenario where the system analysability is favoured without compromising overall performance. The Ada Ravenscar profile [6], of which ORK+ run-time provides a complete implementation, perfectly suits our purpose as it defines a run-time infrastructure following a fixed priority dispatching policy and supporting sporadic task activation and deadlock-free synchronization on protected resources. At the same time, system analysability is guaranteed by enforcing staticness restrictions on task creation, communication and synchronisation.

We attack the problem of injecting time composability into ORK+ in two steps, incrementally addressing what we singled out in Section 2.1 as characterizing properties for a time-composable RTOS. As a first step, reported in Section 3.1, we focus on time management and scheduling primitives, under the simplifying assumption of a simple periodic task model; then in Section 3.2, we reason on whether and how our preliminary solution can be extended to also cover the remaining properties within a more realistic task model.

3.1   Time Composability within a Simplified Task Model

In our attempt to concretely inject the zero-disturbance and steady timing behaviour principles in the ORK+ run-time we first made a set of simplifying assumption on the task model. Although ORK+ provides full support for sporadic tasks and interactions via protected objects, we decided to focus our attention to the management of periodic tasks only, as their disciplined behaviour admittedly makes the job much easier for us. We therefore excluded from our model sporadic task activations, interrupts and timing events, as well as shared resources and the inter-task communication subsystem in general[2]. This simplified setting however must be conceived as a stepping stone to extend our implementation to support sporadic tasks as well.

In this restricted setting, we knew from [4] that the representation and management of time in the system and the scheduling routines defined to order and dispatch processes (properties 1 and 2 in our enumeration in Section 2.1) are among the most critical aspects with bearing on time composability in a RTOS. As such they have been the primary concern of our investigation.

Non-intrusive Time Management. Keeping track of the passing of time in the OS kernel is heavily dependent on the underlying hardware components available to this purpose. In parallel to our effort of injecting time composability within ORK+, we also committed ourselves to porting the run-time – which was originally available for the LEON2 processor (i.e., SPARC architecture) – to the

---

[2] As already observed, both communication and I/Os should be in principle handled as access to shared resources.

PowerPC 750 board in the PowerPC family [9]. The porting effort was motivated by the poor support offered for time representation by the LEON platform, which made a zero-disturbance implementation of time management very hard: the SPARC platform does not offer any better than two 24-bit resolution timers, which alone cannot provide the clock resolution required by Annex D of the Ada Reference Manual [11]; the PowerPC 750 platform provides a 64-bit monotonic time base register and a 32-bit programmable one-shot timer. ORK+ cleverly copes with the LEON hardware limitation by complementing the 24-bit timer by software to obtain the accuracy of a 64-bit register [28].

As observed in [4], time composability may be easily disrupted by tick-based time management approaches that may inattentively interrupt and cause disturbance on the user application. Time composability instead is favoured where the hardware platform provides accurate interval timers that operating system can exploit to implement time management services with as less interference as possible. On the one hand, ORK+ embraces this principle by basing its scheduling on a programmable interval timer, implemented as an ordered queue of alarms; on the other hand, ORK+ is forced to use a periodic timer to handle the software part of its interval timer. Although the tick frequency is not likely to incur significant interference in the current ORK+ implementation we still prefer a pure interval timer solution (i.e., with no periodic ticks) as it better fits our call for zero disturbance and is facilitated by the PowerPC hardware.

Constant-Time Scheduling Primitives. Scheduling activities include maintaining a list of active tasks and keeping it ordered according to the applicable dispatching policy: in the restricted periodic task model we are considering, scheduling decisions are taken according to the fixed-priority preemptive scheduling policy and can occur only at task release and completion. In ORK+ an activation event is managed by programming a dedicated alarm to fire at the time a task needs to be activated; ready tasks are then stored in a unique priority queue, ordered by decreasing execution priority and activation, where dispatching is performed by popping the head of such queue. At task termination nothing more than dispatching the next ready task needs to be done.

Although common practice, such an implementation has the undesirable effect of incurring highly variable execution times on accesses and updates to the involved data structures. In particular, having the alarm queue ordered by expiration time makes the insertion of a new alarm highly dependent on the elements already present in the queue (i.e. the number and value of the pending alarms at the time of insertion). This behaviour clashes with the mentioned principle of steady timing behaviour of OS primitives, with the risk for user applications to be exposed to variable – and only pessimistically boundable – interference from the execution of such primitives.

We re-designed the base ORK+ scheduling structures in a way to avoid this kind of interference. As additional requirement we assume that tasks cannot share the same priority level. Since in our initial setting periodic tasks are not allowed to interact through protected objects, no priority inheritance mechanism is needed, and thus a task can never change the priority level it has been assigned to at the time of declaration. Our constant-time scheduler performs task management operations with fixed overhead, by leveraging on elementary operations over bit-masks.

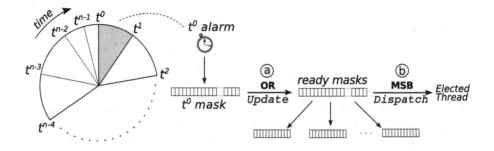

Fig. 2. Constant-time scheduling in ORK+

As shown in Figure 2, the two basic scheduling operations are (a) the task insertion into the ready queue at the time of release, and (b) the election of the next task to dispatch, which could either happen at the time of release of a higher priority task or upon task completion. The only required data structure we need to maintain is a 256-bit mask, where each bit corresponds to one of the priority levels defined by ORK+: under the restriction that tasks should take distinct priorities, a 1 in position n means that the task with priority n is eligible for execution, 0 otherwise[3]. Our implementation consists of a 2-layered hierarchical data structure: the bit-mask itself is represented as a collection of eight 32-bit unsigned integers, and one additional 8-bit mask is required as root, in which a 1 is present in position k if the k-th child mask has at least one bit set to 1.

As a preliminary activity, during system start-up we initialize the alarms corresponding to all the task activations occurring during the hyper-period of the task set. Besides the timestamp of an event, each alarm also tracks which tasks need to be activated at that time, by keeping a mask with 1s set to the corresponding positions. Alarms are then organized in a circular linked list, similarly to [25], which will be looked up as execution time elapses to update the task states and set the next alarm. As soon as one alarm fires to signal the activation of a task, the following actions are performed:

(a) The mask corresponding to the fired alarm is bitwise OR-ed with the corresponding child bit-mask: in this way a 1 is set in the position corresponding to the task to be released.
(b) The task to be dispatched is identified by the most significant bit (MSB) set in the complete 256-bit-wide mask: the corresponding child mask can be identified in turn by looking at the most significant bit set in the root mask.

---

[3] A value of 0 is assigned also in case task at priority level n has not been defined in the considered task set.

Performing step (b) above consists of finding the most significant bit within the base-two representation of an integer, once for the root mask to identify the leftmost non-empty child bit-mask and once to find the most significant bit within the child mask. This can be easily done by applying the constant-time deBruijn algorithm [13] to both masks, thus guaranteeing constant-time latency in thread selection. At task completion nothing needs to be done for the terminating task, since alarms for next activations have been set at system initialization; the election of the next task to dispatch is performed similarly.

Single-level bit-mask structures have been previously exploited by the O(1) scheduler [15] (in the Linux kernel up to version 2.6.23) to provide a constant-time dispatcher. That solution, however, only applies to a strict time-slice model that acutely clashes with our idea of zero disturbance. By exploiting bit-masks also in the time model we are delivering a more generic constant-time task activation mechanism that can be in principle extended to handle sporadic activations.

3.2   Envisaged Extensions

Modifying the kernel by addressing only a subset of the requirements we set on the RTOS, as described in the previous section, is sufficient to enforce time composability within the boundaries of a restricted periodic task model. Extending the proposed solution to meet the remaining requirements is not straightforward as a RTOS with support to sporadic run-time entities, programmable interrupts and protected objects is much less prone to time composability. Those extension, however, are definitely required for a comprehensive RTOS, and especially so for Ravenscar compliant systems where, for example, shared resources are the only permitted construct to provide task synchronization.

In the following we discuss the impending extensions that must be implemented to comply with all the requirements we set for a time-composable RTOS, and anticipate the problems we are expecting.

Flexible Task Model. Admitting sporadic task activations, the first natural extension of the task model, is difficult to accommodate in a time-composable manner. With the introduction of sporadic tasks, in fact, there is no longer static knowledge on tasks' activation time only a minimum inter-arrival time is known for them. The static activation table determined at system start-up works well for periodic tasks but can easily treat event-triggered sporadic activations by simply allowing update operations on the ready task bit-mask. Nevertheless, sporadic tasks need a prompt reaction (low latency) by the kernel when their release event occurs: prompt acknowledgement of sporadic activation events cannot be had without producing intrusive and disturbing effects on the user applications.

Besides acknowledgement, the fact that each sporadic task activation may be followed by a task preemption runs against the concept of zero disturbance as the effects of preemption on a task do not follow a (more predictable and accountable) periodic pattern any more[4]. Although it is widely acknowledged

---

[4] The same problem arises from low-level interrupts.

that preemption allows in the general case to improve the feasibility of a task set, we are interested in limiting its occurrence so as to minimize its negative effects on composability. In fact, recent studies [7, 27] have demonstrated that (carefully) limiting task preemption does not only preserve the task set feasibility but may also improve it.

The deferred preemption framework in [27] provides the theoretical foundations to the intuition that in certain circumstances it is possible – and actually beneficial – to delay the activation of a higher priority task in favour of the continuation of the currently running task, without compromising the feasibility of the task set. In our case, this intuition perfectly applies to sporadic tasks, whose release could be deferred as long as their statically-determined *tolerance* allows, so that system feasibility is preserved. It is understood that deferring task preemption by means of non-preemptive regions does not remove the source of interference, as the preemption will eventually take place; its effects, however, could be tempered as the number of preemptions would be significantly reduced when not minimized.

Further complications may rise owing to the introduction of programmable timing events. The programming abstraction of timing events in Ada allows to explicitly define code to be executed at a specific time instant, without the need to employ a dedicated task. They are permitted within a Ravenscar system with the limitation of being declared at library level. At a closer look, the problems we may expect from timing events are quite assimilable to those related to sporadic tasks in terms of intrusive effects of the applications. In addition, timing events are somehow assimilable to interrupts in that they have stringent requirements in term of responsiveness, which can be hardly met within the deferred preemption framework. On the other hand, however, timing events are a lightweight mechanism in so far as no dedicated thread or context switch is required to execute an event handler: they are by definition short pieces of code that are directly executed by the clock interrupt. Hence, whereas massive resorting to timing events should be clearly discouraged, we may venture suggesting that their limited disturbing effect could justify an occasional use, as long as they are statically guaranteed not to exceed the available system slack.

Composable Inter-task Communication. The problem of providing a time-composable communication resolves in providing a proper mechanism to control the access to shared resources, either software or hardware (via software). Protected objects allow tasks to share resources. The Ravenscar Profile prescribes the use of the ceiling locking protocol. This choice is motivated by the effectiveness of the ceiling locking protocol in placing a strict bound on the longest blocking suffered by tasks as well as in preventing deadlock by construction. However, it requires using dynamic priorities, which in fact breaks our one-to-one association between tasks and priority levels within our bit-masks. Fortunately, our bit-mask solution can be easily extended beyond the current implementation to manage dynamic priorities by adopting an additional set of bit-masks to distinguish between base and active priority, without compromising the scheduler complexity. A more lightweight approach would consist in enforcing distinct priorities for each task and/or shared resource as we would be able to exploit the resource priority position in the bit-mask.

Further critical issues can arise from the combination of shared resource access protocols and the deferred preemption approach we suggested as a practical means to reduce the effects of inter-task interference. In this case in fact it is not clear how non-preemptive regions and critical sections may coexist, whether disjoint or in overlap. Although in principle limited preemptive approaches can be automatically applied to dynamic priority schedulers, we should carefully consider the implications it may have on mutual exclusion. The fine-grained interaction between the access protocols and limited preemptive scheduling is indeed part of our ongoing work.

Selective Hardware Isolation. Although the hardware-to-software axis of composition is out of the scope of this paper, a mechanism to prevent the RTOS execution from polluting the hardware state of the user applications is strongly required by the zero-disturbance principle. With respect to caches, for example, software partitioning [16] approaches may help in achieving isolation without any requirement on the underlying platform. Again on caches, interestingly, an advanced cache management API was already implemented in ORK+ for the LEON2 platform and can be easily ported to any other target.

4   Experimental Results

In this work we focused our implementation efforts on the provision of non-intrusive time management and constant-time scheduling primitives. To assess the effectiveness of our approach, we performed a preliminary evaluation of the modified kernel primitives against their original implementation in ORK+. It is worth noting that although ORK+ was not designed with time composability in mind, at least it has been inspired to timing analysability and predictability. For this reason, the original ORK+ was already well-behaved with respect to time composability and the effects of our modifications may not stand out as in the case of less educated operating system [4].

We conducted our experiments through a set of measurements on well-designed test cases running on top of a highly-configurable SocLib-based PowerPC 750 [9] simulation platform. As a common experimental set-up, we configured the simulator to operate with 16 KB, 4-way set associative and 16 B line size instruction and data caches and Least Recently Used (LRU) replacement policy, in consideration of its predictable behaviour [20]. Since zero disturbance was one of our guiding principles towards time composability, we generally took advantage of an automatic cache disabling mechanism available in the simulator as a quick workaround to isolate the effects of the RTOS on the user application cache state. We are aware of the potential implications of this solution on the overall performance and we are willing to implement and evaluate a limited form of software-based cache partitioning approach to prevent that kind of side effects by reserving a piece of cache for the RTOS.

We exploited measurement-based timing analysis, despite its known limitations, as we observe that the assessment of the steady timing behaviour and zero disturbance properties can be more easily conducted by means of measuring a small number of examples. On the contrary, we think that the use of a safer static analysis tool would have made it more complicated to perceive the execution time jitter. We used RapiTime [19], a hybrid measurement-based timing analysis tool from Rapita Systems Ltd., to collect and elaborate the timing information from execution traces. We performed an exhaustive set of measurements under different inputs or different workloads so as to highlight the weaknesses of the RTOS services with respect to time composability.

We wanted to observe the timing behaviour of the task management primitives in isolation as well as the disturbing effects that the latter may have on an end-to-end run of the user applications. It is worth noting that no measurements have been made on time management services in that, as observed in Section 3.1, both implementations, though different, incur no interference.

Kernel Primitives. We focused our experiments on those kernel primitives that are responsible for updating the ready queue in ORK+. The ready queue is accessed by the *Insert* and *Extract* procedures that are respectively invoked upon task activation and self-suspension (at the end of the current job). Task selection, according to the FIFO within priority dispatching policy, is done by exploiting a reference (thus trivially in constant time) that is constantly updated to always point to next thread to execute.

The *Insert* and *Extract* procedures are also used to access the data structures involved in our modified implementation and are thus directly comparable with their original version. In addition, thread selection in our implementation does not consist any more in dereferencing a pointer but uses a dedicated procedure *Get_First_Thread* to extract this information from a hierarchical bit-mask. However it was not necessary to measure the *Get_First_Thread* in isolation as it implements a constant-time perfect hashing function and its execution time is included in the invocation of both the *Insert* and *Extract* procedure.

Figure 3 contrasts the timing behaviour of the scheduling primitives from the original ORK+ (left) with that obtained from our modified implementation (right). The jittery execution time of the *Insert* procedure in ORK+ stems from the nature itself of the data structure: the position in the queue in which the task will be inserted depends on the number and priority of the already enqueued tasks. On the contrary, the implementation based on bit-wise operations exhibits an inherently constant behaviour and a remarkably low execution bound.

The *Extract* procedure instead already exhibits a constant timing behaviour in ORK+, as it simply consists in dereferencing a pointer. Our implementation, again relying on a bit-mask structure, is still constant though slightly less performing than its original counterpart. Yet, the performance loss is negligible in our reference platform, as the constant-time operation takes less than 100 cycles.

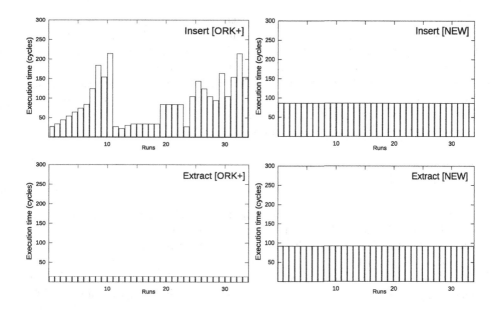

Fig. 3. Experimental results on scheduling primitives

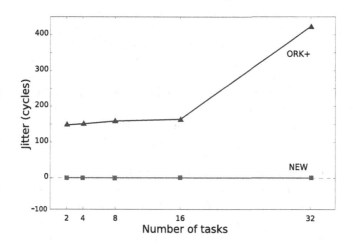

Fig. 4. Execution time jitter as a function of the task set dimension

Application-Level Induced Jitter. When it comes to gauging the effects of different implementations of kernel primitives on the application, we measured the same synthetic application when executing under different workloads (form 2 to 32) of strictly periodic tasks, each performing though at different rates, an identical set of constant-time operations. We measured the end-to-end execution time needed to complete each task's job and the scheduling operations, without including the cost of the low-level context switch itself.

Results are shown in Figure 4, where each point in the graph represents the difference between the maximum and minimum observed values along more than 1000 runs. The jitter, though bounded, in ORK+ grows proportionally to the number of tasks in the system, as a consequence of the variable size of its data structures, whereas our implementation performs in constant time regardless of the workload. The jittery timing behaviour is explained by the variable execution time of the insertion of a new alarm in the ordered alarm queue, which is required to program the next activation of a periodic task.

5   Conclusion

Timing composability resembles the holy grail in the eyes of hard real-time system engineers: although the state-of-the-art compositional approaches to the software development and qualification silently rely on timing composability, the latter seems to be hard to guarantee without placing exceedingly strong restrictions on the system architecture (e.g., partitioned systems). The real-time operating system appears to us as a key enabler of time composability: being a natural mediator between user-level applications and between applications themselves and the underlying hardware, it is the outpost from which the sources of inter-dependences can be attenuated or even eliminated.

In this paper, we take a first move towards the adaptation of a comprehensive real-time kernel with a view to bring it to conformance with the zero disturbance and steady timing behaviour principles, which we identified as characterising features of a time composable operating system. As expected our kernel of choice (ORK+) seems to be already beneficial with respect to time composability, most likely as a consequence of its compliance to the Ravenscar profile and its globally wise design choices. The good quality of ORK+, however, still allow for some improvements and did not prevent us from identifying some preliminary modifications, which we have experimentally proved to effectively improve the original ORK+ in terms of time composability.

The work reported in this paper represents just a first step towards the definition of a comprehensive time-composable RTOS, with no restrictions other than those imposed by the Ravenscar profile. Our immediate plan for future work is thus to further extend our investigation by attacking the challenging problems of managing sporadic task activations and timing events with no harm on time composability.

Acknowledgements. The authors wish to acknowledge Rapita Systems Ltd. for their gracious supply of the RapiTime tool as well as Juan Zamorano, Ángel Esquinas and all the Real-Time Systems and Telematic Services Architecture group at the Technical University of Madrid for their kind support on the porting of ORK+ to the PowerPC platform. The research leading to these results has received funding from the European Community's Seventh Framework Programme [FP7/2007-2013] PROARTIS under grant agreement 249100.

References

1. Altmeyer, S., Maiza, C., Reineke, J.: Resilience analysis: Tightening the CRPD bound for set-associative caches. In: Proc. of the Conference on Languages, Compilers, and Tools for Embedded Systems, LCTES 2010 (2010)
2. APEX Working Group: Draft 3 of Supplement 1 to ARINC Specification 653: Avionics Application Software Standard Interface (2003)
3. Baldovin, A., Graziano, A., Mezzetti, E., Vardanega, T.: Kernel-level time composability for avionics applications. In: Proceedings of the 28th ACM Symposium on Applied Computing, ACM SAC 2013, Coimbra, Portugal (2013)
4. Baldovin, A., Mezzetti, E., Vardanega, T.: A Time-composable Operating System. In: Proceedings of the 12th International Workshop on Worst-Case Execution Time Analysis (2012)
5. Blackham, B., Shi, Y., Chattopadhyay, S., Roychoudhury, A., Heiser, G.: Timing analysis of a protected operating system kernel. In: 2011 IEEE 32nd Real-Time Systems Symposium, RTSS, pp. 339–348 (2011)
6. Burns, A., Dobbing, B., Vardanega, T.: Guide for the Use of the Ada Ravenscar Profile in High Integrity Systems. TR YCS-2003-348, University of York (2003)
7. Buttazzo, G., Bertogna, M., Yao, G.: Limited preemptive scheduling for real-time systems: A survey. IEEE Transactions on Industrial Informatics 9(1), 3–15 (2013)
8. De la Puente, J.A., Zamorano, J., Ruiz, J., Fernández, R., García, R.: The design and implementation of the open ravenscar kernel. Ada Lett. XXI(1), 85–90 (2001)
9. Freescale: PowerPC 750 Microprocessor (2012), https://www-01.ibm.com/chips/techlib/techlib.nsf/products/PowerPC_750_Microprocessor
10. Hansson, A., Ekerhult, M., Molnos, A.M., Milutinovic, A., Nelson, A., Ambrose, J.A., Goossens, K.: Design and implementation of an operating system for composable processor sharing. Microprocessors and Microsystems - Embedded Hardware Design 35(2), 246–260 (2011)
11. ISO SC22/WG9: Ada Reference Manual. Language and Standard Libraries. Consolidated Standard ISO/IEC 8652:1995(E) with Technical Corrigendum 1 and Amendment 1 (2005)
12. Kosmidis, L., Quinones, E., Abella, J., Vardanega, T., Cazorla, F.J.: Achieving timing composability with measurement-based probabilistic timing analysis. In: Proceedings of the 16th IEEE Symposium on Object/Component/Service-oriented Realtime Distributed Computing, ISORC, Pandeborn, Germany (2013)
13. Leiserson, C.E., Prokop, H., Randall, K.H.: Using de Bruijn Sequences to Index a 1 in a Computer Word (1998)
14. Liu, I., Reineke, J., Lee, E.A.: A PRET architecture supporting concurrent programs with composable timing properties. In: 44th Asilomar Conference on Signals, Systems, and Computers, pp. 2111–2115 (November 2010)
15. Molnar, I.: Goals, design and implementation of the new ultra-scalable O(1) scheduler. Linux Kernel, Source tree documentation (2002)
16. Mueller, F.: Compiler support for software-based cache partitioning. In: ACM Workshop on Languages, Compilers and Tools for Real-Time Systems (1995)
17. Puschner, P., Kirner, R., Pettit, R.G.: Towards composable timing for real-time software. In: Proc. 1st International Workshop on Software Technologies for Future Dependable Distributed Systems (March 2009)
18. Puschner, P., Schoeberl, M.: On composable system timing, task timing, and WCET analysis. In: Proceedings of the 8th International Workshop on Worst-Case Execution Time Analysis (2008)

19. Rapita Systems Ltd.: Rapitime, http://www.rapitasystems.com/rapitime
20. Reineke, J., Grund, D., Berg, C., Wilhelm, R.: Timing predictability of cache replacement policies. Real-Time Systems 37, 99–122 (2007)
21. Sangiovanni-Vincentelli, A.L., Di Natale, M.: Embedded system design for automotive applications. IEEE Computer 40(10), 42–51 (2007)
22. Schneider, J.: Why you can't analyze RTOSs without considering applications and vice versa. In: Proceedings of the 2nd International Workshop on Worst-Case Execution Time Analysis (2002)
23. Universidad Politécnica de Madrid: GNAT/ORK+ for LEON cross-compilation system, http://polaris.dit.upm.es/~ork
24. Vardanega, T., Zamorano, J., de la Puente, J.A.: On the dynamic semantics and the timing behavior of ravenscar kernels. Real-Time Systems 29(1), 59–89 (2005)
25. Varghese, G., Lauck, A.: Hashed and hierarchical timing wheels: efficient data structures for implementing a timer facility. IEEE/ACM Trans. Netw. 5(6), 824–834 (1997)
26. Wilhelm, R., et al.: The worst-case execution time problem: overview of methods and survey of tools. Trans. on Embedded Computing Systems 7(3), 1–53 (2008)
27. Yao, G., Buttazzo, G.C., Bertogna, M.: Feasibility analysis under fixed priority scheduling with limited preemptions. Real-Time Systems 47(3), 198–223 (2011)
28. Zamorano, J., Ruiz, J.F., de la Puente, J.A.: Implementing Ada.Real_Time.Clock and Absolute Delays in Real-Time Kernels. In: Proceedings of the 6th International Conference on Reliable Software Technologies, pp. 317–327. Ada Europe (2001)

Worst–Case Execution Time Analysis Approach for Safety–Critical Airborne Software

Esteban Asensio[3], Ismael Lafoz[1], Andrew Coombes[2], and Julian Navas[1]

[1] Airbus Military – EADS
Control Systems Software Department, Air to Air Refuelling Systems
John Lennon Av., 28906 Getafe, Spain
{ismael.lafoz,julian.navas}@military.airbus.com
[2] Rapita Systems Ltd.
IT Centre, York Science Park, York YO10 5NP, United Kingdom
acoombes@rapitasystems.com
[3] GMV Aerospace and Defence
On–Board Software and Validation Division
PTM, Isaac Newton 11, 28760 Tres Cantos, Spain
easensio@gmv.com

Abstract. The fundamental problem in building a system with hard real–time characteristics is guaranteeing that it will deterministically perform its required functionality within specified time constraints. Determining Worst–Case Execution Time (WCET) is key to predictability, that is to ensure that temporal behaviour of the system is correct and hence safe. Furthermore, it is an objective to meet by verification when development of airborne software shall be compliant with DO–178B objectives. Different approaches to WCET analysis could be taken. This paper presents the experience automating such analysis for a Fly–By–Wire system by means of a hybrid approach aiming to combine features of measurement and static analysis. Several challenges arise when integrating the analysis workflow withing the software development process, especially those regarding to instrumentation overhead. Control mechanisms need to be developed to mitigate the drawbacks and achieve realistic WCET estimations to assess temporal correctness of the system.

Keywords: Airborne Software, Safety-Critical, ARINC 653, IMA, DO–178B/C, Worst–Case Execution Time, Predictability, Verification, Hybrid Approach.

1 Introduction

This document is a summary of the return of the experience automating the Worst–Case Execution Time (WCET) analysis by means of a hybrid approach that aims to combine features of measurement and static analysis whilst avoiding their pitfalls. It was used within the Fly–By–Wire system of the Advanced Refuelling Boom System (ARBS) designed, developed and commercialized by

H.B. Keller et al. (Eds.): Ada-Europe 2013, LNCS 7896, pp. 161–176, 2013.
© Springer-Verlag Berlin Heidelberg 2013

Airbus Military. Such system has been successfully installed in the A330 Multi-Role Transport Tanker (MRTT), which is a conversion of a basic airliner aircraft into a tanker aircraft to transfer fuel in–flight from the main fuel tanks to receiver aircrafts. The ARBS consists of a telescopic mast or boom, attached to the underside fuselage of the aircraft, and the relevant electronic and mechanical systems, which make the mast deployment possible from the stowage position, its extension and connection with the receiver aircraft, the supply of fuel and, after the refuelling, the mast disconnection, retraction and stowage.

The document is organized as follows. Sect. 1 presents an overview of the system and explains why timing analysis is required. Sect. 2 reviews the approach to the WCET analysis that was initially used to verify temporal behaviour of an airborne safety–critical software system. Sect. 3 gives a description of a WCET analysis based on a hybrid approach implemented by an on–target verification tool developed by Rapita Systems; the rationale of the approach, the characteristics of the tool and its workflow are presented as well. In Sect. 4, the integration of the analysis workflow within the software development process is presented. The challenges related to the integration of the tool analysis workflow within the airborne software system and the mechanisms developed to address them are outlined in Sect. 5, together with the main results obtained during the analysis of a safety–critical airborne software performed onto the real aircraft target. Finally, Sect. 6 draws the conclusions, pointing out the goals achieved, the lessons learned and the future work lines envisaged.

1.1   System Overview

The core system of the ARBS is the Boom Control and Computing System (BCCS); a redundant control/monitor architecture which comprises four computers. The basic functionality of the BCCS is to receive inputs from the operator, sensors and aircraft systems, to compute the flight control laws and to determine the system operational mode, and to control and monitoring the actuators, which are mainly connected to the aerodynamic surfaces. Additionally, the BCCS manages the control and monitoring of the extension/retraction system and the control and monitoring of the hoist and uplock system for raising/lowering and locking/unlocking the boom. The BCCS is also in charge of providing the failure detection, recording and isolation system and managing the redundancy mechanisms. Instruction operations are also allowed using two flight control sticks in order to provide training capabilities when the boom is in flight.

The system architecture defined is a partitioning, ARINC 653 compliant architecture [1] (see Fig. 1). It is based on a Real–Time Operating System (RTOS) that supports the mentioned specification. ARINC 653 standard is widely used for integrating avionics systems on modern aircrafts. It allows to host multiple space and time isolated applications of software, even with different criticality levels, onto the same hardware in the context of an Integrated Modular Avionics (IMA) architecture. The major part of the application software included in such partitions is manually implemented using Ada95, but there is also some C

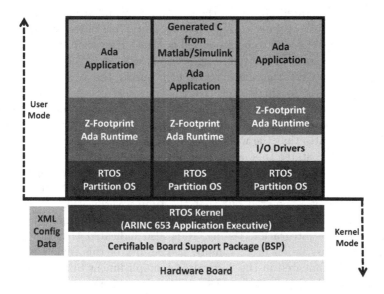

Fig. 1. The BCCS software architecture

code automatically generated from models. The safety assessment of the system defined the Design Assurance Level (DAL) of the BCCS as Level A, so all the development processes, the architecture, the implementation and the verification must be performed in order to be compliant with the DO–178B [4] certification standard for embedded software for avionics systems and all its objectives for Level A software.

1.2 Why Timing Analysis Is Needed

Due to the safety–critical nature of the functions performed by the BCCS, it is considered a Hard Real–Time (HRT) system and therefore, its correctness relies not only on functional correctness but also on the timely delivery of the computed results [2]. The control frequency of the system must be ensured at any time. A failure in the punctuality of the BCCS response (even if it is functionally correct) could result in fatal consequences, hence the need of a rigorous timing analysis to verify that the temporal behaviour is exactly as expected. The timing analysis relies on the determination of the WCET. Simply put, the WCET of a computational task is the maximum length of time the task could take to execute on a specific hardware platform. This excludes any time spent executing other tasks or interrupts [3]. WCETs are typically used for schedulability analysis and timing assurance in reliable real–time and embedded systems, especially in safety–critical HRT systems. A very common use of WCET in avionics industry and in IMA in particular (as it is the case presented in this paper), is to ensure that the pre–allocated timing budgets in a partition–scheduled system are not violated.

Furthermore, as stated above, all the development and verification processes for this project must be fully compliant with DO–178B objectives in order to seek for certification credits to be presented to the Certification Authority (CA). In particular, the focus of the following sections will be set on DO–178 objectives related to WCET that need to be met during the verification process. In DO-178B there is no single objective that is solely concerned with timing. However, as explained below, two objectives include timing considerations. In addition to verifying that the software requirements relating to timing have been met, DO–178B states that the worst–case timing should be determined. Section 6.3.4f of DO–178B states that as part of meeting the verification objective of the source code being accurate and consistent, the worst–case timing should be determined by review and analysis for this Level A software. Besides, in Table A–5 of DO–178B it is pointed out that the timing verification is a task concerned with reviews and analysis of the source code and with requirement–based hardware/software integration testing. It is also indicated that independence in verification must be ensured. Finally, the results of this review and analysis should be documented in the Software Accomplishment Summary (SAS) as timing margins (Section 11.20d of DO–178B). In addition, it is important to highlight that the WCET analysis and the establishment of the timing margins of the software are required as well within last issue, that is DO–178C [5], which in section 6.3.4f is considering the determination of the WCET and path, and in section 11.20i is requiring the inclusion of the analysis results SAS. More references to WCET analysis can be found in DO–248B [6], where it is stated that the worst–case timing could be calculated by review and analysis of the source code and architecture, but compiler and processor behaviour and its impact also should be addressed. Timing measurements by themselves cannot be used without an analyis demonstrating that the worst–case timing would be achieved.

As pointed out above, WCET is a key concept to deal with when addressing timing analysis in the context of HRT systems development. It is also a critical objective to be met when developing safety–critical airborne software under DO–178B.

2   Initial Situation

2.1   A Measurement–Based Approach to Timing Analysis

As stated in Sect. 1, the software architecture is based on a partitioning architecture compliant with the ARINC 653 standard, which offers space and time partitioning in safety–critical RTOS. ARINC 653 defines a scheduler consisting of a major frame comprised of a sequence of minor frames which specify the execution time of an individual partition for a fixed duration; at the end of the major frame the scheduler repeats. Therefore ARINC 653 scheduling implementation is deterministic, i.e. the next partition should start its execution at the exact time predefined in the ARINC 653 scheduler. From the point of view of the temporal behaviour analysis, the timing isolation caused by the time slot scheduling of the partitions was fully taken into account. This feature allows to split the WCET analysis of the complete system into individual analyses for each partition thanks to the determinism of the partitions scheduling. In other words, the whole system timing behaviour and its WCET determination can be performed statically when the different partitions analyses are completed. So the focus of the temporal verification must be placed in the different partitions. Also in terms of safety, given that the scheduler is preemptive, these violations of the time slots are the only possible source of temporal failures.

At early stages of the project, in order to perform the verification process with regard to worst–case execution timing, a manual, measurement–based approach was initially followed. This approach aimed to ease the obtaining of execution time measurements during the testing of the application software so that it could be possible to quickly get an assessment of whether or not the pre–allocated timing budgets assigned to each partition were violated at any activation. The WCET determination process consisted on a very simple tracing system of the source code execution. A small and fixed number of system calls were located within the source code of every partition as a simple form of instrumentation. This mechanism was able to collect timestamps during the execution of the code. At the end of the partition root function, a procedure calcutated easily the time gap between these timestamps and the whole execution time for the partition task(s).

The source code was estimulated by means of the high and low level testing infrastructure. This infrastrucute is based on the target architecture, but in the case of the Partition Testing infrastructure there are only two partitions: one containing the test harness and other including the Partition under Test (PuT). The mechanism was completely embedded in the source code, therefore the only requirement to extract the timing information was to define new signals outputting both the partial times and the whole execution time through the test harness infrastructure. It must be noted that, to meet with DO–178 objectives, a manual review of the source code attempting to identify worst–case paths through the code were performed as well, which is an effort–intensive task. Moreover, the set of test cases executed for the timing analysis achieved a 95% of MC/DC structural coverage. A high structural coverage is a necessary but not sufficient condition to be confident that the testing was able to estimulate the worst scenario in temporal terms. So it was also necessary a final review ensuring that the set of tests were driving the code through these paths. Finally, another important characteristic of the approach is the fact of keeping the real–time during the execution of the tests.

2.2 Outcome of the Initial Solution

To summarize the main results with regard to the initial approach to WCET analysis of the system, a list of advantages and disadvantages are presented next.

Advantages:

– A manual, measurement–based approach provides an initial indication of the execution time performance of the software components to quickly assess the correctness of the pre–allocated time slot for the partitions.

- Execution time measurements are easy to obtain during testing with few changes in the current testing infrastructure.
- The measurements are observations of the timing behaviour of the system code running on the actual hardware, so there is no need for modeling the processor and its advanced features.

Disadvantages:

- During testing, it is difficult to guarantee that the worst–case path has been taken.
- It is also difficult to ensure that the functions and loops on a given path have exhibited their WCETs simultaneously. Moreover, for complex software, running on advanced microprocessors, the longest observed end–to–end execution time is likely to be less than the actual worst–case time, which could result in an optimistic WCET.
- Measurements alone are rarely sufficient to provide high levels of confidence in the worst–case timing behaviour of the system and need effort–intensive manual reviews of the code and the test cases which is, in many cases, an unfeasible task in terms of time and/or budget.

3   Automating WCET Analysis Based on a Hybrid Approach

Although a purely measurement–based approach to timing analysis is widely used in avionic applications, the disadvantages (discussed above) led to other approaches being considered.

Other approaches (i.e. not based on measurement) for timing analysis do exist, for example, simulation or static analysis. These other approaches introduce risks of providing timing data that do not accurately reflect reality. Possible causes of this include an inaccurate model of the CPU, or a model that is not configured in the same way as the target hardware. Furthermore, with these approaches it is difficult to confirm the timing data against the real system – unlike a measurement–based approach, where measurements taken are clearly representative of actual hardware.

The approach that was selected for investigation was a *hybrid approach*, as embodied by the RapiTime execution analysis tool.

3.1   Description of the Tool

In this approach a series of detailed measurements are made, and correlated with a structural model of the source code. The measurements and structural model allow an analysis to be made that:

- Predicts the path through the code which, if executed, results in the WCET.
- Identifies maximum loop iterations and maximum observed execution times of code sections to be included in the WCET prediction.

– Allows comparison between the predicted WCET and the longest observed test case.

The two biggest challenges with a measurement–based approach are:

– How to construct a test case that represents the longest feasible path through the code. In aerospace environments, a required practice is to identify WCET. Indeed for civil aircraft, as seen, this is an objective of DO–178B and it is commonly manually performed through engineering judgement and the analysis of the possible operational or functional scenarios. Achieving a reasonable level of confidence that something close to the WCET has been demonstrated in testing is an extremely difficult task for any but the simplest software.
– Minimising effort in finding the execution time. As implied above, identifying the worst–case test case is time consuming. Another cause of effort being spent is actually making the measurements: instrumenting the source code and interpreting the results can be time consuming, particularly if any level of detail is required from the measurements.

Based on the assessment of available solutions, RapiTime addresses the disadvantages identified for a purely measurement-based approach. The recommended workflow for using RapiTime guides the user in creating tests that execute a worst–case path through the code. Furthermore, RapiTime's automated instrumentation of source code and analysis of the results makes a significant reduction in the effort required for a comparable manual process.

3.2   Tool Analysis Workflow

When using RapiTime to support the construction of test cases following the worst–case execution path, a particular process is recommended. This process is based upon the use of two values that RapiTime will produce: the high water mark (HWM) and the predicted WCET (both described below). Iteratively improving testing and analysis leads to these two values converging, which in turn results in the tests being constructed that result in the worst–case path being executed.

As mentioned above, the two key values reported by RapiTime are:

High water mark: represents the longest observed end–to–end execution time from testing. This is a property of an entire execution path, rather than a single part of a path.
Predicted WCET: represents RapiTime's prediction for the longest possible execution time for this software. This prediction is based upon the combination of a structural model of the source code with measurements corresponding to segments of source code. Combining these two values allows RapiTime to perform an analysis roughly analogous to a critical path analysis. In addition to obtaining a predicted WCET, this approach also leads to RapiTime being able to show the path taken through the code that leads to the WCET value.

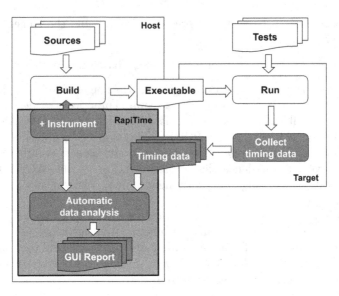

Fig. 2. RapiTime's build–execute workflow

RapiTime extends the traditional build-execute workflow by adding three automated activities (as depicted in Fig. 2):

- Instrumentation. As part of the building process, RapiTime will automatically insert instrumentation points (Ipoint) into intermediate versions of the application source code. The purpose of the instrumentation is to show that specific points in the source code have been executed. When executed, each Ipoint shows that the program has reached a particular location in the code at a specific time. Although the most detailed results are obtained from instrumenting every decision point, it is possible to configure other instrumentation policies, meaning for example that Ipoints could be placed less frequently. As the instrumentation is performed, RapiTime also builds up a model of the structure of the code, which is used in the analysis phase.
- Data collection. The executable is loaded onto the target and the tests are run against the target. When the application is executed, the instrumentation code will result in execution data being generated – this needs to be collected for analysis at the next step.
- Analysis. Once the timing data and structural models are available, they can be combined to provide WCET predictions and other information.

4   WCET Analysis Workflow Integration within the Safety–Critical Software Development Process

4.1   Building Process

The integration of the timing analysis workflow within the BCCS Software architecture was based on the incorporation of the timing analysis toolchain within the actual Partition Testing infrastructure. As seen in Sect. 2, this infrastrucuture consists on an ARINC653–compliant architecture with two partitions, the test harness and the partition under test (PuT). It allows the injection of test vectors, the recording of results in real–time and the on–target tests execution.

From the point of view of the building process, some changes were required in the *makefiles* of the software compilation to integrate the timing analysis. The modifications aimed to automatically generate the preprocessed and the instrumented source code and to generate the structural analysis during the building process of the partition binary to be loaded on the target so that, such binary included the instrumented source code. The integration pursued the maintenance of a normal compilation mode, and the inclusion of a timing analysis mode option. It must be noted that compilation options should be identical in both modes to ensure a realistic analysis. Besides, both modes should be compatible allowing to select between them in one single *makefile*.

Due to the target features, an approach based on a memory buffer was selected. A shared memory region between the PuT and the test harness was created in the configuration of the execution platform to be the mechanism used to manage the timing information of the Ipoints during the execution of the tests and, after the test execution finalization, to create the output trace file. This shared memory region required an instrumentation library specifically developed for this purpose, jointly designed by Rapita and Airbus Military. This library defines the required types and procedures to incorporate the Ipoints mechanism into the software, as shown below.

```
-- RVS Ipoint declaration
type RVS_Ipoint_Type is record
   time : Unsigned_32;
   id : RVS_Ipoint_Id_Type;
end record;
pragma pack(RVS_Ipoint_Type);

-- RVS Ipoints Buffer declaration
type RVS_Ipoint_Buffer_Index_Type is
     range 1 .. (RVS_Buffer_Bytes_Available / 6);
type RVS_Ipoint_Buffer_Type is
     array ( RVS_Ipoint_Buffer_Index_Type ) of RVS_Ipoint_Type;
type RVS_Data_Type is record
   Current_Buffer_Addr : System.Address;
   Start_Buffer_Addr   : System.Address;
   RVS_Ipoint_Buffer   : RVS_Ipoint_Buffer_Type;
end record;

-- RVS Ipoint routine
procedure RVS_Ipoint( I : RVS_Ipoint_Id_Type ) is
   t : Unsigned_32;
   Reserved_Addr : System.Address;
begin
   System.Machine_Code.Asm
```

```
("1:;" & -- label to retry if write fails
 "lwarx %0,0,%2;" & -- load buffer pointer and reserve
 "mfspr %1,<Performance Counter>;" & -- get timestamp
 "addi 0,%0,6;" & -- calculate next position and store in r0
 "stwcx. 0,0,%2;" & -- attempt to store next position
 "bne- 1b", -- retry if write fails
 Outputs => (System.Address'Asm_Output
                ("=&r",Reserved_Addr),
             Unsigned_32'Asm_Output("=&r",t)),
 Inputs => System.Address'Asm_Input
             ("r", RVS_Data.Current_Buffer_Addr'Address),
 Clobber => "r0",
 Volatile => True);
declare
   Reserved_Buffer_Access : RVS_Ipoint_Type_Access :=
        RVS_Ipoint_Type_Access
           (Addr_To_Ipoint_Buffer_Access.To_Pointer
              (Reserved_Addr));
begin
   Reserved_Buffer_Access.all.time := t;
   Reserved_Buffer_Access.all.id := I;
end;
end RVS_Ipoint;
```

4.2   Analysis Process

Once the integration of the analysis workflow within the build–execute process is done, the timing analysis can be performed. It consists of the following steps (explained in Sect. 3):

1. Instrument and build
2. Run tests
3. Analysis

The process combines the execution data with the structural model to derive a HWM and a predicted WCET/worst–case path. If the HWM is significantly less than the predicted WCET, there are two possible actions (not mutually exclusive):

– RapiTime may have made assumptions about the execution that make the predicted WCET pessimistic. For example, it may be that RapiTime indicates that the worst–case path is executed if A and B are true. However, A and B could be mutually exclusive. In this situation, it is possible to add "analysis annotations", which improve RapiTime's prediction of the worst case. Once annotations are added, the analysis can be rerun (it is not necessary to execute the tests again).
– RapiTime will show the predicted worst–case path through the code. If the test cases do not execute this path, it might be worth adjusting the test cases to cause this path to be executed. The test cases will be executed again.

In the ideal case, when the computed WCET path corresponds exactly to HWM path, the process is complete. However, in general these paths will not correspond and it will be important to identify and justify the reasons why.

5   Integration Process Challenges

5.1   Instrumentation Overhead

As stated in Sect. 4, important consequences must be faced because of the choice of a tracing mechanism based on a shared memory region. The main issue caused is the Ipoint routine overhead that it is inevitably included in the trace information. Some actions shall be taken and some mechanisms shall be developed in order to mitigate it.

The execution trace is created by calling an Ipoint routine at specific places in the program execution. The time taken by this routine increases the measured execution time for the function where the routine is called from. Although the instrumentation library is optimized as much as possible, the writing of the time information in memory during the routine execution implies a non negligible overhead.

To account for this additional execution time, a constant deinstrumentation parameter may be applied when processing the trace with the appropiate tool of the analysis toolchain. This specifies an amount of time to remove from the trace at each Ipoint in order to generate a more accurate timing information. The process of determining the deinstrumentation parameter is known as "Ipoint calibration" and involves three simple stages:

1. Creating a program that make successive calls to the Ipoint routine. Since the integration was already established, a sequence of Ipoints is manually inserted (by means of annotations) into the source code near the start of the application main loop.
2. Measuring the execution of this program on target.
3. Calculate the Best–Case Execution Time (BCET) for the routine to be used as deinstrumentation parameter. This was done by calculating the differences between the Ipoints in the sequence.

This is not a complete solution to control the instrumentation overhead so it can result in some overestimation for the WCET (all the variations of the Ipoints execution time above the BCET will be present in the measured times); but it is conservative in terms of safe timing margins.

5.2   Level of Instrumentation

Very tightly coupled with the last issue, there is also an effect related to the number of Ipoints that are included into the source code, which represents the level of instrumentation. The smaller the function instrumented is, the more the instrumentation affects to the WCET estimation so it must be taken into

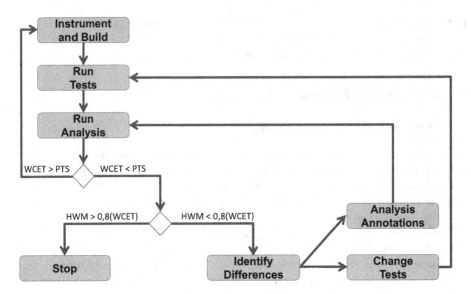

Fig. 3. The modified analysis process

account with utmost carefulness. It is not only a problem with the overhead itself, but also with regard to the fact that these functions overhead is very high compared to their execution time themselves. This problem appears especially when the number of statements of the functions is very low (1-5 statements).

To deal with this situation, some modifications to the normally recommended process need to be made. The following iterative process (summarized in Fig. 3) based on the instrumentation profiles and annotations has been followed, aiming to find a trade–off between the instrumentation overhead and the detail of such instrumentation.

Firstly, an initial WCET estimation must be calculated according with the process described in Sect. 3. To obtain this initial estimation, a standard instrumentation (START_OF_SCOPES profile) is used. This profile presents a good balance between the detail of the instrumentation and the number of Ipoints inserted (with their known overhead).

The main modifications made to the process are the actions to be taken after the analysis of the report and the estimations.

- If the estimated WCET is over the pre–allocated Partition Time Slot (PTS), it could be eventually be caused by issues related to instrumentation overhead and so, a new instrumentation of the source code must be done, controlling not to instrument the small functions. The process must be then repeated from the generation of the instrumented binaries.
- On the contrary, if the estimation of the partition WCET is under the PTS, the comparison between HWM and predicted WCET must be made.
  - As stated in Sect. 4, in the ideal situation, HWM and WCET will correspond. This means that the longest observed execution of the code,

end to end, will be the same as the longest possible path as determined from the intermediate measurements and so, the process ends. However, for complex software, it is not always possible to execute the estimated worst–case path. A threshold must be defined then to stop the process. For this investigation, it has been considered that a HWM greater or equal to the 80% of the predicted WCET is close enough and has exercised the worst–case path sufficiently. Therefore, if HWM surpasses such threshold, the process ends as well and the remaining difference is formally justified through reviews of the test and the code.

- If HWM is below the threshold, then the actions explained in Sect. 4 must be taken to improve the convergence between HWM and worst–case paths.

Finally, as a demonstration of the impact of the instrumentation level, some obtained results are presented in Table 1. It shows a huge gap between HWM (which keeps quite unaffected by the number of Ipoints) and WCET for high levels of instrumentation. For these levels, (almost) every function within the source code is instrumented and the negative consequences of the overhead affect deeply in the WCET calculation. This impact is especially important for the small functions, as stated. Leaving the smallest functions out of the instrumentation has, as shown in the data evolution within the table, positive effects in the WCET calculation which converges with HWM as the number of instrumented small functions decreases. Hence, it is not only a matter of Ipoints number but also of the place where the IPoints are located.

Table 1. WCET estimations for different instrumentation levels

Ipoints(#)	Ipoints Cov.(%)	HWM	WCET
836	98 %	0,367 ms	3,240 ms
358	92 %	0,340 ms	2,471 ms
189	89 %	0,332 ms	1,579 ms
140	97 %	0,332 ms	1,197 ms
66	98 %	0,334 ms	0,971 ms

5.3   Interrupts Handling

In Sect. 1, it was stated that the WCET excludes any time spent executing other tasks or interrupts. So another important challenge is the accounting for the effects that an eventual interrupt during the code execution could be caused in the measured execution time.

Due to the partitioning architecture, it is ensured that only the tasks of one partition can execute. Furthermore, because of the determinism required by DO–178B, each partition application software has been designed with only one task in the majority of cases (just in one partition there are more than one task, but keeping the determinism between them). However, it could happen that the

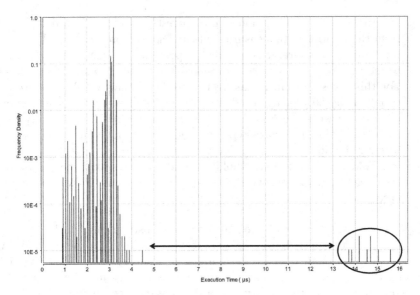

Fig. 4. Execution times of a tight loop affected by an interrupt

Table 2. Impact of an interrupt during a tight loop execution

Min. ET	Avg. ET	HWM ET	Max. ET	WCET
0,880 μs	2,018 μs	1,962 μs	15,597 μs	385,394 μs

execution of the application software is interfered by a kernel interrupt and it is required to account for the time the interrupt handling routine takes to run.

The effects of this are depicted in Fig. 4, where it is shown a critical situation where the execution times of a tight loop in the source code under analysis are mostly grouped from 1μs to 4μs but there are some executions significantly higher which are likely due to the presence of an interrupt.

Moreover, Table 2 contains the corresponding timing information. It shows an average execution time (ET) for the loop of about 2μs. The HWM is very close to such value as well, which suggests that when the longest end to end execution of the code under analysis (the partition in this case) took place, the loop execution time was not affected by any external effect. However, in one or more executions, and probably due to the interference of an interrupt, the execution time for the loop was unexpectedly high (see the difference between average and maximum ET). Even if it happened only for a single part of the loop code, this fact has obvious, direct consequences for the WCET estimation. In a very simplified way, and regardless of any other factors affecting the estimation, we can suppose that all the parts could be eventually affected the same.

A mechanism to distingish the time associated to the execution of the interrupt handling routine from the time of the function that were running when the interrupt took place is required. This mechanism is based on instrumenting such handling routines. This action would permit to take the time coming from the routines into account and not to incorrectly increase the measured time for the code. It is therefore necessary to modify some procedures within the Board Support Package (BSP) interfacing the RTOS kernel and the hardware.

6   Conclusions

To summarize the main conclusions on this investigation, it can be stated that, from the point of view of the required effort to perform the WCET analysis and the confidence on the obtained results, the integration of a hybrid approach (as it is the one implemented by RapiTime) means an important goal achieved. As seen, the approach automates critical processes during the verification from instrumentation to data analysis. Another achievement is the workflow proposed that is fully compliant with the particularities of the safety–critical airborne development environment and offers a systematic, repeatable process for revealing and explaining the execution time behaviour of the software. It also helps in the design of specific temporal tests focused on estimulating the worst–case path.

The memory–based implementation selected for the tracing system presents significant consequences in the instrumentation overhead that must be taken into account with specific mechanisms. Also the eventual presence of interrupts during the code execution must be controlled, as explained. Another critical input in a timing analysis would be the loop bounds. However, it has been out of this study scope due to the fundamentally sequential nature of the code and the bounds static definition of the not many loops in the code.

A careful hardware selection allowing less–intrusive tracing mechanisms (i.e. I/O ports, data buses) from the early stages of the project, would ease the integration process of the WCET analysis workflow. It also impacts critically in the control of the instrumentation overhead.

For future investigations, an unique, integrated timing analysis for a source code composed of C and Ada code would be an achievement in terms of reduction of effort and quality of the obtained timing information. Also mechanisms automating the instrumentation level by analysis of the functions sizes would be very helpful in the overhead control and should be investigated.

Finally, for future projects, an important conclusion drawn is that the earlier the WCET analysis is addressed in the software life cycle of HRT systems, the more useful its results are, not only in terms of timing assurance but also in terms of optimization of the source code implementation and the software design.

References

1. ARINC Specification 653: Avionics Application Software Standard Interface. Aeronautical Radio Inc. (1997)
2. Bernat, G., Colin, A., Petters, S.M.: WCET Analysis of Probabilistic Hard Real–Time Systems. In: Proc. 23rd IEEE Real–Time Systems Symposium, RTSS (2002)

3. Wilhelm, R., et al.: The Worst–Case Execution Time Problem – Overview of Methods and Survey of Tools. ACM Transactions on Embedded Computing Systems (2008)
4. RTCA DO-178B: Software Considerations in Airborne Systems and Equipment Certification. RTCA Inc. (1992)
5. RTCA DO-178C: Software Considerations in Airborne Systems and Equipment Certification. RTCA Inc. (2011)
6. RTCA DO-248B: Final Report for Clarification of DO–178B Software Considerations in Airborne Systems and Equipment Certification. RTCA Inc. (2001)

Author Index

Alonso, Alejandro   127
Asensio, Esteban   161

Baldovin, Andrea   143
Bicchierai, Irene   95
Botcazou, Eric   65
Brandon, Carl   51
Bucci, Giacomo   95

Carlisle, Martin   81
Chapin, Peter   51
Coombes, Andrew   161

de la Puente, Juan A.   127
de Miguel, Miguel A.   127

Fagin, Barry   81

Gutiérrez, J. Javier   1

Hilbrich, Robert   35

Lafoz, Ismael   161

Mezzetti, Enrico   143
Michell, Stephen   17
Moore, Brad   17

Namin, Akbar Siami   109
Navas, Julian   161
Nocentini, Carlo   95

Pérez, Héctor   1
Pinho, Luís Miguel   17

Quinot, Thomas   65

Salazar, Emilio   127

van Kampenhout, J. Reinier   35
Vardanega, Tullio   143
Vicario, Enrico   95

Xue, Xiaozhen   109